how soon is
never?

also by marc spitz

We Got the Neutron Bomb: The Untold Story of L.A. Punk (coauthored with Brendan Mullen)

marc spitz

THREE RIVERS PRESS · NEW YORK

how soon is
never?

A NOVEL

Published by Three Rivers Press, New York, New York
Member of the Crown Publishing Group, a division of Random House, Inc.
www.randomhouse.com

Three Rivers Press and the Tugboat design are registered trademarks of
Random House, Inc.

Printed in the United States of America

DESIGN BY ELINA D. NUDELMAN

Library of Congress Cataloging-in-Publication Data
Spitz, Marc.
    How soon is never? : a novel / Marc Spitz.—1st ed.
1. Young men—Fiction. 2. Jewish youth—Fiction. 3. Children of divorced
parents—Fiction. 4. Long Island (N.Y.)—Fiction. 5. Lexington (Ky.)—Fiction.
I. Title.
PS3619.P67 H69 2003
813'.6—dc21
                                                                    2003013117

ISBN 0-609-81040-5

10 9 8 7 6 5 4 3

First Edition

for victoria

contents

To get back my youth I would do anything in the world,
except take exercise, get up early, or be respectable.

—OSCAR WILDE

I get to live the rest of my life like a schnook.

—RAY LIOTTA IN *GOODFELLAS*

how soon is
never?

hello, i am the ghost of troubled joe

My name is Joseph Green. I don't like the name Joseph. Prefer Joe, but that comes with some heavy pop cultural baggage. If you don't know already, I'll get it over with . . .

From 1969 to 1981, 6´4˝, 280-pound Mean Joe Greene (number 75) was the fearsome defensive tackle for the Pittsburgh Steelers.

My legacy: not much, really.

His legacy:

Team MVP in 1970.

NFL Defensive Player of the Year, 1974.

Four Super Bowl championships.

One award-winning 1980 Coca-Cola commercial ("Hey, kid . . . catch!").

Inducted into the Hall of Fame in Canton, Ohio, 1987.

I think he also played Sasquatch on *The Six Million Dollar Man*.

And then, although few pro-ball enthusiasts point this one out: there's his unchallenged, three-decade run as an unholy source of my profound social awkwardness and tandem substance abuses. Yeah, to this day, even though I'm skinny, 30, Caucasian, and pretty even-tempered when sober, the utterance of my name to new acquaintances, bank tellers, hotel front desk clerks, and, worst of all, eligible women between the ages of 27 and 40 provokes the question:

"*Mean* Joe Greene?"

Each one acts as if I've never heard it before. It's made me pretty fucking mean.

This is one of the reasons why I tend to hang out with 22-year-olds lately. My new social circle consists of kids just out of college. They're members of Generation Y to my arrested X. That eight-to-ten-year age difference can catch you on a mean snag if you're not careful. And it's caught me. Since Miki, I haven't even tried to pursue a steady girlfriend my own age. One of those wife-and-mother-of-your-baby candidates. I don't have any pets. I can't even keep a plant alive. A cactus died on me.

I go out every night with party-crazed kids who don't have the same level of internal decay that I do. They can drink and snort and pop prescription drugs till five in the morning every night, then hop out of bed and do it again the next day. In an effort to keep up with them, I sometimes subject myself to daylong mornings-after that might only be cured by Keith Richards–in–Switzerland-style total blood transfusions. Twelve hours of smoking and moaning, prayer, and guzzling gallon jugs of Ocean Spray cranberry juice cocktail also works and is much more affordable. Most of the time, I'm grateful that the new breed has accepted me as one of their own. When I'm feeling mean and spiteful and jealous of their youth, I fuck with them. After a dozen years of partying, my tolerance has become a brutal thing, and since I'm trying to be more honest than usual here, I'll tell you that it does fill me with pride whenever I drink a 21-year-old down to the puke-slimy tiles and walk away.

Occasionally one of these young girls with their fine skin and goofy wide eyes will go home with me. They're good-looking and hungry for experience. I tell myself that they like me, they're not just "experiencing" me. I do my 10,000th line of blow with them while they're all excited about snorting up their first. After last call, I travel home to the Williamsburg, Brooklyn, loft they share with four other recent college grads. I ride with them on the L train. I'm so wired and paranoid that I'm convinced everyone is staring at me like I'm some child molester who looks a lot like the guy on the cover of Jethro Tull's *Aqualung* album. I wonder if the roommates are laughing at me while I try to fuck their friend in the next bed but can't get a hard-on. Sometimes the girl rides home with me and I hear 15-year-old R.E.M. and U2 songs on classic rock radio in the back of taxicabs while I reach under their T-shirts to squeeze their impossibly smooth tits. Those tits by the way are heaving things that feel like they've never, ever been touched by anybody else before but that doesn't make me feel very special somehow. It makes me feel dirty. So when we get to my place, I drink away the rest of my chances of getting anything resembling an erection. Instead, I put on an LP. They ask, "Is this Dinosaur Junior?" I tell them that it's actually Sonic Youth and smile even as I notice that they're wearing a Sonic Youth T-shirt. This makes me drink even more. These girls get out of my bed the next day and bound into the street to take over the fucking city with their ridiculous energy. I get out of bed two and a half hours later and sit in my shower trying to steam the toxins out of my pores because I read somewhere that Frank Sinatra and the Rat Pack used to do that after a night of ring-a-ding-dingin' with the Jack Daniel's. In addition to the cranberry juice, which I also heard somewhere is a boon to organ rejuvenation, I buy Fleet enemas along with my Camel Lights at the Rite-Aid pharmacy on Hudson Street because I pray they will purge the remaining poisons out of my ass. I'll do anything to feel clean and reverse what I did to myself the night before. What I did to them too. And while everyone else my age is at work or with their wives or their kids, I find myself in the tiny bathroom of my overpriced apartment in Manhattan's West Village. The bowl is full of cigarette butts. The floor is full of old copies of *New Musical Express* and porn. The television is playing continuous reruns of *The Golden Girls* but I've had the sound muted for about two years. Unless there's a plane crash or some other manner of "special report" heralding the end of the world, the old gals' wisecracks remain muted through the night and day. The TV light keeps the roaches away. Sometimes, I cry. Most of the time, I ignore my editor's e-mails and phone calls demanding the 300 words that I have to file on Cute Band Alert, a Williamsburg, Brooklyn–based quartet of self-described "art terrorists" who dress in parachute pants and Members Only jackets, play Casios and Keytars, have withering body odor, and somehow still get to fuck models. Their lead singer is also ten years younger than me. He has a record deal and a mullet, and he says things like "I don't really feel comfortable in most social situations. With this music, I'd really like to destroy society as we know it." I interviewed him over sushi and martinis at the Tribeca Grand Hotel. I was too intimidated by his youth to grab his skinny little neck and snap his head off. Instead, I nodded and said, "Yes. I understand." Then he asked me if I had any pot because he was heading off to England in a few hours and didn't have time to make a call.

Some days, I go back to the house I grew up in and root through the cardboard box of my stuff that my mother keeps in the attic . . . like the mementos of the dead. The stored black-and-white marble journals that meant so much to me in high school are now no different from the plaster handprint of my little monkey-sized paw from a kindergarten art class in 1974 or the broken ventriloquist's dummy clown that I used to play with. I look for meaning but everything I find just makes me feel older and sadder. Still, I snatch some artifacts and bring them back to the city, hoping they'll ward off some demons. But soon, there are more bad-sex stains on the only pair of sheets I've ever owned, and the next little girl has gone again, and instead of porn or expensive English music magazines, I read my high school yearbook wistfully on the toilet. As painful as high school was, I've reached the place in life where I'd happily saw off my nuts to go back for just an hour so that I could be that person with untouched flesh and easily filtered pores and a virgin liver, wondering what my first fuck or my first line of coke or the first time I hear a song that changes my life is going be like. I'm not sure if I have to shit or puke but I opt for puking cause there's a plastic enema bottle up my ass.

Yes, I am vain. Yes, I am immature. Yes, I enjoy complaining. But before you assign me general admission seating in that especially torturous place in hell reserved for 30-plus-year-old guys who still hang around their old college town, let me clarify something here: I work in rock 'n' roll.

I don't sing or play guitar, drums, or organ. I couldn't even shake a tambourine with conviction. But my job, writing about rock 'n' roll for *Headphones* magazine, makes this generation slumming and the blow jobs from women who still remember what was on their college lit reading list a lot less damnable than they might be. Naturally, this is the first real job I've held for more than six months. I get paid to write about pop music. I don't like to say that aloud for fear that someone will find me out as an unqualified sham. (But really, who *is* qualified to write about rock 'n' roll besides the kids who have no interest in writing about it because they're too busy really connecting with its energy?) Still, for four years now, I have been exchanging my thoughts on rock for actual U.S. currency . . . and health insurance. I suspect such arrangements drove rock critic legends like Lester Bangs and Nick Kent to their fatal and near-fatal abuses, respectively. Even if you're good at what you do, and some say that I am, you're still *writing* about rock 'n' roll. If I could identify a blues scale, it might make sense that a large corporate magazine pays me money to listen to records and go see bands but I doubt it. I don't want to end up like Lester Bangs, dead at 33. Hence the enemas (which was going to be the alternative title for this book). I want a wife and a child and a beige four-door Volvo and a house in the country. Or at least I tell myself I do in the morning when it feels like a pig has shit in my head. But, to paraphrase Jim Morrison, no one here gets the Volvo.

They sell a T-shirt in the tourist shops on St. Mark's Place in the East Village that says Rehab Is for Quitters. Every time I pass it, hanging in the window, it makes me shudder. I may be a lot of things but I ain't no quitter. I understand the pride, pathetic as it is, therein. I'd never wear something as goofy as a pop slogan across my chest. T-shirts are for the band merchandise table, unless you happen to be 22. Then they're designed to ironically promote companies you've never worked for or varsity sports teams you've never played for, like Peachtree Tractor Repair or Davenport High School Wrestling Squad (preferably, these are well worn with a hole or two on the neck or under the arm). There's a popular saying in rehab that there are three outcomes if you keep getting high and living irresponsibly: jails, institutions, and death. That's your destiny.

Jails.

Institutions.

Death.

What they don't tell you, and they really fucking should, is that there's a fourth destiny (call it a hidden track).

Number four: working for a major rock 'n' roll magazine.

Let's put aside death here, cause even if you don't drink and smoke and do drugs and blast Metallica's "Master of Puppets" at four in the morning, you're gonna die like everybody else one day, right? So then there's jail. I've spent a night in jail, after a bar fight. They let me out in the morning. I've been institutionalized. Rehab. Where I heard the fucking saying in the first place. Got out. Signed some papers and walked away. The fourth outcome, that's the trap. It doesn't look like a trap. It looks like salvation. It looks like a dream job. It looks like something that might enable us to thumb a nose at convention forever. But after a few years, we can't stay in this business either. Not without the fear. Rock writers don't mature, we just get older. We get ever-deepening lines around our eyes. Our hair starts to gray and thin. We "ache in the places where we used to play," as Leonard Cohen once sang. We become ugly vampires. Not the suave, cocksure Anne Rice vampires, but cool-thirsty desperadoes trying to grab and stick the greased pig of cultural relevance, then drink deeply. We are aging on the outside but emotionally retarded for eternity.

Stay cool.

Stay hip.

Sell ads.

Sell magazines.

Suck blood.

Give the kids what they wanna read. In order to really do that well, we have to think like a kid. In order to think like a kid, we have to travel with the kids. In order to travel with the kids, we have to act like they do. We are pop narcs and New York's Lower East Side is our beat. Or rather, it used to be our beat. It's their beat now, we just haunt it. The better we can pull this off, the greater the reward. I've been promoted. My salary has nearly doubled. My byline has gotten more prominent. Publicists and doormen and even rock stars have started to recognize me. I've already mentioned the little girls' form of endorsement. I should also mention the free promotional CDs. They come in the mail daily. They are essentially free money to further subsidize the expensive freezing process if you've got some truck with the buy/sell/trade guys. Free money! Still, there's no amount of compensation for what this life does to your soul if you let it. What good is any of it if I can't listen to a record just to listen to it anymore? Why go to a show if I can't just be at a show? When I can't make eye contact with the young lead singer of a band I admire like the Strokes without putting $150 worth of vodka down my throat because he's the real thing and I'm just wearing the same clothes. He's Bob Dylan in *Don't Look Back* and I'm that hack dictating in the phone box. Describing the authenticity of the new youthquakers with their "eyeshadow and undertaker makeup . . . they are there . . . they are with it." I remember when I was with it. Now, I've just had it—mod trousers and collarless leather coat or no . . . But still, when it comes time to put them on the cover of *Headphones,* I get the job because nobody else at the office who is experienced enough to handle a cover story looks remotely like a 22-year-old hipster. I'm akin to a professional athlete and drinking and smoking and playing air guitar are my training. If you're a good player, nobody will stop you and say, "This is not how a thirty-year-old person behaves." Nobody will say, "Get a life or a wife already. You're an adult." Nobody will even say, "Why are you wearing that stupid fucking leather jacket?" They're just glad you're successful at second-guessing the new fave raves. I can truly say from experience that snorting one line of smack is less soul-destroying than sitting in a huddle in a corporate conference room, wondering if the tattooed assholes from that crap band Crazytown are worthy of a feature profile.

"Is it good?"

"Do you like it?"

"I don't know. Do *you* like it?"

"The kids like it."

"It's on MTV every minute."

"Oh yeah? Well, it's kind of catchy. The kids like them?"

"I think so."

Have you ever seen those old newsreels from the early '60s where the socialites slummed it downtown to the Peppermint Lounge so they could do the twist and feel sexy? That's us. If you think the Who look foolish limping onstage at nearly 60 to sing "I hope I die before I get old," think about the rock writers who can't justify it all and buy trout farms in the English countryside. No, most of us buy cocktails instead. Cocktails and blow. I know what you're thinking now: *God, what a drama queen! He's only 30.* Thirty is young for lawyers. If you're a rock writer, fucking retire. Besides, in bright light, I look 40. In bar light, I can pass for 19. I still get carded at certain clubs. I know it's the law, but really, it's hard to keep from kissing the doorperson in a fit of gratitude.

I don't want you to worry about reading on because you're convinced that this is going to be a total fucking downer. This is a story about hope, man. No, really. First of all, I swear that one day I'm going to start a support group for "fourth destination" people like me. We'll meet in the grimy basement of the Mercury Lounge on Houston Street and wear crisp Brooks Brothers shirts and navy blue wool ties. We'll drink decaf coffee from paper cups. We'll confess our rock 'n' roll sins.

"My name is Joe Green and I've got Lester Bangs disease."

"Hi, Joe."

And they'll only ask me if I'm Mean Joe Greene once or twice. And it'll be okay.

Second, I'm committed to blindly truck on and try not to imagine myself alone and culturally predatory at 35 or 40 or 50 with a stack of Just for Men hair products in my medicine chest and a velvet blazer at the dry cleaner's being let out "just a little" for the fifth time. I won't think about the possibility that the girl who'll be in my bed then hasn't even been born yet. I'll snatch some peace of mind here and there. When especially blue, I'll tell myself that a special report is going to interrupt *The Golden Girls* one of these long, spinning afternoons and none of this is going to matter. And I'll turn up the volume and listen to the world end and feel something real, even if it's utter terror. Until then, I'll file my 800 words on the four 19-year-olds who call themselves the Kissing Disease. I'll convince myself that their debut album, *Cold and Hurty*, rocks . . . or at least the kids say it does. I'll take care not to call them an emo band because emo kids find it confining and insulting. The effort I make to avoid revealing myself as a pretender will momentarily distract me from the shame of having to write the piece in the first place. I'll search for a similar term because I can't write about what I really hear: noise, blank death-rattle noise. Metal machine music. The wheezing drone of my own self-hatred.

*   *   *

Third and finally, I haven't really lost the music at all. Or rather, I've recently regained it. When it all gets to be too intolerable, I'll break the emergency glass and pull out a record by the one band that I can still hear and feel. And then even the spontaneous interruption of *The Golden Girls* and the screams of the air raid sirens will not rattle me.

"My name is Joe Green and I love the Smiths."

If you don't know who the Smiths are, that's fine. Just picture your mother or your father or your husband or your wife or your child. Think about how you love them. My love for this band is as strong. It's the only real love I've ever known. And because I love them so completely, they provide me with my only hope that one day, I can feel the same way about something that's not a song they've written and sung but a real person. Maybe even someone my age, like Miki is. I know this because a while ago, I couldn't even love these songs. They were too pure. Now, I can listen again. When these songs make me laugh and cry and smile or even want to drink, I know it's a real impulse. I laugh. I cry. I drink. Even though the band ceased to exist more than a decade ago, the Generation Y kids love the Smiths too, but they can't have them. They are my band. Nothing can corrupt them anymore. I know this because Miki and I tried to corrupt them ourselves just a couple of years ago. I will tell you now how I reclaimed my rock 'n' roll soul, but in order to do that, I'm going to have to go back a bit and recount how I got that soul in the first place. Rock 'n' roll soul doesn't grow on trees. And it didn't grow at all on Long Island in the early '80s.

two

have you seen your father, baby, standing in the shadows?

Long Island got its name because it stretches about 120 miles from west to east. Oh, and because it's a fucking island. Its width is approximately 20 miles. In other words, it's a big place, full of universities, museums, wildlife preserves, farms, and nuclear power plants. It wasn't settled by upper-middle-class Jews but rather by mammoth-slaying proto–Native Americans who migrated downward across sheets of ice from Siberia and other frigid, northernmost points. The English and Dutch colonists came next, I believe. By 1981, however, there was a vast racial, cultural, and economic demographic: working-class Italian American and Irish American and African American families. Hispanics, Asians. There was also John F. Kennedy International Airport, one of the nation's largest. My childhood home was beneath the departing flight path, and I could see and hear flights bound for Sydney and Paris and Tokyo and Los Angeles soaring past me daily. Despite all this, it remained quite easy for a pre-adolescent like me to believe that the entire world consisted of a scattering of a few hundred comfortable Jewish families. I knew that my parents were the grandchildren of immigrants who had come to Ellis Island from Russia and Poland and scraped and sweated for their fortunes, but I forced myself to believe that we were here first and always. I assumed that we had always had shelter and heat and food on the table. We had always owned French poodles. We could trust our neighbors because their cars and clothes and noses and dogs looked just like ours. And nobody could hurt us. I watched plenty of television and loved reading *Newsday*, the Island-wide paper. I knew this was a bullshit assumption. I knew it was the height of ignorance. At the time, I had my reasons for narrowing my worldview until it included no more than a series of tree-lined blocks full of big white clapboard houses with shiny Cadillacs in the driveway. I had cause for being afraid of getting hurt or corrupted by the troubling, unfamiliar influences that lay beyond all those white picket fences. I'll give you two biggies.

Reason Number One: The Inevitable Nuclear Holocaust

It was the thick of the Cold War. Ronald Reagan was in the White House with his finger on the button. We lived on the brink of nuclear war every day. At night, as I tried to sleep, I could almost feel the Russian missiles pointed at our houses. Our Cadillacs. Our poodles. And ours were pointed at theirs. All someone had to do, on either side, was accidentally lay an elbow on the button and it was all over. I had nothing against Reagan. He seemed very personable and charming with his jelly beans. I had nothing that could be mistaken for political awareness. I just didn't trust *anyone* with the button.

"Doomsday," my nutty old grandfather Chaz called it whenever he'd visit us. He'd intone the word like an angel of death. "Doomsday!" Chaz had seen a lot. He'd built the fortune that we all benefited from. He'd turned a modest lumberyard into a major construction-supply empire with branches all over the tristate area. He was a good man who loved his children and grandchildren. I don't believe he was being malicious in his antagonism. Although there was something about the way he smiled when he'd shout "Doomsday." It was almost as if he wanted to see it happen. He wanted to exit under the mushroom cloud with everybody else. I guess nobody wants to die alone. Chaz was in his mid-70s and knew that he wasn't going to be around much longer, and in the same way I mess with the new postgrads today, he seemed to delight in rattling me with details of the coming apocalypse. I was easily rattled. So my suburban ostrich-in-the-sand mentality was a reaction to the inevitability that I was destined to be vaporized with Grandpa Chaz before I ever even got a chance to grow up and experience life. My mother, Susie, was petite, with frosted hair, a high-pitched voice, and kind brown eyes. Whenever I'd have nightmares about Chaz' prophecies, she would calm me. It was only after these dream visions that I'd run to her, screaming for an explanation for bringing me into a world wired to explode.

"Your grandpa's just playing around with you, Joseph. There's no such thing as nuclear war."

Susie, with her thick Long Island accent (she pronounced war as "waw-uh"), brought uneasy comfort with her own brand of blindly optimistic logic. "It's never going to happen."

"How do you know, Mom?"

"Because the way things are set up, both sides would annihilate each other. Do you understand? There can never be a war now because nobody would win. Now go do your math homework."

When I wanted it to, it made perfect sense. The "waw-uh" wasn't coming soon. At night, when it was so quiet that I could almost hear the chatter of the air travelers as the jets flew over my house, I told myself they were only traveling as far as Cedarhurst, the next town over, where everyone was the same as we were. And there was no danger.

Reason Number Two: Sid

The way I figure it now, and I've got the references to figure it, my father, Sidney Green, so confounding back in the '80s, was at the time little more than one of those classic stuck-in-the-'70s suburban white Superfly wanna-be cokeheads. He had bushy black hair and wore a thick mustache that resembled Yankee captain Thurman Munson's. He was especially proud of his lime-green suede trench coat. He wore it up until around '91 or '92. I'd like to get my hands on it now. I'd totally wear it.

A mama's boy Canarsie Jew (my paternal grandmother slathered his knishes with deli mustard well into his 40s), he dreamed that he was a street-talking Italian and then became one (to paraphrase Neil Diamond's "I Am I Said," which I won't do again). He even nicknamed himself "Sonny" after James Caan's doomed character in *The Godfather*. Sidney liked to gamble. He picked it up from his father, Dr. Lou Green, an old-school general practitioner who kept a .38 in his black bag, frequently shot himself up with B_{12}, and made house calls to the local wiseguys. When Lou died, he left my dad a solid gold horse's head with a ruby eye. This gambler's good-luck charm was strung on a thick gold braid. Supposedly, it aided in the handicapping of ponies.

"When I die, you'll wear this," Dad used to promise me, stroking the thing.

There are old Super-8s of me being wheeled through the track in my stroller. I don't recall that. I do remember being dragged through the parking lot and into the smoky, congested floors of Aqueduct and Belmont Park once I could walk. On days when he couldn't get to the races, we'd go out for eggs and home fries, then hit up the Off-Track Betting outlet. We'd wait on line at the greasy OTB window, my father passing me the printed-out ticket to hold for luck while we watched the results on the high-mounted television sets. He'd snatch the paper from my hand when the horse broke and choked. Actually, he'd snatch it from my hand when his pony won too. I was too small to reach the window and cash the thing anyway. When we were up, he'd duke me a $10 bill on the sly and warn, "Don't tell your mother." Ten bucks bought a lot of candy and baseball cards with their chalky slats of bubble gum back in the day. When luck (he'd call it skill) was with us, I'd lord it over my pre-Ritalin schoolmates, the sugar-pusher king of the cafeteria.

Still, for all the spoils, the track fucked up my little head as bad as Reagan and the Commies did. I'd never seen shrunken old men with tattooed skin like hanging deli meat . . . or hairy-faced women smoking cigars. I'd never seen so many African Americans and Puerto Ricans in one place. I'd never seen them drunk and cursing either. Our housekeeper, Sylvia, a balding beanpole of an old woman, was black, but she never cursed . . . and she was all alone.

Sid loved everything about this beat-down world. Susie abided it for a while. She allowed him to dip into the family lumber fortune, not work, and stay high. But you can't, as I've come to know, slum anywhere evil too long and return to your safe, clean home without incurring some domestic static. That broke-down gangster voodoo shit sticks to you . . . and it costs you. In the summer of 1980, it cost Sid his wife. My mother must have realized the party was over years earlier when her shopping and lunching cash started looking more and more like crumpled window tickets. There were signs. She quit drinking and smoking. She started eating yogurt. She broke up her weekly canasta klatch. Gambling had become increasingly unkosher. Their fights would start after dinner. I'd hear them through the walls of my room as I tried to focus on *The Muppet Show*. Afterward, they'd apologize to me and insist that they loved each other and loved me and everything was going to be fine. And I believed them, even though I knew something bad was coming.

Sid didn't even pursue custody. He just slipped out the back, as one does when an ugly scene is made at a rapidly fizzling party. Chaz' money made for a tidy divorce in terms of division of assets. Susie asked for nothing. She knew Sid had nothing. Once Chaz assured her that he would provide for keeping Sylvia on the payroll and raising me in a clean home without depending on an absent breadwinner (or loser) for child support, she just wanted him gone. Happily, this left Sid free to go to the track all day, every day, and snort coke all night without worrying about my needs. The divorce was quick too. There was no trial separation. One afternoon, while I watched from the driveway, Sid loaded up a borrowed and battered silver Datsun, then piled on top of several other refuse-to-give-up-the-party divorced men in a weedy, musty bachelor pad in Atlantic Beach. Sid's new family consisted of bald, skinny, mustached, hunchbacked Will, a shoe salesman; Afro'd, bespectacled Koz (a dead ringer for the young Elliott Gould, as he'd remind people constantly); and twitchy, slightly retarded Martin (shag haircut, denim cutoffs with one testicle always drooping below the fringe). With no sensible "bitches" around, the lot of them started smoking the coke out in the living room. And the party swung on.

*   *   *

how soon is never?

Atlantic Beach was just over the Atlantic Beach Bridge, only three miles from my childhood home. It might as well have been five hundred. During the summers it was a teeming resort community, boasting a strip of private clubs that offered exclusive access to the white sands and warm ocean surf. In the off-season, it was desolate. A slip of water divided them but the lifestyle schism would have been as wide even if Sid had moved next door. Susie had the evergreens and willow trees in the backyard, the aforementioned French poodle curled up on the overstuffed couch in front of the fireplace, and the cream Seville in the long driveway. Sid lived on cocaine and cold cuts ordered in from Abe's Deli. Abe was an unintelligible concentration camp survivor with three missing fingers and sauerkraut breath who would frequently shout "No problem!" at people with no provocation. Sid loved Abe. Perhaps he admired his resilience. Or maybe he just loved being assured there was no problem.

In the months immediately following the divorce, I'd ride my bike across the bridge to visit my father. I'd find Sid in his underwear, doling out sticky red spare ribs to an equally half-naked and super-stoned teenage girl whom he'd introduce as my "new mother." I had about seven or eight "new mothers." I don't know what I was doing there. Most of the time I was ignored or treated like a pet. I guess I just felt like I should be with my father once in a while since I knew where to find him. But I had no idea where he was, even when he was stretched out on the couch snoring. When extremely bored or scared, I used to wield the old man's base pipe torch like a light saber. I'd swing the thick blue jet of flame around my head, shouting, "Luke, I am your father!" from the recently released *The Empire Strikes Back,* until he'd snatch it out of my hand and sternly inform me that it wasn't a "fucking toy." Sometimes I'd try to rehabilitate him. I attempted to make him more like Susie in order to get some kind of equilibrium with which to traverse the new zones they'd delineated. I'd let myself in unannounced (the door was never locked). I'd throw out his porn and cigarettes, clean up his room, and fold his clothes (one T-shirt sticks in my memory . . . mall-style glitter iron-on with the message A Friend with Weed Is a Friend Indeed). One day I found a rusty old manual mower in a ditch and spent an entire Sunday afternoon hacking down the thick growth of lawn, which hadn't been trimmed since the '60s. I didn't find anything precious buried under the overgrown vegetation, a gold watch or a lost and confused dog. Still, there were treasures on that property amid all the troubling decay.

One of the wired floppers Sid lived with back then was a guy named Nick Davis. Nick was a stringy-haired tweaker who made a killing selling quality leotards and unitards. What he was doing bunking with a rotating crew of divorced men a decade his senior, I still don't know and won't guess (it was the coke). Sometimes I'd find a stack of Nick's *Creem* magazines or issues of *Rolling Stone* and lose myself for hours, reading about music I'd never heard. I'd wonder, who was Lou Reed? Who was Johnny Rotten and why was he so angry? Why did they all look so weird? Was there something out there, beyond the suburbs, that had gotten to them? Was it going to get me? Part of me wanted to find out more about these people and hear their music and solve their mysteries because I wanted to avoid their fate. Another part of me was just fascinated that they seemed to have endured large quantities of blackness and negativity and, like Abe the deli owner, they'd survived. They seemed genuinely crazed and I wanted to know why they hadn't perished yet. Maybe there was hope for my father, I thought. I'd honestly never seen a pop star frown before. I was obsessed with how these figures could so obviously have trawled through some slimy hell and emerge smiling. Was there a device or a philosophy that would enable me to grin while inhaling nuclear fallout or secondhand free-base smoke? My obsession grew so strong as I plowed through the late-era works of Lester Bangs and Dave Marsh that in the summer of 1981, when Nick grabbed my shaking, sweaty left hand, led me into his room, and sat me on the bed, I didn't resist. This was a big deal, and not just because I looked up to him as some kind of older-brother figure. Nick's room was always locked. He paid the bulk of the rent with his unitard salary, fortified us with much of the Abe's Deli fare. Nick seemed the improbable alpha male among Dad and the other loser lodgers. His private room, unlike the rest of the pad, was very neat. He had his own separate entertainment console. Television set, turntable, 8-track tape player in the shape of a diving helmet.

"What are you looking for?" I asked, a little fearful, as he dug through his closet, tossing out Peter Frampton and Boston albums, and more spandex tights than a man should really keep.

"I wanna play you something."

"Why?" was all I could say in response. Had I done something wrong? Right? I don't even think my father had crossed into Nick's sanctum.

"Cause your fucking old man won't stop with that fucking R & B shit. You don't give a shit about the fucking Spinners, right?" Sniff.

He was right. I didn't give a shit about the Spinners. Or the O'Jays. Or the Stylistics. I like them now but at the time, it did nothing to help me understand my world.

"Fucking Dionne Warwick. That's old-people music. You and I are young. Right?"

"Right."

"I want you to listen to this and tell that motherfucker that this is 1981 and he should get with the fucking times, all right?" Sniff. Snort.

"Don't call my dad a motherfucker."

"Joe, I love the guy but he's a motherfucker. Do you know what a motherfucker is? It doesn't mean he fucks your mother, cause he doesn't fuck your mother anymore." Sniff.

I shifted and looked at the door. Tried to transport myself through it, mentally.

"I have to go to the bathroom."

"No, you don't."

I could see the crack in Nick's pale, freckled ass as he leaned over the contents of the closet. He finally found what he was searching for and held it up to me.

"You have to listen to this."

He pulled the record from the sleeve and placed it on the turntable. Then he put the needle down and handed me the sleeve.

"I'm gonna go take a shit and read the paper. Now, I don't want you to come out of this room until you've listened to the whole thing. I mean it. If I see you leave this room, you're not allowed back in this house ever again. You got that, Joe?"

"Okay." I was near tears. He grabbed my shoulder and gave it a hard but affectionate squeeze and walked out. He doubled back and grabbed a copy of *Newsday* off the bed. It was then that I first heard what I could only identify as "the strange." The thumping bass intro was ominous, and the lead singer's voice quavered and barked as he keenly detailed the doom and panic I'd suspected, and strenuously denied, up until that moment. I couldn't pretend it wasn't out there anymore. He sang like he had been inhaling toxic fumes so long that he'd learned how to breathe them:

how soon is never?

"The ice age is coming, the sun zooming in, meltdown ex- pected, the wheat is growing thin . . ."

This was confirmation of my fears. This wasn't Dionne Warwick asking the way to San Jose. Or Paul McCartney won- dering why you said goodbye when he said hello. This was some guy—who was, I surmised as I scanned the sleeve, named the Clash—blowing away my mother's fuzzy logic about the impossibility of "a nuclear error." I stared at the cover. An angry man was smashing his bass guitar on the floor of a concert stage.

What the fuck is really going on in the world? I wondered. *Why are they telling me not to prepare for destruction? This is the sound of destruction and it's pretty fucking convincing.*

I instantly knew that this guy—this *thing* called Clash—was right and my mother was wrong, but I was too young and scared to do much about it. I put the record down and ran out- side, past Nick on the shitter. I jumped onto my bike and ped- aled wildly over the bridge, back to the safety zone, where London wasn't calling and phony Beatlemania had not yet bit- ten the dust.

Nick never enforced his ban. Sky-high, he'd probably forgotten I was ever there. Yet after a while I didn't visit the bachelor pad very much. I decided to bury my spinning head even further into the sand, so as to avoid it being strewn with the golden horse head and lordship over a dark world where I had multiple mothers and a stinging contact high. I decided that blunt anonymity was crucial to my salvation. As I rolled into the seventh grade, circa 1982, I wanted and needed to look like everybody else at Lawrence Junior High School. I bagged up any traceable evidence of Sid's ties to the subculture, which, on my mom's side of the bridge, fortu- nately amounted to little more than a few Chicago LPs, a fringed jean jacket, a beaded belt, and a funky old suede hat that inspired my father to call me "Leroy" whenever I wore it. I disposed of any trace of Sid, whom I blamed for keeping me just left of the center where I belonged. I assimilated with a vengeance. I became a JAP or Jewish American prince. By the way, Jewish American princes or princesses happily referred to themselves as JAPs. It was hardly an ethnic slur. How could it be? We were all of the same ethnicity. It was our identity. And I was happy to have one.

The JAPs had a uniform. Foremost, we had to own Ralph Lauren polo shirts in every color. If an outlet ran out of them, you drove to the next town to stock up. They were not flattering on my still-pudgy body ("husky" was my suit size, I recall), nor do I think they look good hugging the nicest of upper torsos in any situation. Still, the corridors were lousy with them. A plague of happy tints and hues, they came in peach, lavender, pink, turquoise, candy stripes. Everybody had at least two dozen and rotated them because you couldn't wear the same one more than once a week. Whether knit in a waffle weave or straight combed cotton, there was also an unspoken way of wearing these horrible shirts: bottom button always fastened, top two loose, collar up. I remember the obscene polo player stitched into the breast, as if we moneyed suburban trash had been astride a pony, swinging a mallet, any more than those poor sweatshop workers who made them by the thousands each day. The sneakers had to be K-Swiss tennis shoes, unscuffed white. While I was fortunate enough to wear the real deal, the poor kids wore knockoffs from Fayva or Shoe Town discount stores and were reminded of this every day. They'd never be free from ridicule with a tiger or a quail or a porpoise or a pack mule sewn into the breast of their polo shirts. They had to have a white man on a pony, swinging a fucking mallet. I had my ponies, and for a time, I was safe, if uninspired and secretly ashamed. It wouldn't last. You can take Sid out of the picture but once you've heard London calling, eventually you're going to have to answer it. Besides, I may have been through with Sid, but he wasn't ready to cash me in.

puberty love

I'd been having some problems at school. Well, the problem was, I'd stopped going to school. It became increasingly difficult to fit in. I felt smarter than my classmates. I may have looked just like them, but their language had become foreign. One morning, I woke up and decided that I'd had enough. I can't really say why. It's almost as if my conformity had been egg-timed. I was a late bloomer and still hadn't gone through puberty but something was stirring. Just like cats and dogs can anticipate an earthquake, I felt harbingers of pubes and zits and a breaking voice. Do you know that feeling you have just before you make an ultimate decision and you know that things could not go any other way? Like just before you break up with someone, before you even broach the subject, you know that you're never going to see that person again? That's essentially what I went through at the end of my first year of high school. I knew I would never be a JAP again. Clothing aside, the change wasn't cultural at first. Believe me, I was still rocking Journey and Styx and Billy Joel on my new Sony

Walkman. It was . . . hormonal. I was poised, biologically, for something different and you know, I could insert any manner of caterpillar-to-butterfly metaphor here but fuck it. It's true. They had me when I was a scared baby, and I was about to aggressively outgrow them.

Sid had gotten himself into some trouble in New York and split for Lexington, Kentucky, in early '83. On holidays, or sometimes late at night, he'd call Susie and coolly ask to speak to "my son." I'd take the phone and listen to him rave.

"Have you ever seen bluegrass? You can drive down the highway and look out at these rolling hills and everything is blue. As far as you can see! This is God's country," Sid rhapsodized over the phone. "God's fucking country." I remembered how my father used to drive the Datsun, whipping the stick shift in pantomime like it was a horse's flank. I had no desire to occupy that passenger seat ever again. But out on "Wrong Island," as I'd started calling it, everything was blue as far as I could see too. I didn't miss the old man and his mayhem. But I couldn't face the prospect of rising, dressing, and inserting myself into my suburban routine for even one more day. I started to feign illness, not wanting to call attention to this encroaching emotional shutdown (which, like everything else, scared me witless). When I couldn't stretch my false cold and flu symptoms any longer, I'd board the school bus, get out in front of the building, and ditch, through the ball field, behind the hedges, and over the chain-link fence. I'd walk all the way down Broadway to the docks, sit on a splintered bench, and watch the black water roll in and out as gulls circled overhead and pigeons strutted underneath. It's hard to describe the hours you pass when you're living inside your head. You don't think about much that's concrete. You replay memories, songs, movie dialogue. Sometimes you just count as high as you can.

* * *

Susie had started dating a Corvette Stingray–driving schoolteacher named Dick. Well dressed in a tweedy sort of way, handsome, and athletic, Dick took her out for long Italian and Chinese dinners . . . to the movies . . . to bed. He didn't get high. He liked fine wine. He knew he wasn't Italian, and he didn't gamble. She was being romanced, distracted. She was happy. I had a few weeks there, during their initial courtship, where I could have committed horrible acts of vandalism and all kinds of antisocial carrying on right there in her living room and she wouldn't have noticed. Eventually, though, a formal letter arrived from the principal informing Mom that I'd missed nineteen school days and inquiring whether or not I'd transferred. I had indeed. I just didn't know where to.

"I want you to talk with Dick," she said calmly after calling me into her room and gesturing to the letter with a look that said, *You know what that is, don't you?* Although she once broke a plastic hairbrush on my ass when I was seven or eight (can't remember the crime, but to this day I don't brush my hair), Susie didn't lose her temper much with me since the divorce. She probably felt guilty about the fights with Sid that I had overheard.

"Why?"

"He's a teacher. If you're having trouble at school, he'll understand."

"I don't wanna talk to Dick. I'm fine."

"You're not fine. You've turned down every single bar mitzvah invitation you've received, Joe."

It was true. The year that I turned 13, there were literally hundreds of bar and bat mitzvahs going down. Somber ceremonies marking Jewish man- and womanhood followed by lavish thematic receptions (Roller disco! Smurfs!). I RSVP'd "I will not attend" to every one and opted out of having one of my own. Susie didn't push it on that point, but snubbing my friends' expensive parties outraged her.

"Well, *Dick* wants to talk to you. He's on his way over."

"Fine, I'll talk to Dick."

"You'll like Dick, Joe."

"Why?"

"He's nothing like Sid."

Dick arrived and it was decided that he'd take me for a drive in the sports car and we'd chat man to man. He *was* nothing like Sid. Rather than coke and sweat and monosodium glutamate and sex, Dick smelled like expensive cologne. He wore brown leather driving gloves. Wool sport coat with suede elbow patches, khaki shirt and trousers, braided brown calfskin belt. Loafers. No socks. Evidently, he tore down the highways blaring Paul Simon on the 'Vette stereo system. The problem was, I needed Sid. Instead, I got . . . Dick.

"I think I know what's going on in your head," Dick informed me. I had no clue myself, shutting down every day as the waters lapped in and out and the birds wondered whether or not it was finally time to swoop down and peck my corpse. But evidently, Dick knew.

"You're worried that I'm gonna take your mom away from you. That she's gonna leave you just like your dad left you. Well, you don't have anything to worry about. I'd never do that."

"Thanks, Dick."

"I couldn't do that even if I wanted to. Your mom really loves you. Do you know that?"

"Yes."

"Do you have any friends at school, Joe?"

"Yes."

"You do?" Dick's incredulity was a bit insulting.

"Yes! I'm very popular." And I was. I was so good at moving with the herd that they rewarded me appropriately. "It's not that," I said, my defenses up.

"Well, what's going on in there?" he asked, laying a gloved palm on my head and mussing my hair. "You can tell me."

"I hate them."

Dick pulled into the neon-lit Sherwood Diner parking lot and we went in and took a booth. He bought me a grilled cheese sandwich and a root beer. Ordered a patty melt for himself and sent it back twice because it was cold, then "still cold." He wanted a scalding melt, that Dick.

"Your mother tells me you're a smart kid."

"I guess."

"She tells me you read the newspaper every morning. That's pretty rare for someone your age."

"I'm worried about the Russians."

"I wouldn't worry about them, Joey."

"Joe. I don't like Joey."

"Sorry, Joe."

"There's never gonna be a nuclear war. And do you wanna know why? I'll tell you why . . . here's the thing . . ."

By the end of the semester, my bags were packed and I was ready to become "Sid's problem" for the summer. He was a little reluctant to welcome me into God's country for any long period of time. He had business to do. Committed to self-employment after his divorce, the guy had developed a real thing for get-rich-quick schemes. While still on the Island, he'd been marketing 14-karat-gold Menudo necklace charms. This after being hipped by his Puerto Rican track buddies that the eternally teenage singing and dancing sensations were ready to blow up *muy grande*. Shortly after making it to the country, he devised a way to spend most of his days at the track and turn a buck or two at the same time. Another all-things-equine-obsessed friend of his had invented a portable horse-leg whirlpool. This nameless thing, which Dad referred to more than once as a "self-contained horse leg fixer-upper that shoots water on the part that's fucked up," was a plastic tub fitted with various PVC tubes and plumbing sockets and jets that pumped water over a racehorse's sore leg muscles. The things retailed for six or seven hundred bucks. According to Sid, they practically "sold themselves."

I found out as soon as I landed that Dad eliminated the middleman by assembling these goofy-looking contraptions himself in the garage of his one-bedroom apartment. He'd get crazy high on glue fumes. Soon, he'd be chasing some tiny flying Pegasus across the bluegrass. This was something to see, especially if you'd been helping and caught a bit of huff yourself. The Steve Miller Band, singing their big hit of the previous year, "Abracadabra," would play on the transistor radio and the old man lunged for Pegasus like every other elusive prize he'd tried to snare in his luckless life. His street-dandy rap was gone, his guard way down. This was Kentucky, it didn't play here anyway. The look on his face was guileless and giddy. He seemed almost innocent.

"I wanna reach out and grab ya."

A 40-year-old man, a long way from home, trying to glue together some dubious wares to sell, momentarily sidetracked by magical Pegasus and everything it represented.

"Abra-abracadabra," he sang along with Steve.

"Maybe we should open the door?" I asked.

"No, he'll get out! Grab it, Leroy! Grab it!"

"Grab what?"

"The fucking horse, Leroy!"

"Don't call me that, Dad."

"That's your name, boy."

"My name's Joe Green."

"That's the name your mother gave you. I wanted to name you Leroy. She wouldn't let me name you Leroy."

"Well, I guess I ought to thank her someday."

"Do you see him, Leroy? Help me grab him."

"Grab what?"

"I wanna reach out and grab him!"

On days when the old man was peddling around the stables, I'd walk into town and shop with the money he'd leave on the table, next to the spare key. Not a lot of money. A couple of dollars, maybe a ten. Enough for a combination breakfast/lunch or some groceries at the Kroger supermarket, maybe a magazine. I didn't know it when I first arrived but Lexington, Kentucky, is a college town. The University of Kentucky, to be exact. This meant that in addition to the racetrack and the swimming pool supply store, where Sid was screwing the homely proprietor in exchange for valves and gaskets and the glue, there was a punk rock record store.

At first, I was reluctant to go in. I heard loud, angry music playing. I could smell incense and must and cat piss. The only record store I'd ever been in up until then was Platterpuss on Central Avenue in Cedarhurst. It was run by a stooped, middle-aged woman and her sickly, always-absent husband. I remember in addition to records, they sold harmonicas and banjos and other folk-related instruments, as if there were a big market for that sort of thing in our socially aware community. Platterpuss's stock, as I can look back now and place in educated context, was a perfect study in substitution. Their reggae section (which was actually labeled "Reggae") consisted of Stevie Wonder's album *Hotter Than July* (which contained the reggae homage "Masterblaster [Jammin]") and Eric Clapton's *461 Ocean Boulevard* (which featured his cover of Bob Marley's "I Shot the Sheriff"). Their rock section had the basics: Elvis, Beatles, Stones, Van Halen. Vinyl Jockey Records on South Limestone Avenue in Lexington, Kentucky, was different. This was God's record store.

The first thing I saw when I walked in was a huge hanging poster for *London Calling* by the Clash. I stepped backward. It took up most of the wall, behind the register, sharing space with promotional posters for bands I'd never heard of: X, Black Flag, the Germs, Adam and the Ants, the Stranglers, Siouxsie and the Banshees, the Buzzcocks, Public Image Limited, Duran Duran, Kate Bush, the Birthday Party, Human Sexual Response, and Depeche Mode. I began to feel dizzy. The second thing I saw was Jane. She was only 18 or 19, with a pretty, cherubic face, but she already had the broken blood vessels along the sides of her nostrils that drunks get in their middle age (I have them now). In each ear, she wore a small, plastic naked Kewpie doll, impaled on a hook. Her hair was naturally blond but ratted high and strewn with thin black silk ribbons. Her T-shirt was also black. It read "The Misfits" across her large breasts, and proclaimed Bullet just above her exposed navel (which was pierced with another Kewpie doll). It depicted the JFK assassination in all its brain-matter-soaked gory glory across her slightly paunchy belly. Her pants were red plaid and super-tight. She chain-smoked and fiddled with a Rubik's cube that had been spray-painted jet black (entirely, yes).

"It's all right, hon. You can come in. I don't bite," she said in a thick local accent.

I took my Walkman headphones off and stepped onto the moldy, old wood floor. Stared at the 10 rows of vinyl, layered in plastic and filed, unalphabetically, in milk crates.

"But watch out for the kitty, hon. He'll bite ya. What's your name?"

"Joe."

"Whatcha listening to, Joe?" she asked, winking.

"Nothing." I was listening to Hall and Oates.

"Well, then, you're in the right place, hon. I'm Jane. Like the song."

"What song?"

" 'Sweet Jane.' "

Nothing from me. If she'd said, "Look at me, I'm Sandra Dee," I could have responded.

" 'Sweet Jane'?" she repeated.

"Oh."

"The Velvet Underground?"

"Who?"

"You've never heard the Velvet Underground?"

"No."

"Lou Reed?"

"Oh. Lou Reed. I know about Lou Reed."

"You're not from around here, are you?"

"No. I'm here visiting my father."

"I could tell. You're a little young for college, and you certainly don't dress like one of us. What do you call that style you're wearing?"

I called it shame! Absolute, undiluted, burning, combed-cotton, pull-it-off-and-run-into-the-woods-naked shame . . . I thought. I felt clownish. Foolish. Do you remember the very first time you felt uncool and couldn't catch up fast enough? This was it. Jane just smiled. She gestured to my black and white striped top. Polo, of course.

"I like the top. Cut off that silly pony and it's very New Wave."

"New Wave?"

"Come here."

I slowly approached the counter. She leaned in. Her breath smelled like beer, cigarettes, and meat. She took my hand. Her palms were soft and wet. She pulled me closer. Took out a pair of scissors. I stepped back.

"What are you doing?"

"Hold still, Joe."

She moved the cutter toward my chest and deftly removed the red polo pony like it was a malignant tumor and she was the world's foremost punk rock surgeon.

"There, that's better."

My hairless nipple poked through the circle. I stared down at it. I wasn't angry. I wasn't even scared anymore. In fact, I was significantly less ashamed.

"I hate those things, don't you?"

I shrugged. "It's just a shirt."

"It's not just a shirt. It's a personal statement. Do you want it to be your personal statement or the Polo guy's?"

"Ralph Lauren."

"Whatever his name is. You should think about that stuff more, Joey."

"I don't like Joey."

"Why not? You've got the same name as Joey Ramone. You should be proud."

"Who?"

"Oh, boy," she sighed sweetly. Then she snatched away my Walkman and investigated the contents.

"You're right, hon. This really is nothin' you're listening to," she said as she casually pulled all the tape ribbon from my plastic Hall and Oates cassette. "But don't you worry. You're in the right place. I think we should start with the basics. Come back here."

I didn't move. I couldn't figure out why someone like Jane was interested in me at all. I felt certain that I had absolutely nothing to offer her. I was a child. Maybe that's what she wanted. She looked like she'd been through something that had left her old and a little beat up.

"It's all right. There's no one else here. Don't be afraid."

"I'm not afraid."

I was afraid. She pulled me around the counter and sat me down on a beanbag chair.

"You walked in on your own. You're looking for something, aren't you?"

"No."

"Joey, are you my friend?"

"No."

"Yes, you are. You are now."

"Okay."

"So why you wanna fib? Tell me the truth. Why are you here?"

"I don't know."

"Well, I know. Couldn't be more obvious."

She mussed my hair.

"Why do you wear your hair like that?"

She spit in her hand, rubbed her palms together, and proceeded to spike my shaggy, feathered cut. "That's better. Now, are you wearing anything under those shorts?"

It seems silly now, but as soon as she asked me that question, I turned and ran out of Vinyl Jockey Records as fast as I could. I ran all the way home to my father's house and spent the rest of the day pacing. Sid walked in around eight and asked me if I was hungry. I told him I felt sick and wanted to go to bed. He asked me if I needed any pills.

"Do you have anything that will make me go to sleep?"

"You wanna sleep?"

"I wanna sleep fast."

"Why?"

"I want today to end and tomorrow to begin."

"You're a fucking strange kid, you know that?" he said as he removed his muddy boots and walked in stained white sweat socks to the john. He emerged with a prescription bottle.

"Here, eat this," he suggested, and handed me a little blue pill.

how soon is never?

"What is it?"

"It's a V."

"A V?"

"It's a fucking Valium. Eat it. You'll sleep. I'm gonna call the Chinks. I'll order you some egg rolls."

"No, I'm not hungry."

"You eat today? You shouldn't take that on an empty stomach."

"Dad?"

"Yeah?"

"Do you know who Joey Ramone is?"

"Who's that?"

"I don't know."

"Are you talking to strangers? I don't want you talking to strangers."

I swallowed the pill and crawled onto the couch, waiting for the Valium to start working. Sid called the Chinks. I couldn't tell Sid, but all I really wanted was for it to be morning. I already missed Jane.

The Valium kept me out until three in the afternoon. I was still in a state of extreme lethargy when I awoke. Still, I hurriedly got dressed in my black Polo T-shirt and blue jeans. I searched the old man's medicine cabinet and found a pair of mustache clippers and a few more V's, which I pocketed. I cut the polo pony off the breast cloth myself, then took a handful of his shaving gel and spiked my hair. I stared at myself in the mirror. I wished my cheeks weren't so chubby. It looked beautiful on Jane but it made me look like a fucking baby. I remember worrying that she'd know I had no hair on my balls.

When I got to Vinyl Jockey Records, Jane was behind the counter, dressed in a T-shirt that said Dead Kennedys.

What's with this girl and the Kennedy clan? I wondered. The Kewpie dolls had been replaced by glow-in-the-dark skulls, and her hair was in a ponytail tied with a silver ribbon. She was smoking and petting the kitty that bit.

"I knew you'd be back. Nice shirt." She smiled and stared at my self-exposed nipple. "Come here."

I walked toward her, now with a little trepidation.

"He don't really bite . . . unless I tell him to," she explained. "This is Iggy, my pussycat."

"Iggy?"

"Yeah, like Iggy Pop."

"Oh."

"You don't know who I'm talking about, do you?"

"No."

"I don't know what I'm going to do with you, Joey!"

Then I said it. I don't know where it came from. From the docks . . . from my want of puberty . . . from the passenger seat pit of Dick's silver fiberglass Corvette rolling off a cliff while Paul Simon sang, "Someone told me it's all happenin' at the zoo."

"Do something with me! Please."

She paused. I was, after all, the boy who'd run away yesterday.

She laughed. Her angel face dimpled up and her eyes glowed mischievously.

"Okay, Joey. Now, you know when I asked you if you were wearing anything under those shorts yesterday, I wasn't trying to get fresh with you. What are ya? Fifteen? Sixteen?"

"Yeah," I lied.

"Well, which is it?"

"Sixteen."

"Yeah, well, I think you're lying to me but I'll be your friend anyway."

"You will?"

how soon is never?

"Look around, Joey. It's dead today. Nobody here but you and me and Iggy. You know how I knew you'd be back?"

"How?" I asked.

"I don't know. I just did."

I moved closer to her without being invited. She put her arm around me. She leaned into my ear. I could feel her warm, smoky breath and the faint touch of her lips as they parted and said, "Hall and Oates are really bad, Joey."

That afternoon, Jane and I ate Valiums and drank beer and smoked cigarettes. I'd never had a drink or a smoke before. I didn't care for the taste of either, but I liked the feeling of lightness, of possibility they both gave me. My senses were numb, my defenses down, my fears out the window. I didn't protest when she drew symbols on my jeans, then told me they stood for anarchy. I protested a little when she informed me that she wanted to put a hole in my ear. A kiss on the cheek and a promise that it would only hurt for a second (chased with another beer) left me helpless. She violated me that afternoon with a Bic-lighter-sterilized safety pin and then removed her left skull and penetrated the hole. I wondered if I was her new pet or something. Maybe she thought I was one of those Kewpie doll earrings come to life.

While this consensual culture rape was going down, she played me the new album by my namesake, Joey Ramone. It was called *Subterranean Jungle*. She asked me what I thought and I told her that I liked the one about "psychotherapy."

"It's better than Hall and Oates, isn't it?"

"Yeah."

"So you like punk now, huh?"

Punk? This was punk? What the hell was she talking about? These were pop songs. As catchy—no, fuck that, catchier than anything Daryl Hall or Lionel Richie wrote. They weren't about death and contagious disease and world war. They were about being young and stupid and bored, like I was. The Ramones left me feeling a rush and a high, like I wanted to stay out all night and break windows, and they were funny! If the Ramones were punk rock, I decided that I could handle Johnny Rotten. He'd been placed in context too.

"Why are you staring like that, Joey? Close your mouth, you'll catch flies."

"This is . . . punk?"

"Yeah! These guys invented punk rock."

"This is . . . *punk?*"

"I think you should splash some water on your face, hon. You're looking a little dizzy."

I could see that Jane was a little zooted herself, and felt proud that I could keep up with her. I'll say it right now: I felt cool and proud. Prouder and cooler still when she threw the two or three customers the cold shoulder in favor of laying all her punk rock maternal attention my way. I was king of the prepubescent studs when she burped and drawled, "I like you, Joey. I wish you were a little older."

"I like you too, Jane."

Sid screamed as I walked into the house, drunk, stoned, ripped, pierced, graffitied, and holding a copy of *Raw Power* by the namesake of Jane's cat.

"What's that shit on your jeans?"

"It's anarchy, Dad."

"Anarchy? What the fuck is that?"

Sid continued, reading my jeans.

"Did you join some fucking devil cult or something? What happened to your shirt? Take that shit out of your ear. Take that shit out of your hair!"

What was going on here? Sid was acting like Susie. Mr. dick-swinging/coke-snorting/racetrack-strutting Superfly was scared! This was some powerful shit, punk rock. His deep voice, with its Canarsie accent . . . it was quavering.

"Who the fuck did this to you?"

"Lou Reed."

"Where the fuck is he? I wanna talk to him!"

"I don't know, Dad."

He sat down on the couch and stared at me. Ten long minutes passed before he said anything. Finally, he turned his eyes to the floor, lit a cigarette, and looked up again.

"I had a bad day. I almost had a sale. The guy was writing out the check! He had the fucking pen in his hand."

"I'm sorry."

"I was gonna take you out for dinner," he said sadly.

"That's all right. We can eat in." I moved closer to him. He actually moved away. What had I become? I'd liked it before, but without Jane it felt lonely. I was repellent. I realized then that you really needed a gang to pull off this punk stuff.

"I can't take you anywhere looking like that anyway."

"Dad?" I asked, putting my arm on his shoulder. This was the first time I'd touched him since I was a child.

"Yeah?"

"Can I have a cigarette?"

Soon my old man came around. He had no choice, really. He'd never been a disciplinarian before and had no real interest in becoming one. And every morning, despite his warnings to stay away from "that fucking devil cult," I'd go into town and sit with Jane as she worked. I'd come home with a new hairstyle every day. Sid actually grew to like the attention I'd get when we'd go out to eat. He'd even take me with him to the track in an effort to spark conversation with prospective whirlpool customers. Would even deign to put away the tubs and the glue to take me to the record store because it had the word *jockey* in its name. Jane thought Sid was a first-class villain. To her, he must have seemed the embodiment of everything her generation was trying to bury. He was a swingin'-single, coke-tootin', polyester-rockin' '70s throwback with a stack of Fleetwood Mac vinyl. She actually laughed aloud when I first pushed him through the shop's doorway. I laughed with her and felt guilty.

"You're the devil worshiper who's fucking with my son's head, huh?"

"That's right."

He nodded toughly, then shook his head in disgust as he scanned the room.

"You better be careful. Anything happens to him, they'll never find you. Understand?"

"Sure do!" she chirped, then shot him a flirty wink. God, I loved her. I crawled under her armpit as Sid backed away with a curt "I'm gonna wait in the car." Iggy hissed at him as he left. We had a gang. He had none.

If the devil sent Jane to shake up my world, that was nothing compared with what he really had in store for me. I'd been feeling pain in my bones for weeks now. I figured it was a by-product of all the pills and booze and nicotine ingestion. It wasn't. One night in August 1983, I went to sleep bald with a short and chubby body. I woke up four inches taller, several pounds thinner, and a whole lot hairier. I swear it happened almost overnight. My entire frame had elongated. I couldn't believe it. The first thing I did was run to the bathroom to experiment with myself. I jerked off excitedly, thinking about removing Jane's black clothes, laying her down on a Union Jack–draped bed, and penetrating her with my brand-new penis. I did this for an hour and a half until I came into my raw hands.

"Oh, my fucking God!" Jane exclaimed as I proudly walked through the door with a pocketful of Valiums and my new body under a Black Flag *Damaged* T-shirt.

"I can cum!" I shouted, not realizing that unlike most days, Vinyl Jockey was full of customers. Iggy purred. Jane cackled. I blushed. Everybody else either laughed to themselves or pretended not to hear me. We swallowed the pills down with beer, and Jane spent that afternoon just staring at me like I'd grown a second but extremely handsome head. That night, she took me out to a local college bar called Sticks.

"You're not gonna hear any Styx there, hon," she kidded. Our goal was to see if I could indeed pass for a young adult. I got through the door without being carded. I was nearly six feet tall and looked like a punk. Sticks had peanuts in large bowls and discarded shells all over the floor. They also had a Bally Kiss pinball machine and a jukebox full of punk rock. Jane ordered round after round of Jack Daniel's, which we downed one after the other. We toasted my new pubes each time until she and I were both plastered.

"I wanna see 'em!" she slurred.

She dragged me into the bathroom and pulled down my jeans. I modestly held tightly to my drawers, but she was stronger than I was, even with my new muscles.

"Wow! Those are pubes all right."

The transformation had hit so fast and forcefully that I'd already sprouted nearly twice as many of the fair brown hairs as I'd had earlier. Jack Daniel's! It'll put hair on your nuts. She pushed me against the wall and kissed me. I could taste the bourbon that had temporarily pickled her tongue. I liked feeling a tongue in my mouth. A kiss, your first kiss, shrinks your vast, strange world down to something you can touch and put in the pocket of your jeans. It instantly makes you realize you're part of the human race, where before you felt like some kind of lonely hermit.

"That's all you're gonna get, hon."

She laughed and wiped her lips.

"I'm too old for you. It wouldn't be proper."

Jane was only seven years older than I was. If I was *only* seven years older than the girls I sleep with now, I might not feel so filthy all the time.

Proper? I thought at the time. *What happened to punk rock freedom?* I wanted more.

"Can I see you too?"

"What?"

"I wanna see," I demanded.

"You've never, have you?" she asked sweetly.

"No. Just my dad's porno," I slurred, and slipped my trembling fingers into the loops of her black denim skirt.

She laughed and unbuttoned herself.

"Well, that doesn't count, hon. Those aren't real women anyway. They're space aliens."

"I know." I burped.

"You can look but you're not touchin' nothin'!"

She opened her red lace bra and exposed her large, pale breasts, with faint blond hairs dotting her erect nipples. I, of course, touched them immediately . . . and got a hard smack in the face.

"What'd I say, fucker?"

"I'm sorry."

"Watch it!"

She laughed and shimmied out of her skirt. Pulled down her black cotton panties and stood before me.

"There. These are my tits, and this is my pussy. That's your new dick. Happy?"

"Yeah."

"Are you talking to me or my pussy?"

I lifted my head away from her magnetic field and stared into her half-closed eyes.

"Wow!"

how soon is never?

It was all I could say. Even now, when I first see a new one, somewhere in my head, I say, *Wow!* Who doesn't? They're a wow, aren't they? Pussies.

There was an abrupt knock at the door.

"Shit, pull your pants up now. You're gonna land me in jail, Joey," she said as she fumbled with her bra. We walked out of the bathroom past a shit-faced punk in an army jacket. He was itching to drain himself of cheap beer.

"What's up, guy?" he asked as I passed.

"What's up?" I echoed confidently. I'd just seen my first pussy and been accepted as some kind of brother by an actual punk rocker. It had been another really good day!

Jane drunk-drove me home and peeled out wildly after a quick kiss on the lips.

"Don't tell no one about this," she warned.

"Okay, Jane."

"And stop smiling, fucker!"

Sid was passed out on the couch. He'd been at the track all day and had no idea that he was now the parent of a full-grown punk. I shook him awake gently. He stared up at me like I was some kind of fully mature home invader.

"Who the fuck are you?" he mouthed sleepily before rolling over and falling asleep again. I didn't have a chance to respond, but for the first time in my young life I knew the answer.

gudbuy t'jane

I'd never seen Sid worry about a thing. If he ever did, he never let on. It was his shield, the by-product of acting cooler than you actually are for decades. But when summer was dog-daying it and it came time for me to return to New York, he began to openly fret about exactly whom or what he was sending home to his ex-wife.

He'd recently sold a horse whirlpool to a loaded Saudi Arabian horse owner's extremely gullible trainer. The poor mark was no match for an old Canarsie street rap. Sid was a little flush, so, with uncharacteristic concern for popular decorum, he bribed me into getting a very short haircut.

I guess he wanted something Jane couldn't spike or dye. So I took the money and instructed the barber to shave my head. Sid said I looked like I'd been in Auschwitz. Jane said it made me look like Ian MacKaye, the lead singer of the D.C. punk band Minor Threat. Then she played me their EP *In My Eyes*. I loved it and congratulated myself for making a damn good deal with Dad. But Sid wasn't finished. A few days before I was set to depart, he sat me down in the living room and informed me that he'd splurged on two front-row tickets to see my old favorite Phil Collins at the Rupp Arena out in Louisville. I informed him with more than a bit of insouciance that I simply could not feel it coming in the air tonight anymore.

"What do you mean? You love Phil! He's the fucking man!" Sid yelled, drumming out a backbeat against the chipped wood coffee table with a rolled-up *Daily Racing Form.*

"Abacab, doo doo doo, you really care. Doo doo doo doo, you're really there," he sang, botching those super-insightful lyrics.

"I don't like him anymore."

"Well, why the fuck not?" The old man was crushed. I was somehow personally insulting him *and* Phil.

"He's retarded, Sid."

"Am I your father?"

"Yeah."

"Am I your fucking father?"

"Yes."

"So you fucking call me Dad."

"Fine."

"I know I haven't been around much, but I'm always gonna be your father. Your mom and I made you and I'm telling you, Phil Collins isn't retarded. You know who's retarded? *You're* retarded. You come off the plane a normal kid, maybe you got a few problems, so I take you in, I feed you . . . but I still gotta go out and make some money. Right? Right?"

"Right, Dad."

"And now you're a retard! I turn my back on you to go make some money so you can eat and now I gotta send you back to your mother a fucking drug addict retard Auschwitz boy who worships the fucking devil and doesn't like Phil Collins!"

"I guess."

"She's not gonna recognize you. You're too fucking skinny."

"Skinny is good!" I hated being chubby.

"You don't look like yourself."

"That's good!"

"What good? You know that fucking bitch is gonna blame this on me!"

"It's not your fault. It's puberty, Dad!"

"Nah, it's not puberty. It's those drugs you're on, and all that devil shit you're listening to. I should have been more of a discipliner."

"Disciplinarian."

"Shut the fuck up!"

"Fine."

"I can hit you, you know. I'm your father. I'm allowed."

"I know."

"If you listened to Phil Collins, you wouldn't have those pimples all over your face, I'll tell you that!"

"*It's puberty!*"

Yeah, I screamed. He'd hit a sore spot. Just like a hangover, the giddy delirium of my vagina-inspecting, bone-stretching transformation had produced some truly embarrassing side effects. I'd sprouted a few die-hard zits in the weeks since. Jane called them "perfectly natural" and showed me photos of Sid Vicious with a face full of big red pimples. ("They call them 'spots' in England," she said.) She even let me pop one of hers into the ladies' room mirror at Vinyl Jockey. It wasn't quite sex but it was legal, and to this day, I haven't experienced anything quite as intimate. But Sid really kicked the dog with that one. I exploded. I foamed. My red zits disappeared as my cheeks flushed up with rage.

"Fuck you and fuck Phil Collins and fuck this fucking stupid place!"

I threw his *Racing Form* up in the air, scattering the pages, each one neatly circled with pony-handicapping shorthand.

how soon is never?

"Don't you use that fucking language around here!" he spat back. "I'll shove your fucking head down the fucking toilet. Show you where you fucking learned to talk that shit. You hear me, boy?"

I got up and pulled my suitcase from under the fold-out couch.

"What the fuck are you doing?"

"I'm leaving now."

"Where do you think you're going?"

"Jane's."

"Oh yeah? With what? You have no money."

"You just gave me a hundred dollars for the haircut!"

"Shit!"

He threw a beer against the wall. It didn't shatter. He picked it up and smashed it on the table. It still didn't break. He yelled "Shit!" again, this time raging at his own paternal impotence or the resilience of the bottle glass or the failure of Phil Collins to keep me under his Abacabby spell.

"You walk out of here and I'm not your father. Do you understand?"

"Yeah."

"You walk out of here and you got no father. I'm telling you!"

"Fine."

"You walk out of here and you can tell everyone you're an orphan."

"I'm not an orphan. I have a mother."

"She's not your mother!"

"What?"

"All right, she is your mother, but you walk out of here and—"

I walked out of there.

I could hear him still trying to break the bottle as I left. Clunk. Bang. Ping. "Shit!" Nothing shattered.

*　　*　　*

It was late but after a quick pay phone call, Jane picked me up in town. She was dressed down . . . undone. She wore a Pep Boys T-shirt that said Manny, Moe, and Jack on it and was covered with hair dye stains. She had on ratty sweatpants and flip-flops but still looked beautiful to me, even without the punk rock adornment.

"Now, you can stay with me, but you're sleeping on the couch."

"Why?"

"Because if you sleep in the bed, something will happen, and you're just too young, hon."

"It's not because I'm ugly?"

"You're not ugly. Shut up."

"These zits won't go away, Jane."

"They'll go away when you're a little older."

"Great. It's like everything I want is gonna happen when I'm a little older."

"No, it won't, hon. You better believe that too."

Jane was not her usual happy, drunken, punk rock wild self that night. She had the blues.

"I wanna sleep with you now. What if there's no tomorrow?" I asked.

"What if there is?"

"What if there isn't?"

"I'll tell you what, hon."

"What?"

I was excited. I smelled another bargain. I probably had a hard-on, but I had one every 30 seconds back then. I have one every 30 days now.

"If you can produce proof that there's no tomorrow," she continued, her voice too heavy and sad to be sly, "I'll let you do whatever you want with me, Joey. You can do whatever you want to my li'l old body, and you can run and tell everybody. Tell your crazy daddy. Tell the police."

She frowned. I was pissed.

"Aren't we supposed to live like today's the last day of our lives?"

"Yeah. Sure."

"What about Patti Smith? What about Johnny Rotten? What about him?"

"What *about* Johnny Rotten?"

"He said there's no future. He said it! You played it for me."

She slowed the car down and turned carefully down her street, stopping at the stop sign we'd blown through a hundred times that summer.

"He was just singin', hon. Believe me, if there weren't no future, Johnny Rotten would be as upset about the whole thing as everyone else."

"But what about punk rock, Jane?"

"I'm not gonna sleep with you cause of punk rock."

The rest of the drive was quiet.

"Here we are," she said flatly as we pulled into her weedy driveway.

Unlike my father's store-bought, cheap but neat furnishings, Jane's apartment was cramped with thrift-store furniture. A bulbous orange lamp with a broken white shade glowed in the corner. An overstuffed canary-yellow velvet couch with cigarette burn holes was pushed up against the wall, facing a round glass coffee table. Stained *Happy Days*–themed drapes with cartoon Potsies and Ralph Malfs and Fonzies with quotations like "Aaay!" and "Sit on it!" kept the light out, night and day. Records were piled up everywhere, mostly punk or kitsch by Jackie Gleason's orchestra or Jim Nabors or Sammy Davis Jr. Awful paintings of whales and clowns and big-eyed bear cubs hung on the smoke-yellowed walls. Iggy the cat's smell was thick in the air despite an array of scented candles and a big incense burner. Jane placed my bag on the couch and yawned a real dead yawn. Something vital had been drained from her. I prayed it was temporary. I wondered if it was my fault. I just wanted to drink some beers and listen to *Germ Free Adolescents* by X-Ray Spex and make out like we'd done a dozen times in the Vinyl Jockey parking lot or the dusty, cozy stockroom. Now that she'd finally allowed me into her home, I was keen to do the same, then see where it went from there. I hoped it would lead to her bed.

It wasn't gonna happen.

"The couch is pretty comfortable if you look out for the loose spring. You'll find it. Get some sleep, Joey."

She pulled off her flip-flops and padded wearily into her bedroom without another word. I sat down on the couch and stared at the pile of books and magazines on the coffee table. There were *Vogues*, *Cosmopolitans*, lots of supermarket fashion magazines with tips about applying makeup and how to keep your men. Jane was a good person. She'd taken me in because she hated my father and knew I had nowhere else to go in that strange city. But she didn't want me to see things like this. Normal shit. She wanted to keep living the illusion that she was free and wild and full of piss and anarchy when she was really just an alcoholic girl who worked in a college town, watching students come and go every semester. Maybe she'd fallen in love with one or two of them before. Had she watched too many of them graduate, then move away to the city and leave her consulting these magazines, wondering what she did wrong? I walked to her refrigerator and opened it. Beer. Cheese. Coca-Cola. More normal shit. I grabbed a beer and popped it open, then walked toward her closed door and knocked on it. There was no answer. I knocked again.

"Jane?"

"I'm sleeping, hon," she said weakly. I could her the rickety sobs in her throat.

I turned the knob and walked in. She was naked, half covered in a ratty cherry-red terry-cloth robe. Her knees were pulled up to her belly and her thick, pretty feet were splayed out, exposing her rough heels and chipped toenail polish. The bedroom also smelled like a scented candle . . . and cat piss.

"Did I do something wrong?" I asked.

"No."

"Then why are you crying?"

"I can't tell you."

"Why not?"

"Cause you'll try to get in my pants if I do."

"You're not wearing pants, Jane."

"Fuck off!"

She pushed me away harder. I could see her nipples as she shoved me. I tried to cover my 155th hard-on of the hour.

"I'm trying to lighten things up. That's all. Come on!"

"Don't. Just go to bed. Then go back to New York, okay?"

Go back to New York? What the hell was happening? We'd fantasized for days on end about schemes that would enable me to stay.

"I don't want to go back to New York. I want to stay here with you."

"I want you to stay here with me too, Joe."

"You do?"

"God, you really don't understand anything, do you?"

It never occurred to me, not once, that Jane was carrying on like this because she was genuinely pissed that she couldn't sleep with me or be my girlfriend. That even though she'd already cruised in and out of puberty years ago, the fact that I was about to turn fourteen was a major bummer for her too.

"Well, why can't I?"

She rose slightly and raised her voice, then took it down to a defeated whisper again.

"Cause you're too fucking young! And you don't belong here."

"I don't belong anywhere."

"Yes, you do. You belong in New York with your momma and your friends."

"I don't like them. And they don't like me."

"It doesn't matter. That's just the way things have to be."

I didn't dare bring up punk rock again, but in my head, I thought that there was something wrong with this logic. Hadn't protopunk Jerry Lee Lewis married his 13-year-old cousin because they were in love and fuck the world? It would be another few years before I grasped the concept of a poseur and how crucial elements of the pose were to any punk's very survival. I was just too fucking pure. I believed it all. I was Lexington's most authentic fucking punk and I didn't even know it. And Jane . . . she might as well have worked down at the supermarket. It was the same gig. Just louder and more colorful. It made me sad. I felt less alone when I didn't have her in my life. Relating to one person is much more dangerous than not relating to anybody at all. You never get let down the other way. I swear, this memory of Jane, who is probably married and fat with three healthy kids and the beige Volvo full of baby toys and Celine Dion CDs, is one of the reasons why I remain single. She was my first real love, my first taste of sex, and my first disappointment. I kissed her on the cheek and she pushed me away. I got up and walked toward the door. I wonder now if these idealistic little girls who leave my apartment in the morning are disappointed that I'm no longer pure. There's cheese and beer in my fridge. There are GQs and Esquires on my coffee table too, with advice on how to be a fucking man and keep a woman happy. I could confess that for all my getting stoned and running around, I sometimes consult their advice columns and surveys. I could tell them that I was . . . and I could pinpoint for them where the very first crack began, right there in Jane's stinky bed.

"Turn out the light on your way out."

how soon is never?

That was the last thing Jane ever said to me in person. I picked up my bag, walked to the door, looked back once, and tried to take a mental snapshot of her feet. They really were beautiful feet.

I would like to say that I contemplated life and its many conflicting dimensions and troubling ironies as I walked back to Sid's place. I didn't. I cried my eyes red like a self-pitying little baby bitch boy. By streetlight, I bawled and bawled and bawled through the strange city, thinking self-pitying teenage shit like *Everybody I ever love is gonna leave me*. This, of course, segued into self-righteous shit like *Nobody in this world is gonna get what they want because they don't have the courage of their convictions like I do now*. Even though I no longer have anything resembling any kind of courage of conviction, I still have walks and thoughts like that when I'm drunk and I can't afford cab fare. I don't have to tell you it's no longer sweet.

Sid was surprised to see me in the morning, sleeping on the couch with my newly thin cheekbones slathered with tinted Clearasil. But being Sid, he kept his cool.

"You hungry?"

"No."

"You should eat."

"Yeah."

"You use too much of that stuff. It's gonna dry out your skin," he said, gesturing to my caked benzoyl peroxide mask.

"It makes the pimples go away faster."

"You in a rush?" he laughed meekly.

"Yeah."

He sat down on the couch. Touched my leg, then pulled his hand away awkwardly.

"Why don't you get cleaned up? We'll go for breakfast."

"Fine."

"You know, your mother always used to say that. What the fuck does that mean, 'fine'?"

"It means 'okay,' I guess."

"You look more like her than you look like me now. You're all bony. Your mom was bony."

He often spoke about her like she was dead.

"I guess."

"You're still my son, though."

I went with Dad to see Phil Collins at the Rupp Arena that night. We sat in the front row. Dad bought me a T-shirt (in a tribute to Johnny Rotten, who once famously vandalized a Pink Floyd T-shirt, I'd later scrawl "I Hate" above his silk-screened bald pate). That night Phil wore a cheesy white suit and sang all his big hits. The crowd in the sold-out arena ate it up. Sid copped a loose joint off a super-stoned teenage girl in an acid-wash Loverboy jean jacket and proceeded to get super-stoned himself, whooping loudly as Phil did his thing. Rising and holding his lighter aloft with 19,999 others when Phil sang "In the Air Tonight." I sat in my chair the whole time, arms folded. I thought about Jane. I worried about being the one holdout there. I was about to go home to a place even more homogeneous than this rock concert. Not only did I feel different, I looked different. And I thought differently. I wondered what that meant for my future. The only thing that felt familiar was the numbness of being alone again.

belligerent ghouls run long island schools

I would have gone back to public school. It never even occurred to me that I might do better in a different academic environment. I thought, *School is school, just like a kick in the balls is a kick in the balls.* Was there any way to sweeten the experience? Susie and Dick had been conspiring while I was away stretching my bones. In addition to foreign policy, Dick knew much about education. It was Dick who picked me up at the airport. At first, he ignored me when I deplaned and walked through the gate, looking for Susie's face. I was still buzz-cut and dressed in tight black jeans, which Jane had showed me how to shrink so they fit my legs like a second skin. I had on combat boots from the army surplus store and Jane's precious glowing skull in my ear. A Motorhead T-shirt clung to my skinny torso. To be fair, I walked right past Dick once too. I couldn't figure out why he was there instead of my mother. Dick didn't seem nonplussed by my appearance. He'd probably seen worse on the job. I was a little disappointed.

"We've enrolled you in Woodmere Academy," he told me

flatly once I was loaded into the 'Vette. "It's a small private school with an excellent reputation. The student body is extremely creative."

"Who's we?"

"Your mother and I."

Susie nearly fainted when she saw me. When I grabbed her arm and said, "Mom, how are you?" she responded with a series of "Oh, my gawds" and some long, shaky hugs. After she splashed some water on her face and gave me a meal, I was taken into the living room and given the news in full.

"Who decided that I was going to transfer? Don't I have any say?"

"Dick and I decided. We've been doing a lot of thinking about your future, Joe."

"Since when is Dick making plans for me?"

"Well, Joe, Dick is living with us now. We're engaged."

"Oh. Listen, if you're going to tell me that I have an adopted Asian baby brother waiting for me upstairs, I'm gonna have to have a smoke before I meet the kid, okay?"

Dick sat down next to me and put his arm on my shoulder, then reached into my back pocket and pulled out my pack of cigarettes.

"You can't smoke in here, son."

He continued, "I know this is a lot to take in, Joe, but you don't have to swallow it all in one day. You've got ten days."

"Ten days?"

"You have to report for orientation on September first," Susie warned.

"Woodmere Academy? What is it, like a military school?"

"It's a regular school. Just like Lawrence High School. Dick and I just thought you'd fit in better with people who were more like you."

"You mean weird people?"

"No."

"Tall people?"

"Joe!"

"What kind of people, Mom?"

"Creative people."

"So it's an art school?"

"No, it's just a really good school," Dick interrupted. "There's nothing to worry about."

"Nothing?"

"No, nothing. Well . . ."

"Well, what?"

"There *is* a dress code."

Woodmere Academy was really only fifteen minutes away from my house by bus. It was a massive brick building situated atop a squat green hill. It was not an art school, nor was it "arty," as Susie and Dick swore (their self-comforting new description for anything I did that was infuriating). It did have a small art room. I entered it accidentally on my very first day, not in hopes of enrolling in an art class but rather to find a place to artfully rend my school uniform to shreds before orientation began. My summer adventure had taught me that the most severe punks were remarkably scared and insecure. The more frightened and awkward they were inside, the more garishly hard their exterior became. These fucked-up kids were like bugs scurrying around under the thick, bright shells they'd evolved. The disorienting colors telegraphed the message "Don't eat me, I'm poisonous" to would-be predators. I was terrified of being eaten. The navy blue woolens that we were made to wear did nothing to indicate to predators that I was, in fact, very poisonous. So I ducked away to quickly evolve a harder shield. The art room wasn't too arty either. It was lit by fluorescent tracks and heated with a hissing, old radiator. Paint chips were peeling off the wall. The piss-yellow shelves were stocked with dusty canisters of tempera paint and paste.

I used the paste to spike the hair on my spinning, sweaty head, which, like the hair everywhere else on my spinning, sweaty body, had grown back quickly and thickly. A few long Formica tables and orange Eames chairs occupied the white linoleum floor space. There was a crummy stereo system in the far corner. The room seemed like it had originally been designed to harbor some kind of young salon society. Then, artwork was constructively criticized while music played and the enlightened student body of Woodmere Academy unbuttoned their white collars and loosened their black-and-gold ties for a few hours. I could almost hear the chatter of long-graduated students. Now, everything was covered with a quarter inch of dust. As soon as I walked out into the hall, it became apparent that these enlightened souls now profited little from their forefathers' artistic visions. The institution's intelligent student body, just like the same type of kids in public school, were an oppressed minority. They were scrawny and pimply and virginal and routinely tortured by . . . JAPs. These JAPs wore blue wool suits here but they were otherwise identical to the ones I'd left behind. The only thing that distinguished these private-school JAPs was that they seemed even more ornery and intolerant of any kind of physical weakness or lack of confidence. I witnessed an example of this almost immediately. As I walked out toward the front steps to try to sneak a cigarette, I watched a short, weedy kid named Jerome being strangled by a jocky JAP named Mitchell. I knew this because Jerome was screaming, "Please, Mitchell, it hurts!"

"Hey, welcome back, Jerome. How was your summer?"

When Mitchell asked this, I could tell that being facetious was taxing his minimal intellect for all it was worth. The way he smiled made me want to hurt him. He was proud of himself for being clever. He wasn't smart or funny. He deserved to get hurt for trying to lay claim to wit. After all, wit was all the weird, smart kids had. I wanted to smash his skull with the heel of my combat boot. I just watched. I was all alone. If I had been with Jane, who had no tolerance for bullying whatsoever, we would have broken that shit up, gotten our four clenched fists bloody if we had to. And we would have found his silver Porsche later and keyed it good.

"It was okay. Please stop!"

Why did he even answer? It wasn't going to turn into pleasant conversation. They weren't catching up.

"You suck on a lotta dicks over the summer, Jerome?"

"I don't suck dicks. Stop!"

"I bet those braces feel really good on a dick."

"I'm getting them off next week. Please stop!"

It was awful. Worse because this bill of goods had been sold to me by Susie and Dick as an alternative. Scared and angry and now guilty for my cowardice, I retreated to the art room once again and painted Jock Nazis Fuck Off! and the symbol for anarchy on the back of my new blue school jacket. Shorthand for "Don't eat me."

Mr. Bertel, whom I called Bert because of his pointy head, pallor, and thick unibrow (he resembled the famous Muppet), was Woodmere Academy's headmaster. He didn't notice me as I emerged from the art room and filed into the auditorium with its cheap velour stadium seating for 300 and chintzy gold-sprayed Greek columns on either side of the elevated stage with its wood-paneled podium. I kept my head down and prepared to climb the stage, shake his hand, and hear him announce my name like he'd announced the name of every other new student that morning. As I found my place on line, I saw some blond girl with permed hair and a bobbed nose point at me and turn to her friend. Her thick Long Island patois was shrill and very audible.

"Uch, what's he been doin? Finguh-painting?"

"Look at his hay-uh!" her identical-looking friend shouted.

I kept my head low and pressed my back against the chest of the horrified kid behind me. He was an H, I guess. The F's were up. The G's were next.

"Fellow Wolverines, welcome Andrew Feld!" Bert boomed.

Wolverines as in the Woodmere Academy Wolverines. The wolverine was our school mascot, and that was how we apparently referred to ourselves at moments of great pageantry such as orientation. The crowd applauded and accepted Andrew Feld, and the kid just beamed. He was now a proud Wolverine. I later learned that the scientific name for the wolverine is *Gulo gulo*, "glutton." It's a truculent rodent, so named for its unabated consumption of garbage.

"Wolverines, meet Mr. Joe Green."

I stepped up and held out my hand for him to shake. I could hear the beginning of the question well in his throat like a vaudevillian loogie. "Mean Joe Greene?" He was gonna ask it. He was. It had been over ten years. I knew when they were about to ask it. I had Spidey sense for that shit. Which is why I felt good preemptively striking his ass. I turned my back to the audience and displayed my colored shell. *Don't eat me!*

"Mr. Green? What is that?"

I paused. I couldn't look at the crowd. I only stared into Bert's eyes and smiled.

"What's what?"

"What's that on your jacket, Mr. Green?"

"What's it say?"

"I know what it says, Mr. Green. I can read."

The crowd started shifting and whispering.

"Get off this stage," he fumed.

"Okay."

"*Now*, Mr. Green. I'll see you in my office when this is over."

how soon is never?

He shuffled some papers at the podium, calmed that pesky last nerve, the one he was counting on for summer vacation and early retirement, and evenly announced . . .

"Greenberg. Adam Greenberg."

Bert was Wolverine-izing his third Greenberg by the time I'd fought my way out of the auditorium, pivoting and weaving away from each curious monkey finger as it tried to spin me around and get a load of my defiled jacket. I'd later discover that this sensation was not unlike holding your own in a mosh pit.

I was punished with dozens of detentions as the weeks went on. Every morning, I'd willfully violate the dress code and every afternoon I'd be dumped in with the vandals and the pot smokers. These kids considered me soft-core. I was only making fashion statements. Like them, Woodmere Academy couldn't expel me because my tuition check had cleared and they'd probably spent the money on a surplus of navy blue felt *W*'s for the football team . . . who, I admit, scared the shit out of me. Yeah, I know that's funny. Cause of my name, right? Funny.

In addition to the squarehead JAPs, the Wolverines footballing fraternity included the academy's few black students. They were bused in from nearby towns like Inwood and Far Rockaway on athletic scholarships. There were some black girls there too. On academic scholarships, I guess. Some of them were just fucking gorgeous. All of them called me "Big Head." I think it was affectionate. Sometimes they'd ask about the bands I was listening to on my Walkman and when I'd jabber on about Adam Ant or Siouxsie Sioux, they'd get curious and want to check them out. After a few songs, they'd hand the machine back to me like it was a turd. Once in a while the exchange would consist of me listening to their machines and hearing early freestyle tapes from Doug E. Fresh and Big Daddy Kane. They'd try to teach me to pop and lock and breakdance, and they'd flash their warm brown eyes at me before huddling together and laughing as I flailed my gangly limbs against the beat y'all.

"Go, Big Head! Go, Big Head!"

Football practice coincided with my detention, and the jocks and I were sprung around the same time in the late afternoon. They were amped after a few hours of crushing heads out on the field. The sight of me, a skinny, spotty non-Wolverine in a *Give 'Em Enough Rope* Clash T-shirt, wearing his hallowed school tie around his neck like a noose, was just a red flag for the bulls. I did my best not to cross them. There'd been an unspoken fatwa ever since my little orientation stunt. I'd turn myself into a running blur when I saw them coming. On most days, I'd hide in the art room and wait for them to climb into their expensive cars. It was on one of these desperate afternoons that I met John Robertson, and in one unexpected flash, I was no longer alone.

John was a tall, thickly built kid with long brown hair. He looked about 25 (he was 15) and goddamn if he wasn't dressed in a black gabardine trench coat, torn-up black jeans, and black army boots with gold laces. Upon closer inspection, I realized he'd shredded the Woodmere Academy tie and laced up his combat boots with them. I didn't know what to say. What do you say when you meet someone who is going to be your best friend no matter if he turns around and says, "Hitler was all right with me," or "I have the head of an infant girl in the pocket of this black trench coat, wanna play catch"? I didn't care, especially after I noticed that he was actually making art . . . out of the stereo system while it was playing *Chronic Town,* the first R.E.M. EP.

"Who's that singing?"

"R.E.M." He said it in a weary voice, pitched higher and reedier than his build would suggest. He didn't look up.

"It's good."

He put down his paintbrush and waited for the pretty silver filigrees on the black Sanyo casing to dry. He stared at me, clocking that day's violation, a promo shirt for X's new *More Fun in the New World,* one of the few remaining pieces of punk rock booty that Susie hadn't succeeded in "losing" in the laundry (my enrollment at WA coincided with her realization that Sylvia had a washer and a dryer down in her dungeon). I'd also taken pains to fasten about 700 safety pins to the entire left side of my uniform and knotted my school tie around my right arm, Johnny Rotten style.

He smiled. I felt proud.

"I like it. Maybe you could tape it for me? I have a tape."

I pulled my Walkman out and practically shoved a blank TDK at him.

"It's got Oingo Boingo on it but this is a lot better. It's great!"

"Yeah. If you wait around for me to finish, I'll tape it for you. I'll put *Murmur* on the other side. It's longer . . . and even better."

"Okay. Cool. Thanks."

I sat down and watched as he went back to painting with a focus that I immediately wanted too. He made it look vital. When satisfied with his added details, he cued up my tape and rewound his, hit dub, then returned to his work and continued to ignore me.

"I'm Joe."

Nothing.

"Joe Green."

More of the same.

"Like Mean Joe Greene." Believe me, I only used that myself in moments of serious desperation to connect.

"Who's Mean Joe Greene?" he finally replied without turning around.

"Nobody." I smiled, full up with real joy, like Santa Claus had walked in and announced, "Guess what? Nobody will ever get sick and nobody will be sad and none of us will ever die. Ever again! Ha ha ha!" A little glimpse of the impossible.

"I'm John."

"Hey, John."

"I'm Joe."

"You just said that."

I walked over to the Sanyo and turned it up while he was still adorning it.

"You can't really understand what he's singing," I observed bluntly as this new sensation called the voice of Michael Stipe. Why hadn't Jane exposed me to this too? I'd conclude that R.E.M. had been left off my sonic curriculum because it wasn't punk. It was what would come to be called "college rock" and it probably reminded her of all those bookish boys who'd broken her heart before I came and went.

It sounded as if he were singing *"Weeeeeeeel stumble through the yard. Weeeeeel stumble through the ABC. Faaaaaah-thatrainggggggguhhhhhhhh!"*

"You know, I really can't understand what he's saying. D-Do you understand what he's singing?" I stammered, worried that he actually did.

"No."

"Oh. Cool."

"That's why I like it."

We listened to *Murmur*, which was indeed longer . . . better. When he finished the dubbing, he popped out the tape and handed it to me. I quickly jammed it into my Walkman as a gesture of gratitude. If he acknowledged it, it didn't register on his face. Who was this kid? He got up off his knees and screwed on the cap of his paint and instead of returning it to the case of cheap tempera, he carefully pocketed it.

"Is that your paint?"

"Yeah. It's my paint. They don't have paint like this here. You can't get paint like this here."

"Oh."

"You can only get it in the city."

"Do you go to the city a lot?"

"Yeah."

"Cool. For . . . for what?"

"What do you mean?"

"Why do you go to the city?"

"Have you looked around?" he asked. He was arrogant. I liked him even more and wished I'd gone into the city . . . for paint, for anything. Manhattan. In one instant he'd made it seem incredibly attractive. I'd only ever equated it with field trips to the Central Park Zoo and holiday outings to Radio City Music Hall and Lincoln Center when I was small.

"Why are you doing that anyway?" I asked, inspecting his work. This made his posture stiffen a bit. I knew then that he was alone and flailing a bit as well . . . that he was glad I was there too. I felt better.

"Why not?"

He walked over to the sink and started washing his hands.

"I'm gonna have to look at it every day. It might as well be something I wanna look at."

"Are you the new art teacher?"

"No. I'm not a teacher." He laughed and sat down next to me. "I'm fifteen."

"Oh. Cool. Do you go to school here?"

"Yeah."

"Oh, cause I haven't seen you around."

"I haven't been around."

"Oh."

"I'm gonna be around now."

"You're new?"

"No."

"I'm new."

"That's great."

"Are you making fun of me?"

"Yeah."

"Why?"

"I don't know. Do you want me to stop?"

"Yeah." I flushed.

"Why?"

"Cause . . ." I couldn't say it but my look said it and John was kind. He knew what I was driving at. *Cause you just introduced me to R.E.M. and I'm hiding from the football team, who want to kill me, and I want to be your best friend right now!*

"You wanna go do something?" he asked.

"Yes."

"All right."

He picked up his bag, slung it over his shoulder, and walked out.

"Wait." I grabbed his arm and stopped him as he made for the parking lot.

"What?"

"Aren't you afraid of the football team?"

"No."

"You're not?"

"No."

"Why not?"

"Come on." He laughed again and made his exit. I trailed and after over a year of strenuously trying to avoid it, again I was a follower.

The jocks were just emerging from the locker room, grunting. John grooved right past them like they were no more dangerous than the squirrels on the lawn. I stepped up my pace.

"Where are we going?"

"I dunno. You got a car?"

"No."

"I got a car."

"You do?"

"Yeah."

"Can you drive it?"

"Yeah. It's a car!"

"I know, it's just . . . you're fifteen. I can't even take driver's education yet."

"I didn't say I had a license."

"Oh."

"You asked me if I had a car."

"I know, but . . ."

I didn't know which was worse, waiting around for the looming jocks to pin us for two fags or to get into the powder-blue Galaxie 500 with John. At least Jane had a fucking driver's license and a couple of years behind the wheel, but I made my decision and something told me as John peeled out that he'd had a couple of years behind the wheel anyway.

"Those guys don't fuck with you?"

"No."

"Why not?"

"I slashed one of them."

"You did not!"

"Yeah, I did," he said proudly.

"Oh."

I shifted and stared out the window.

"I didn't really slash him," John finally clarified, sensing my intense discomfort.

"Oh. Good, cause I was kind of worried."

"Yeah. You looked worried."

"I did not," I protested, trying again to look tough.

"Slash is more like a side-to-side motion. What I did was more like a stab. Like an up-and-down motion."

"Shit."

"Not a slash. A stab. With a pencil."

"A pencil?"

"A number-two pencil."

"Did you give him lead poisoning?"

"That's just a myth."

"Did you get into trouble?"

"I got suspended."

"Oh. That's why you haven't been around?"

"Yeah."

"But now you're gonna be around."

"Yeah."

It went on like that as we left Woodmere and headed down Sunrise Highway toward the working-class, gentile scape of Valley Stream, past White Castle hamburger joints and car dealerships and motor inns.

"This is a nice car."

"You wanna hear some music?"

"Sure."

He turned on the car stereo and went left on the dial. Suddenly, New Wave music started to pump and we drove faster and farther from my home and my supper. As the sun set over Sunrise Highway, the Go-Go's sang "We Got the Beat," Visage sang "Fade to Grey," Missing Persons sang "Words," Duran Duran sang "Planet Earth," the English Beat sang "Twist and Crawl," Q-Feel sang "Dancing in Heaven," and on and on. Jane had stocked many of these records in Vinyl Jockey but I couldn't believe this stuff could be picked up on a local frequency in my hometown.

"Wait, this is the radio?"

"Yeah."

"This is the *radio*?"

"No, I'm throwing my voice," he laughed, eyes rolling.

"What station?"

"WLIR."

"How long has it . . . been . . ."

"I don't know. You've never heard WLIR?"

"No!" I grabbed his arm with my hand and shook it excitedly. "This is amazing. Is it on like this all the time?"

"Yeah. It's the *radio*!"

"If you can hear my voice, you're listening to the Larry the Duck Show on the world-famous WLIR, ninety-two-point-seven, Hempstead, Long Island. Coming up we've got some Depeche Mode, the new one from Devo, and just to show you our playlist is not alphabetical, we've got the latest from R.E.M."

"That's where you found R.E.M.?"

"Yeah," John confessed. "What'd you think, I went to Athens?"

"They're Greek?"

I was flushed. Practically spitting. I seriously needed to calm down.

"Athens, Georgia."

"My head hurts. I gotta call home."

"You gotta stop bouncing."

"Sorry."

"Or I'll slash you."

"You'll stab me."

We laughed . . . together.

"Keep it here and dare to be different."

As the DJ's signature duck quacks faded into a commercial for a nightclub called the Malibu, I kept my gaze down and fixed on the dial, both embarrassed by my outburst and really fucking eager to hear the promised Devo single.

*   *   *

You have to understand, back then radio was everything. Susie and Dick didn't have cable yet. Within a year, my mother finally installed a cable box, and New Wave videos on TV would enter my living room in all their geometric glory and make things much easier, but before I discovered WLIR, I pretty much had the small clutch of records I'd brought back from Kentucky to inspire me. As a 14-year-old kid in the suburbs with no car, I had no means of replenishing this vital supply either. Not only did LIR provide this in abundance, it encouraged nonconformity. "Dare to be different!" Nobody had really articulated that to me so bluntly. Jane and the punks at Sticks dared to be different but I swear I thought they were the only ones outside of England. I was certain that nobody ever dared to be different on the Island. Nobody dared to be anything at all. Happily, I was proven wrong.

Discovering LIR ranked closely behind puberty as the most significant change in my teenaged life. Tuning in was essential to getting through the day and the night. It was Radio Free High School, telegraphing vital information in an age when it wasn't instantly accessible via the computer. I couldn't even find a current issue of *Rolling Stone* in my hometown but I heard the brand-new Elvis Costello and the Attractions single on the very day it was shipped to the station. I can't overstate how that changed my world and accelerated my absolute love of music.

If I had had more friends, I might not have been so dependent on the radio, but what does it matter when the radio is the best friend you could ever ask for? It nourished me without demanding anything in return except that I sit through a few ads, which were geared toward an alternative sensibility (the jingle for Honda of Mineola, a dealership out in the sticks, was a dead-on parody of a Ramones song). Everything I did from that point was accompanied by an LIR broadcast.

Eating, sleeping, showering, homework. I listened on my headphones when I wasn't near a stereo and I didn't stop for four years. The tunes and chatter provided 24-hour empathy to soothe every bit of sexual confusion, social angst, and apocalyptic nightmare (there was even a heavily rotated novelty song by a band called Made for TV entitled "So Afraid of the Russians").

"Dare to be different . . . dare to be different . . ." I repeated to John.

"Are you okay?" John asked, turning off the highway and down a dark side street.

"Yeah. I'm so fucking okay now!"

It went on like that and by the time we pulled into the parking lot of a pizza place, I had two new best friends. One of them was a radio station. The other one liked me for the same reason I liked him: because nobody else did . . . at first. Encouraged by each other and the music, we would soon collect misfits, like little Jerome with his braces, and overweight, redheaded Richie, who wore thick specs like Bert and did magic tricks and still played Dungeons and Dragons. There was Maria, an academic scholarship beneficiary. Her dad was a cop. Her mom was a housekeeper for Jaclyn Kaplan's family (and Jaclyn Kaplan attended Woodmere Academy—you do the awkwardness factoring). After a few weeks, we were a gang. We had pencils for stabbing football players, and a little fortress next to the gym with a silver Sanyo perpetually tuned to 92.7, WLIR. Someone had superglued it that way, and nobody protested. Before, we were just different. Now, we fucking dared to be different. Soon, over those very same airwaves, we would hear the one voice that made more sense out of all the pain that went along with taking such a dare more than any other: the voice of Morrissey.

the first violent femmes album

I wore a Smiths T-shirt before I ever heard any of their music or even knew what the band members looked like. I know that sounds weird but weird things happen when you cease to be yourself and turn overnight into a giant, lonely penis.

"You don't paint!" Susie shouted.

"I would paint if I could get any good paint!"

"No, you wouldn't," Dick challenged.

"You can't even get good paint here! You can't get shit here!" I raged.

"Paint is paint!" they harmonized.

"Paint is *not* paint!"

This argument really had nothing at all to do with paint.

You see, one afternoon in early 1984, after another spell of driving around the Island in John's car, I decided that I wanted to move to Manhattan. I was 14 years old.

"You have to finish school!" Susie commanded.

"They're gonna expel me."

"They're not gonna expel you! They cashed the check."

It was true. I'd already tried for a few months and surrendered. They were never going to expel me from that fucking school, no matter what I did. I could have burned the Wolverine flag. I could have burned actual wolverines in the middle of my chemistry class, torching their prickly fur with a crudely wielded Bunsen burner, then set them loose and flaming down the hallowed hallways. They wouldn't let me go. And I had to go . . . somewhere. I chose New York City.

"What's in New York City?"

"Paint!"

This type of conversation, which had become a staple of our dinners (moved back an hour to accommodate my postdetention cruises in the Galaxie 500), really had nothing to do with moving to Manhattan either. I lived 45 minutes from the greatest city in the world, but at the time I didn't care. This conversation had everything to do with me not getting laid. Or rather, with me really, really wanting to get laid. I was having wet dreams every single night. They were starting to get to me. When you dream that you have a girlfriend, then wake up to find that she doesn't exist, it screws with your head, especially when you have to shower, shave, cover your zits with tinted Clearasil, and go to school after such dreamy fake sex. I wanted whatever I'd started with Jane to run the course to its natural end. I couldn't get a Woodmere Academy JAP to touch me with a long stick and I hated myself for even wanting to. It went against every new value and discovery that was nourishing my soul, whether it was Michael Stipe or the thrift stores that John and I would pick through after school. I wanted to be touched all over my skinny body by the very girls whose behavior and fashion sense disgusted me silly. Simply,

I didn't want to be alone. I had to drain the blood from this 24-hour hard-on or I was gonna fucking die. I was sure of it.

I spent every day at school listening to the first Violent Femmes album on my Walkman. Over and over and over again. The thing was superglued into the cassette carriage. It had only been out for just over a year but I blasted it so frequently that I once actually caught Susie humming the melody to "Blister in the Sun" while she was straining spaghetti over the kitchen sink. That album has since become so iconic, it's probably the subject of one or more college theses on the teenage angst. The Milwaukee-based trio were all probably in their early 20s but they articulated what was going on in my head and in my nutsack perfectly.

"Why can't I get just one fuck?" Indeed. When I wasn't staining my sheets, I was scribbling some crazed scorecard into my red spiral notebook. Maybe it was Sid's bum gambler genetics at work, but I somehow believed that I could handicap myself into the sack with one of these JAPs.

JACKIE Spanish class. Got there early. Sat next to her. Smells good. Told a joke. Made her laugh. Funny is good.

MICHELLE Let her copy off my test. That counts for something, doesn't it?

RORY I think I heard her fart. Didn't smell but will she avoid me now?

LESLIE Absent again. Where is she?

ELLEN Not as pretty as everyone else. But still so stuck-up.

LISA Told her I'd make her a tape. Was she joking or will she listen? Make tape!

STACEY Not my type. Unless . . .

I would draw cartoons of all of us engaged in various sexual positions. At least, I thought they were sexual positions.

I really had no clue. Sometimes my cartoon dick would be three times the size of my cartoon body. That's the way it felt in real life too. I was convinced that I would never get laid on Long Island. I couldn't go back to Kentucky. I reasoned that there had to be someone in New York City who'd have my virginity. Worse, my new group of friends didn't seem preoccupied with sex at all. They loved the Violent Femmes but nobody ever mentioned what the bulk of their songs were about. When we'd gather in the art room every day between classes and during lunch hour, the conversations were almost entirely about what had been on television the night before. I couldn't be the one to bring up fucking. I was too shy. And John didn't seem to have any hormones in him at all. He never spoke about sex, even within the privacy of the Galaxie 500. He never looked at girls. I once asked him if he'd ever had a girlfriend and he looked at me like I'd asked whether he had a tail. All he cared about, it seemed, was painting, playing his cheap electric guitar (he'd mastered just about all of Peter Buck's fingering), finding missing parts for the Galaxie, and eating anchovy pizza. Then there was little Jerome with his braces. We'd taken him into our group mostly out of pity. Mitchell the jock ceased his daily beatings once he saw Jerome walking down the hall flanked by John. He knew he'd catch a pencil point in the eye or worse. But feeling sorry for someone isn't necessarily the best foundation on which to build a deep friendship. Jerome was 13 but he acted like a 10-year-old child. He even kept the doll he slept with in his locker during the school day. It was a Boy Snoopy, one of those augmented Snoopy dolls designed to cash in on the Boy George craze. Following the success of the third Rocky movie and *The A-Team,* they made Mr. T Snoopys too but Jerome had opted for the cross-dressing beagle. He also never got his braces removed as promised. Still, he was my friend because nobody else would have him. It was important for John and me to walk the walk. We couldn't pride ourselves on being outcasts while shunning all the other socially inept students who wanted in to our little club. Our policy was pretty much open-door. The downside was that I had to sit and listen to Jerome perform some stupid Eddie Murphy comedy routine he'd memorized when all I wanted to talk about were tits.

Maria had tits, but I could never bring myself to ask her to see them. She was just too sad and angry. Once I gave her a tape of the new the The album *Soul Mining* cause she'd mentioned that she thought the single "Uncertain Smile" was pretty. She smiled at me and I thought we had what some people would call "a moment," but I couldn't use her for sex. She depended on me for friendship, leadership even. John's age, his wheels, and the fact that he showed no compunction when it came to stabbing the enemy made him the obvious choice for king of the geeks. I was his first lieutenant. Our only real mandate was that Richie was not allowed to bring his Dungeons and Dragons games anywhere near the art room. Even geeks have to draw the line somewhere. Richie complied. He had no choice. He had nowhere else to go. Richie found a loophole in talking incessantly about slaying some funky-ass demon named Asmodeus or something with a deft roll of his ten-sided die. I don't think Richie and Jerome knew that dicks were for more than pissing.

Sometimes we'd walk into the art room and find two jocks there sitting in our seats, going through our notebooks and tapes in search of something they could steal. Van Halen's *1984* album, maybe. John would just stand there silently with a creepy look on his face until they got up and left, chuckling to themselves. If one of them had seriously wanted to borrow, say, Squeeze's *Singles 45's and Under* or Sparks' *Angst in My Pants* or something like that, we would have been happy to loan it out provided they left some kind of deposit. We didn't hate them. Our open-door policy included JAPs and jocks. Their policy didn't include us. Sometimes, in moments of weakness, I resented John and Jerome and Maria and Richie for keeping me apart from the student body. I blamed them for my virginity. I'd stare out at the cafeteria tables full of good-looking girls and athletic boys and wonder why I couldn't sit there too. Daring to be different would have been a lot easier with just one fuck.

"You really want a ride into Manhattan tomorrow?" John asked. It was another one of those late Friday afternoons that promised nothing but another long, lonely weekend in my room, jerking off (to everything from a sticky old *Playboy* that featured a partially nude pictorial of those cheesy blond Landers sisters, who always guested on game shows, to fucking Smurfettes), when I decided I would run away.

"Yeah. I do. Can you give me one?"

"Why do you wanna go into the city?"

"Why do you need to know?"

"I'm trying to figure out if you want to hang out in Manhattan or if you just want a ride."

"I just want a ride. All right? If you've got a problem with that, I can take the train."

"No. I'll take you," he offered sadly. I'd hurt his feelings. My horniness and the shame that tagged along with it were turning me into an insensitive bastard. John agreed to the lift.

I fell asleep easily that night. I dared imaginary girlfriends to come to me. In the morning it wouldn't matter. I'd have a real one. I didn't know how I was gonna find one . . . but I had a little over a hundred dollars, which I'd saved by stashing small portions of about twenty-five weekly allowances. It was my sex fund. I'd just go to Times Square and wave it around (the money, not my dick). By Sunday morning,

I'd vowed, the constant rattling in my nerve endings, the tape loop of flesh behind my eyes, the metronome tick in my brain that made my dick jump like an upstream salmon and gave me hard-ons when I'd sit over the school bus wheels would be wiped away. I would be normal. We listened to the Femmes as we gunned down the Van Wyck Expressway and across the length of the Midtown Tunnel, heading into Manhattan.

"But the day after today . . . I will stop . . . and I will start!" the lead singer, Gordon Gano, promised.

I didn't tell John where to go once we were let out of the tunnel, so he instinctively headed downtown and east, rather than uptown and west toward Times Square's sex market. I was too embarrassed to redirect him. As he headed down Second Avenue, through the unfamiliar streets, I started to get a little scared. *What if someone tries to talk to me?* I thought. *What if I get lost? The city's restless! It's ready to pounce.* I knew Pennsylvania Station was somewhere near 31st Street and Seventh Avenue, but I didn't know how far that was from the Village. I also quickly realized that it was pretty silly of me to think that it was going to be easy to find someone to just fuck me and toss me back into the world ten minutes later with heretofore unknown peace of mind. It's not like there was a store you could patronize. And if there was, farther uptown somewhere, now that I was actually in Manhattan, I wasn't sure I wanted to lose it that way anymore. I worried she would cut my throat and take my wallet when it was over. Did it matter? Yeah, it did. I didn't actually tell Susie and Dick that I was running away. I just left. I didn't tell John that he was abetting me. It wasn't too late to call it off. There was something else affecting me. The farther downtown we got the more my hopped-up fear was converted into some kind of serious excitement. I liked the look of things.

"Why don't you park it and we can walk around for a while?" I suggested.

how soon is never?

"Don't you have to be somewhere?"

"Not for a while."

"Well, what do you want to do?"

"I don't know. Do you need any paint?"

"No. I've got paint."

"Oh."

Downtown looked very cool. I wanted to explore, but not alone.

"Well, do you know of any record stores?"

"No."

"Maybe we could find one?"

"No. I'm gonna head back."

"Don't. Hang out with me."

"You didn't want me to before."

"Well, now I do."

One of us was the spoiled brat. I'd been indulged for years and had developed the irritating habit of occasionally treating my friends like my mother. I made a note to myself to fucking stop. John was finally persuaded to leave the car, after I'd offered to pay for long-term parking. It was becoming increasingly clear that my cash wasn't going to be spent on flesh. We parked the car on Second Avenue and walked a few blocks south.

"Do you know where we're going?"

"Yeah."

"Where are we going?"

"St. Mark's Place."

"What's that?"

"It's a street."

"Oh, cool." A street in Manhattan.

St. Mark's Place! It was just like Sticks. Full of punks! As we walked west, past the Gem Spa newsstand, I realized that if this was Manhattan, I could have it too. There was nothing scary about the East Village as far as I could see. Nobody had tried to mug me in the past ten minutes, even though I was braced for it. And did I mention there were fucking punks? We might not have looked just like them, but we didn't look like tourists either. So we cruised on by and I can't speak for John but I certainly felt cool.

"Check that out. There's a store called Trash," I said, with a point that probably outed me as a tourist after all. "Let's go in."

Trash and Vaudeville was hot. As in hot pink hair on the hot punk chick in a rubber dress who took John's bag for checking and gave me my ten millionth hard-on of the year. "Goo Goo Muck" by the Cramps was playing loudly as we browsed the racks of ripped T-shirts, studded belts, eyeball rings, and Manic Panic hair dye.

"I'm gonna dye my hair," I announced.

"What color?" John asked.

"I don't know. What would piss off Bert the most?"

"Blue?"

"Blue is good, yeah. Oh, how about flaming pink? Like hers?"

"You might look like Bozo the Clown."

"I don't wanna look like Bozo the Clown."

"Or worse, Ronald McDonald. Pink is good for a girl. Maybe not a boy."

"Blue it is, then. I'm gonna buy this," I said, grabbing the container, "and I'm gonna dye my fucking hair blue." I sang the last line like Dale Bozzio did in the Missing Persons song "Words," altering the lyrics slightly: "Do you hear me? Do you care? Will you expel me? I don't care."

We loaded up on badges next (at the time, we called them "buttons"). Trash represented for all our favorite bands: the Cure, R.E.M., B-52's, Bauhaus, Depeche Mode, and Yaz. The WLIR all-stars were represented in a silver spray-painted wicker basket. Fifty cents apiece.

"I don't wanna stay here. Let's go somewhere else," John said as I tried to drag him toward the back of the store, where I could find a pair of blue shoes to go with my soon-to-be-blue hair. Resigned to my virginity, I'd decided to blow my savings on bullshit instead.

"Why not?"

"Cause I can't afford any of this stuff," he said in one of those responses that really meant, *Do I have to say it, you idiot? I'm not as rich as you are.*

It was true. John had a car but he didn't have $20 to blow. That was food and gas money. Like me, he was a little too young and fucked in the head to be made to hold down an after-school job. Like me, his mother was divorced. His father had split on him around the same time mine did. Unlike me, his mother was a mailman . . . or mailwoman. They lived in a one-bedroom apartment in Valley Stream. John slept on the couch and had converted the building's basement into a personal space where he could turn up his amps and learn the chords to R.E.M.'s "South Central Rain." He was like Maria that way. They both attended Woodmere Academy on full academic scholarships. But their whip-smart intellect shared head space with a shame that I didn't know. Even those times with Sid, who lived beyond his means and borrowed against that, I was never hungry and rolled in plenty of shut-up/divorce-guilt hush money. I was no longer a JAP, but although you can take the boy out of the Polo . . . you know the rest. So every once in a while, my spoiled-brat rearing would clash with John's unexpressed but less-than-subtle poor kid's anger and resentment. After these clashes, I wanted to die from shame. I'd do anything to avoid them, but sometimes they just unspooled, seemingly of their own will. There wasn't any demon between us other than that, but make no mistake, it was a demon. More often than not, I'd mitigate the situation by forking over some cash.

"Is there something you want?"

"Yeah," he said calmly.

"What?"

"Nothing."

"What do you want? I can buy it for you and you can pay me back."

He never did. I never asked.

"Well, I was looking at that T-shirt."

"What T-shirt?"

"There."

He pointed to a black T-shirt with a naked man's torso on it. Beneath that, two words: The Smiths. I walked over to the counter and wordlessly replaced the container of blue hair dye. My light brown spiky head would remain natural. I was going to buy two of them. One for him. One for me. I didn't even know why I wanted one too. Maybe because of the look in John's eye as he stared up at it. I looked up to him. He was my hero. My older brother. And he was just fucking dumb-struck by the thing.

"Is there another one?" I just about shouted to the sales clerk. I was worried that I'd have to buy John the only one.

"You're gonna wear it too?" he asked, more incredulous than annoyed.

"Yeah, I like it. It's cool. Who are the Smiths?"

John didn't answer. I didn't care. The Smiths could have been lawyers. Car repairmen. I just wanted the shirt too. I knew it was somehow very, very important. The pinky sales clerk grabbed a long pole and pulled two tees from the high-up cubby. Mediums. Beefy-Ts. Their freshness a bit rude and incongruous with the message silk-screened across the black cotton. They'd have to shrink a bit. John and I weren't into anything that looked or smelled new. We never washed our school uniform. His was paint-stained. Mine was starting to funk but it didn't matter. I was prepared to wear nothing but this shirt for the rest of my days. I didn't know why, but I had a feeling that if I did, things would be different.

"Who are the Smiths?" I asked the clerk.

"Cash or charge?" she answered.

"Cash."

She put the shirts into a pink bag and we left in silence.

"Who are the Smiths?" I asked as we made our way to Washington Square Park.

"Who are the Smiths?" I repeated as we sat eating lemon Italian ices and hot pretzels and watching jugglers, stand-up comics, roller skaters, cops, children, dogs.

"They're a band."

"Are they good?"

"I don't know."

"How do you know they're a band?"

"You don't believe me?"

"I believe you. I just . . . I mean, how come I've never heard of them?"

"I don't know."

"No, really. How come I've never heard of them? They don't play them on LIR."

"Yes, they do."

"When?" My tone got suspicious. Serious.

"I don't know," he admitted, embarrassed. "I keep missing it."

"Missing what? What do they sing?"

"They have a song called 'Hand in Glove' that LIR played once. I heard the last thirty seconds of it and really liked the guitarist, that's all."

"That's all?"

"Well . . ."

He stared off down Sullivan Street. I thought I saw his cheeks blush.

"Who's the guitarist?"

"I don't know."

"Why not?"

"Cause every time they play it, I always miss it," he answered angrily.

" 'Hand in Glove'?"

"Yeah."

"Well, if you know the title, why don't you just sit in front of the radio until they play it again?"

"I have been."

"You have?"

"Yes." He was definitely a little embarrassed. I was certain of it.

"When?"

"Every day. They're not playing it."

"Why don't you request it?"

"I have."

"You have? When? Did they play it?"

"Yes, but I missed it."

"How could you miss it?"

It went on like this, as it did in the days long before the advent of Web searches and CD burners. John confessed that he had been, for nearly three weeks, secretly obsessed with the last few bars of a mystery song called "Hand in Glove" by a band called the Smiths. He didn't know much about them because he had heard only one snippet of the singer's final verse, then the instrumental outro, but apparently that had been enough to warrant tens of hours staring at a fucking radio.

"Wow!" I said.

"It's not a big deal," he responded.

"John?"

"What?"

"I dragged you into the city so I could get laid. That's why I've been weird today."

how soon is never?

There was something about us having the same T-shirt in a pink bag that made it okay for me to confess anything to him.

"I really need sex and none of those girls at school will give it to me."

John just laughed that warm but slightly condescending laugh he'd patented for occasions where I brought up the subject. I laughed too. I still had my boy cherry but all in all it had been a pretty good day, even though the three record stores we stopped in on the way back to the car did not stock a band called the Smiths. One smart-ass clerk with thick nerd specs and a visible booger in his nostril said, "Sure do," piquing our excitement levels something awful before handing over *Toys in the Attic* by Aerosmith. We decided to burn the store to the ground . . . one day. We also resolved, as we walked toward the car with our new shirts, to dispatch orders to our art room troops: the mission was to capture the elusive "Hand in Glove" on tape by any means necessary.

We didn't play the Violent Femmes on the way home, or much at all anymore after that trip. We spent most of our time imagining what the Smiths sounded like. Anything else just got in the way.

seven

fifteen minutes with you

"I heard it! I heard it!"

The familiar voice was followed by the little gallop of Jerome's sneakered feet.

"I heard it, you guys! I heard it!" he shouted in his still-haven't-gone-through-puberty voice.

John and I sprang up from our drawing paper excitedly.

"Did you tape it?" John asked.

"No. But I totally heard it! I swear!"

"Why didn't you tape it?" I demanded, easily flexing my muscle as number-two geek.

"I couldn't get to the art room in time. I heard it on my Walkman."

"You're suppose to have a tape ready at all times," John said, and pushed Jerome into a seated position.

"I know, but—"

"That's not even a Walkman. A Walkman has to be Sony," I spat.

We were all a little high-strung. "Hand in Glove" had been elusive. For nearly two weeks, we'd been obsessing about it like only teenagers can. I wanted to hear it because John wanted to hear it. Jerome, Maria, and Richie wanted to hear it because I wanted to hear it. And everybody wanted to be the first one to get it on tape and make themselves a hero to the rest. The days of sitting by the radio for hours waiting for the DJ to play one song are long over for me (and you too, thanks to shit like downloading) but damn if it wasn't a perfect, temporary existence for all the frustration it put us though at the time. That rush of anticipation when the ad ends and the start of a new half-hour block of music takes over was amazing. I didn't even know what I was listening for. Just something called the Smiths. I told myself I'd know it when I heard it. You know, I can't listen to the radio for ten minutes now. It's all ads and no rush at all.

"When did they play it? We've been listening for an hour," John interrupted.

"Third period. I wanted to tell you but you were in class. I just got out. I'm done for the day."

"No, you're not," John said.

"Yes, I am." Jerome gritted out the words though his braces.

"You're gonna sing it for us."

"Huh?"

"You're the only one who's heard it. And you didn't tape it, so you're gonna sing it."

"I can't sing, you guys!" he protested meekly.

"So hum it," I offered.

"No way."

"Yes!"

"What are you gonna do if I don't?"

Jerome was spoiled. He knew we didn't beat up our own.

"Nothing," I said cryptically. "But we won't let you hang out with us anymore."

"Oh."

Jerome was scared. I heard him clear his throat. Then he asked if humming it would really suffice.

"You can't remember any of the lyrics?" I asked in a rare moment of practicality.

"Some, yeah."

"Just sing the song. It doesn't have to be any good."

"Come on, guys. Maybe they'll play it again."

"Sing!" John said. Maria put away the brushes she was washing and sat down, awaiting the recital. She and Richie pulled their chairs in closely.

"Sing it, Jerome, you fag," Richie requested.

"Do I have to do it in a British accent?" he pleaded.

"Yes," I said.

"No," John vetoed.

"Okay . . . it goes something like this . . . I think . . ." Jerome took a long pause, sighed sadly, and in a slow, terrified quiver rocked out—even giving us a bit of the Brit inflection.

" 'Hand in glove. The sun shines out of our behinds.' Um . . . 'Hand in glove' . . . something else."

He started to hum the rest of the song. Tears were welling in his reddened eyes and he was choking on the melody.

"The sun shines out of our behinds?" Richie repeated incredulously. "You made that up!"

"Shut up, Richie. What about the chorus, Jerome?" I inquired, still pretty fucking riveted by that very line.

"What's a chorus?" Jerome asked.

"The main part. The hook," John explained.

"Oh. I don't think it had one."

"Every song has a chorus!" I shouted. "What was it?"

"Well, there was a part that went on like . . ." He took an

almost identical pause and resumed. " 'I really don't know and I really don't care.' "

"You're definitely making that up," Maria hissed suspiciously.

"I'm not! That's how it goes. I swear, you guys."

"All right, Jerome. That was good. Make sure you tape it next time," I said.

"I will. Can I go now? My mom's waiting for me."

"You can go."

"I can still hang out here, right?"

"Yeah."

Jerome smiled his metal smile and hotfooted it out the door.

"He's got a great voice," John laughed.

" 'The sun shines out of our behinds,' " I recited.

"It sounds like a stupid song," Richie critiqued.

"Oh, and 'Karma Chameleon' is a smart song?" I attacked Richie, already defending this band I knew nothing about—to the death if necessary.

"You don't like Boy George?" he cowered. Jerome and Richie really loved Boy George. I was convinced that Richie spent most of his waking hours on edge, worrying if that made him a fag. I was about to go off on the Boy when Jerome returned to the art room, the blush of terror drained from his chubby cheeks, a glint of pride in his eye.

"What now?" Maria asked. "You gonna do 'Save a Prayer'?" Maria was a closet Duranie.

"I forgot to tell you. Donna Donna said the singer's name is Morrissey."

"Morrissey what?" John said.

"Or what Morrissey?" I quipped.

A horn honked outside. Jerome turned around.

"It's just Morrissey. One word. Like Madonna. That's my mom. I gotta go."

"We should call Donna Donna," I suggested.

"You can never get through to the DJs," John said.

"Well, maybe we can vote for it for Screamer of the Week. We'll call like five hundred times and it'll win and then at least we'll know when they're gonna play it." The Screamer of the Week was LIR's weekly fave song competition. We voted religiously.

"Or we can get Jerome to sing into a microphone this time," Richie suggested. I hit him. Then John hit him.

"I have to go to detention. Will you be here when I get out?"

John shrugged.

"All right, well, if you hear it again, come grab me. Say my whole family was in a car wreck and I have to go identify the bodies or something."

"Will do."

The sun was setting nowhere near my behind as I sat in Ms. Casper's room, trying to remember what I'd done or if I even had detention. Perhaps I was there out of habit. Ms. Casper, my chemistry teacher, was really pissed off whenever it was her turn to monitor detention. I was always glad to see her, though. Unlike most of my teachers, she was a real hottie. The only chemistry between us, sadly, was the shit in my textbooks. It gave me a headache, and, like my math texts, I hardly ever opened the heavy-ass things. I was a straight-D chemistry student and couldn't even have told you which elements made up water if it hadn't been the title of a Hall and Oates album, but I could describe in detail the outline of her ass cheeks as they pushed against the cheap fabric of her beige skirt. I'd daydream about spanking her naked ass until I actually daydreamed that I got bored. What do you do with an ass after a while anyway? So I'd sit there, frequently alone with my hard-on. But that day I didn't think about sex. I was thinking about Morrissey. One word. Like Madonna. With an incandescent arse of his own, beaming ultraviolet rays at all those who dared trouble him, his love and his glove. Who was his love? Was it a man? Was it a woman? Was it his own hand? That I could have related to. I looked around the room. Nothing but oppression: failed constructions of compounds still on the blackboard with Casper's chicken scratch corrections (boldly hostile, they were) scarring each dunce's attempt to understand chemistry. And Casper raged silently like we should've come out of the womb with full knowledge of the shit. I hated her. I hated school. I wanted to go back to the city. To St. Mark's Place. Wearing my Smiths T-shirt, which I'd wash every night and put on every morning, only reminded me of what I was missing there. I settled for ditching.

"Can I get a drink of water?" I asked.

"What's the compound that makes water?"

"One part oxygen, two parts hydrogen, I think."

"Go ahead, Joe."

As I paced the hallway, I could hear the familiar, high-pitched voice of Mr. Sturmer, the drama teacher, leading some kind of acting exercise for the drama club kids. He'd grunt like a pig, and his loyal retinue of boys and girls would echo it. "Umph. Unk. Umph!" And again. I guess it was supposed to cast out their inhibitions and free up their muscles or something. I followed the noise and soon found myself spying on them. It looked like jive to me.

"Can we help you, Mr. Green? Are you here to try out?" Mr. Sturmer asked.

Sturmer drank during the day. I could smell it on him. He was always trying to get me to audition for his stupid theatrical productions. He'd do shit like reverse the gender of characters in musicals like *A Funny Thing Happened on the Way to the Forum* and act like he was responsible for some kind of radical, creative overthrow. Soon the actors grew self-conscious and stopped grunting.

"Nope. Just watching."

"Well, Mr. Green, this is not a performance. It's a rehearsal. It's not meant for spectators, so why don't you go back to detention?"

He turned away. I tried not to laugh, but he didn't make it easy.

"Now shake it out! Shake it out! Get it out!" he ordered as he marched over to a boom box and hit the play button.

"Hey, sucka! What the hell's got into you?"

I knew the song from MTV. It was Wham!'s "Wham Rap." And it was awful.

"Shake it out! Feel the beat."

He repeated this many times as six of my fellow Wolverines commenced interpretive dancing. They stretched and twisted and shook whatever it was they needed to get out of their systems. Bad theater, maybe. The goofy spectacle made me almost glad that my extracurricular activities consisted of watching Ms. Casper's ass. That is, until I saw Jennifer shaking it out.

Jennifer Rosen was one of the six Wham! rappers. She was the lead, in fact, in that year's scheduled production of *Fiddler on the Roof*. I'd seen her a few times before and hadn't thought much of it. Love at first sight might exist, but this was a case of love at third or fourth sight. Sometimes you just have to see someone shake it out. She was a new girl and like me, a transfer from some public school. Maybe she'd gotten into some trouble like me and was looking for a fresh start. Maybe Sturmer ran into her in some liquor store parking lot and convinced her to take a part. Unlike me, she had quickly become very popular with the JAPs. For the first time, I didn't care whether or not she was out of my league. I needed to make her mine. I fell in love right there. I actually felt it happen. I heard the rush of blood travel from my dick to my heart. It was a classic teenage insta-crush. One minute, you're only concerned with staying out of detention. The next, you're fantasizing about staying together forever, or at least well into the '90s.

Jennifer stood out among the five other dancers, whom I couldn't describe to you right now if you threatened me with a weapon. But she . . . she stays with me. She was 15, one year older than me and a class ahead. She had olive skin and dark brown hair. Bright eyes. Skinny. No tits. No paint on her long fingers and toes. A broad smile that overtook her whole face and forced whomever she smiled at to smile back whether they wanted to or not. It was some powerful, toothy grin. She wore weird green earrings and used a pair of sunglasses as a headband in a way that was hardly fussy. She seemed smart. You can sometimes tell just from looking into someone's eyes, you know. She was barefoot and wearing black tights and a black cotton turtleneck. (That was probably the cause of my affections, in hindsight. No socks, black wardrobe . . . that's enough sometimes.) As she moved to the music, I could tell that she knew what she was doing was ridiculous, but unlike me, she had respect for her teachers. Still, her bony shoulders hunched a bit with insecurity. Or so I thought as I searched my stricken brain for some way to make a serious first impression on her. Soon, I found myself walking toward the stage. Then I found myself onstage. Then I found myself shaking it out. Except I had nothing to shake out. No umph unk umph in me. Still, I got in the middle of the six and started pogoing madly to Wham! Yeah, I started dancing like a spaz to impress a girl. It works. Try it.

"Mr. Green, what are you doing?" Sturmer raged. "This isn't a joke! This is a serious exercise!"

I jerked back and forth, oblivious. Everybody else stopped shaking it out. They were freaking it out. Except Jennifer. I clocked her out of the corner of my eye and caught that smile. It made me shake harder, faster, with even more stupidity. I tried to breakdance but forgot how. I twisted an ankle instead.

"Fuck!" I screamed.

"Mr. Green!"

I tried to stand up. I couldn't.

"Mr. Green! Please leave now!"

"I can't!" I shouted. "Fuck!"

"Mr. Green, please stop saying 'fuck' and please leave right now!"

"I fucked up my foot!"

"Well, perhaps you will now appreciate that this is a method, not a joke."

"I think he's really hurt," someone said. I looked up. It wasn't Jennifer. She was biting her tongue, trying not to burst into a fit of laughter. God, she had a lot of respect. She must have had really good parents or something. I had no class but felt at that moment that I stood a pretty good chance of having an ally. Or at least a lift up. I stretched out my arm in her direction and waited to see if she'd take it. She did. I wrapped my fingers around her cotton-draped forearm and felt her strength as she pulled me off the stage.

"Ow!"

"I'm glad you hurt yourself," Sturmer sniped, and turned off the music.

"I'm glad you hurt yourself"? Who says that? Ever?

"Class dismissed. Mr. Green, you can be sure Mr. Bertel is going to hear about this."

He marched into his office and slammed the door. You didn't need X-ray vision to figure out what he was doing in there. If I'd stuck around twenty minutes or so, I could have counted on him weaving out and applying an Ace bandage to my sprain, breathing his ethanol vapor in my face, and apologizing for his musical selection.

"Are you okay?" Jennifer asked in that half-earnest way, hoping that I wasn't really hurt cause she wanted to laugh badly. I nodded and she promptly laughed her bony ass off, tears and everything. The five other budding thespians left us alone, probably pretty embarrassed they'd allowed themselves to dance to Wham! after all, once some punk rock shmuck pointed out how stupid they looked.

"You're an asshole, do you know that?"

"Yes. I do know that."

"What's your name, asshole?"

"Joe."

"I'm Jennifer."

"Hi."

"Hi."

"How's your foot, really?"

"I'll be okay," I said with mock bravery. "Sometimes you have to suffer for your art."

"That was art?"

"That was art."

"Are you supposed to be in detention or something?"

"Yeah, but they're just gonna give me another one. I've already got more detentions than I know what to do with. So I figure I've got nothing to lose. You want one?"

"No, thanks."

I was standing again. I limped after her as she walked backstage and grabbed her bag. She pulled on her navy blue skirt. It was almost like seeing her undressed, I thought, now that I was watching her dress. She tugged up her thick black workout socks and a pair of clean white sneakers.

"Well, I'm glad you're not paralyzed or anything."

"What does that mean? I mean, if I was, would you like push me around the halls or something? Cause I don't think

anybody else would. Maybe push me into traffic. Are you saying you wanna be my friend? Cause you know if you do,
maybe I can make you an offer."

"Make me an offer?" she asked, a little put out.

It hit me that I was rambling, as one does when one tries
to talk to a really pretty girl who's just pulled on a skirt. I had
to go with it or she'd start to notice my sweaty upper lip.

"Yeah, make you an offer. You know. You can have my late
afternoons. Maybe some weekends if I'm not in the city."

"You go to the city a lot?"

"Yeah. I practically live there."

"Really? Is that where you shop for clothes?"

"That's right. Clothes . . . paint."

"Paint? Are you an art student?"

"No, I'm the quarterback of the football team."

"You know, I find that once someone learns how to be sar-
castic, it can be difficult to stop." So she was smart. I tried to
be smart too.

"Yeah. It's like a drug."

"Do you take drugs?" she asked.

"Only before I dance."

She smiled again at my stupid joke and pushed me. That
smile. It was something. I was falling hard.

"Well, I should go," she said.

"Are you here every day?" I asked.

"Yeah. I'm the lead in this play."

"*Fiddler on the Roof*?"

"Yeah. I play Tevye. But, you know . . . as a woman."

"Right."

She detected my unimpressed tone of voice and was quick
to defend Sturmer's invention as we walked toward the parking lot . . . together.

"I think it makes it more interesting. You don't?"

"I think it's pretentious."

"It's provocative. It's the same thing you're doing with your Smiths T-shirt. You wear it because you know it's going to provoke a reaction. People will probably think you're gay even though you're not."

"The Smiths are gay?"

"Does it matter? Unless it's Mötley Crüe or Journey around here, it's gay."

"How do you know I'm not gay?"

"The way you stare at me. You're blushing now."

She laid a hand on my shoulder.

"I'm sorry. I'm going through some weird hormonal stuff."

"Well, that's the perfect band for you, then, right?"

"Right." I didn't know what the fuck she was talking about.

"Sometimes I think Morrissey just needs a blow job, don't you?" she asked.

Normally, I would have fixated on the words "blow job" coming from her beautiful lips but instead my head exploded.

"Wait . . . you know this band?"

She nodded.

"Tell me about them. Please?"

"You don't know them?"

"No."

"You're wearing the T-shirt of a band you've never listened to? Now that's pretentious."

"I know," I said sadly. "I'm so lame. I've been trying to listen to them. I mean, I want to. They don't play them on the radio here."

"I heard them last night."

"On what? The top-forty station?"

"LIR."

"You listen to LIR?"

"Duh!"

"Nuh-uh!"

I was shocked. I honestly didn't think any of the popular

kids knew the frequency. I mean, there were bands that we shared because they'd gotten so big, we could no longer keep them to ourselves: the Police, Duran Duran, Musical Youth. But the popular kids listened to hit radio stations like WPLJ and Z-100. The old folks listened to WCBS-FM (Sid was a great fan of DJ Don K. Reed's "Doo Wop Shop." It was fucking dogma.)

"Besides, I've known about them for like a year," she boasted. "They're like the biggest band in England right now. They're even bigger than Spandau Ballet."

"How do you know?" I was sweating.

"I was in London all summer."

"Why?"

"I was studying at the Royal Shakespeare Academy's youth program. Getting my iambic pentameter down."

"I was in Lexington, Kentucky," I muttered, wishing I'd been in London. Somehow, wherever I ended up, it just wasn't the place to be.

"They've been on *Top of the Pops* and everything."

"*Top of the Pops*?"

"It's like *American Bandstand*." She laughed.

"Do you have the album?"

"Of course. It's great."

"Do you have it here?"

"No. It's at home."

"Can I go there?"

"Joe, I hardly know you."

"Can you sing it to me? All of it?" I asked, realizing how silly it sounded, even if she was the chick Tevye.

"Sure," she said. I waited. "I'm kidding, Joe. I'm not going to sing it for you."

"Please?"

She laughed and cleared her throat. Draped her arms over my shoulders and leaned in, breathing an exaggerated croon into my ear: "Fifteen minutes with you, oh I wouldn't say no . . ."

She pulled away. I felt like crying. Here was the girlfriend I'd been dreaming of, made real.

And I wasn't in my bed, crusty-eyed and sweaty, a load of wasted seed in my briefs. She was standing before me, singing the Smiths. Then, of course, laughing that she'd blown my cool with the precision one must pick up studying overseas. She pushed me again.

This pushing, what the hell does it mean? I wondered silently.

"Joe, you look unwell," she said in a flawless British accent. "You look poorly. You should tend to that leg."

I tried to find something, anything, to say. I wiped my brow and ran my tongue over my dry lips.

Then she made it easy.

"Listen, I'll make you a deal," she said.

"Okay."

"If you promise not to interrupt any more rehearsals, I'll tape you a copy of the album and bring it to you tomorrow."

"Really?"

"Yes. Now go bother someone else. I've got to get home."

"Where do you live?"

"That's none of your business."

She extended her hand and waited for me to shake it. I stared at her.

"Joe?"

I shook her hand vigorously and continued to stare.

"How come we've never hung out before?" I asked.

"Because I'm popular?" To her credit, she replied in question form, tempering the meanness and rendering Woodmere Academy's unspoken caste system the absurd thing it was. Still, it was true.

"Okay, I'll see you tomorrow, Joe. Stay out of trouble."

I watched her as she walked across the lawn. Her gait was

quick and confident. She climbed into the back of an idling white BMW, waved to me, and rolled her eyes as it sped away. I stood there on the grass for some time, watching the spot where the vehicle had been. I thought about the healing power of blow jobs. I thought about London. I thought about *Top of the Pops.* But mostly I thought about Jennifer . . . until Ms. Casper exited the building and approached me purposefully.

"That was a long drink of water, Joe. I sent a memo to Mr. Bertel explaining that you failed to serve today's detention and recommending that you try again tomorrow."

"I'm sorry, Ms. Casper. I fell down."

Casper got into her red Fiat junker and drove away. I wondered briefly where Casper went after hours, if she drank alone at a local bar or played with her eight adopted cats. Maybe she read romance novels. I suspected that whatever she did, it had nothing to do with chemistry. I quickly forgot about Casper and decided to walk home. I felt high as the sun setting into my behind. *Tomorrow,* I thought, *a pretty girl who's been to London and uses the term "blow job" casually is going to come looking for me, bearing a gift, and I'll sleep well and I'll never have to jerk off again.*

As I moved over the suburban lawns toward another of Susie's hot dinners gone cold, I replayed her voice and tried to imagine her hot, pepperminty breath in my ear.

lullaby

It was a day for losing your cool. I'd sweated out the first three periods, wondering whether she'd forgotten about me. I even passed her in the hallway and didn't approach her. She was surrounded by her friends, a phalanx of sneering JAPs. How did she mix with those people? She'd studied Shakespeare in London? She was Reb Tevye as a woman! Those JAPs had no life in their eyes. No love for the theater or music or travel or anything as far as I could tell. Was she so confident in her gifts and her hungers that slumming with these static cultural retards was no threat? Pondering the connection gave me a fit of shyness and big red hives on my forearm. It overcame my impulse to rush her bones and ransack her book bag. She didn't show up with my imported booty at lunch either. I waited in the cafeteria for her, suffering stares and an inquiry from big jock Mitchell, who seemed to be a perpetual senior. I was sure he was about 21.

"Shouldn't you be in the geek room?" he snickered.

"Shouldn't you be in community college by now?" I answered. It was the best I could do with my horrible distraction. He replied with a forceful push that knocked me backward.

"Dick!" I muttered as he passed, wondering briefly if my stepfather's name had caused him much grief in high school. I saw Maria moving swiftly toward the art room, carrying a tray of franks and beans and a container of milk. I got in her way.

"Where's Jennifer Rosen?" I asked. "You were just in geometry with her, right?"

"Why? Do you have a crush on her?"

"Come on, Maria. This is serious."

She probably saw something flashing in my eyes that said, *Don't fuck around.*

"I saw her heading for the parking lot." She shrugged. "My franks are getting cold, Joe."

"It's your icy grip."

"If I wasn't so hungry, I'd kick you in the balls, Joe," she replied without a smile. I got out of her way. Maria had kicked people in the nuts before. I'd seen Richie go down with a pained squeal.

I reasoned that Jennifer must have gone to the diner with her popular friends. She was eating macaroni salad and drinking egg creams and talking about boys. I didn't belong there.

I mustered whatever patience a lifelong spoiled brat could and followed Maria into the geek room to eat my bagged lunch with John and Richie and Jerome. Ever since she'd divorced Sid and shacked up with Dick, my mother had been straining to get in touch with her inner wholesome housewife. Sid would just slip me some cash so I could get with the franks and beans myself. Susie handed me brown bags every morning, meat loaf sandwiches (unwieldy hunks of ground beef held together with a raw egg and covered with a varnish of ketchup) and baked ziti (with a charred mozzarella covering and the consistency of a swimming pool tarp). She'd cook these horror shows up in her new microwave oven, which, unlike the fairly compact ones that are now readily available, was the size of a small car. It hummed loudly in the kitchen as Susie excitedly watched her creations irradiate. The suburban trash staples—Cool Whip, Squeeze Parkay, Kraft singles, Hershey's syrup—were banished from the fridge when Dick moved in. They'd been replaced with carob, lactose-free soy cheese, and lots of fruit. It was a drag. But she was my mom, so I ate her cooking. That's what you do, even when pickles and macaroni salad and a pretty girl holding the first Smiths album beckon you to disrupt a summit of JAP girls just a ways down the road.

The art room was buzzing with WLIR as usual. Public Image Limited. John Lydon was wailing "This Is Not a Love Song." It might as well have been "This Is Not a Smiths Song" for all the coiled, frustrated energy it created. I didn't tell my gang what I was waiting on, but they could sense that I was distracted as I chewed my meat loaf sandwich.

"What's wrong with you?" John asked, his mouth full of Tater Tots.

"Nothing."

"You never came back yesterday. I waited in here."

"I met a girl."

"Who?"

"Nobody." I shrugged, trying to be cryptic.

"Jennifer Rosen," Maria announced.

"Thanks, Maria!"

She threw a Tater Tot at me. I caught it in midair and ate it.

"That fell on the floor, you know!" she snapped.

"Who's Jennifer Rosen?" John asked.

"She's just a girl," I said. "She's been to London."

He rolled his eyes and got up.

"I'm going to get some cookies," he said. "If they play the song, come get me."

"Okay, John," Jerome promised loyally.

I worried that John was getting increasingly possessive of my time. I didn't really know why. I reasoned that maybe if you clear your mind of all the stupid lust that clutters it up, you get frustrated with the people around you who go chasing after every object of attraction. John really was a teenage monk, I thought. LIR played the Alarm, Aztec Camera, Howard Jones, and Peter Gabriel. Nobody ran to grab John and his cookies. I left to hit my locker before American history class.

"Whatcha got in there?" a voice on the other side of the thin metal door asked. I closed the locker and stared at Jennifer.

"Puppies and kittens," I replied matter-of-factly.

"Let me see," she asked, and peered in.

"Why?"

"I have something for you. It's not as glamorous as all that but I thought maybe you could put it in your locker." She reached into her bag, pulled out a clipping from the *NME*, and handed it to me.

"Who's that?"

"That's him."

"Who?"

"Morrissey."

I stared at the photo in shock. I was almost embarrassed by how handsome this person was, and immediately felt very, very ugly and awkward myself. *It couldn't be,* I thought. He didn't look like I imagined he'd look: ghoulish, freaky, gothic. Instead he was very skinny and bookish with a prominent chin and thick eyebrows. His black hair expertly quiffed up in an almost comical high Elvis style. He wore a button-down shirt, open to the navel, and a cluster of necklaces that seemed to be designed for old English aunties. I felt garish in my black punk rock boots, T-shirt, and splattered, safety-pinned, badge-covered blazer. I closed the locker door, still holding the photo.

"I hear you've been looking for me."

"No," I lied, trying to keep my cool.

"You want your tape, don't you?"

"I don't know. Maybe. Sure."

Again I masked my nerves. I wanted the tape desperately, but I didn't think I could handle it after seeing that photo. It was too much. Jennifer had no idea that she'd unwittingly handed me an archetype. The image of this person instantly became a design for everything I wanted to be. What I wanted to dress like.

What I wanted to express with my own eyes, sharpness and warmth all at once.

How I wanted my hair.

After looking at that photo just once, I decided that I had to burn everything that hung in my closet. I didn't even really know why. I just knew that everything I'd done up until that afternoon had been wrong if only because it hadn't been in-formed by this vision. Morrissey just seemed perfect. I wasn't attracted to him physically. I wanted to *be* him. Or at least the Jewish version. And not just because Jennifer was mad about him either. He just looked perfect.

"What do you mean, you don't know?" She touched my arm with her long fingers. "I stayed up making you this tape."

"Yeah," I answered absently. "Thanks."

"Are you okay, Joe? You look sick."

"Yeah. I'm sick."

"Maybe you should go to the nurse."

"No. I have to go home."

I walked toward the exit to the parking lot, still clutching the photo. She followed, concerned. "You're just gonna leave? You have to sign out. I'll take you to the nurse if you want. Do you want me to take you to the nurse?"

"Yeah," I said, and kept walking.

"Wait!" she called as I opened the door to the lot and stepped into the harsh sunlight. "Don't forget this."

She pressed the cassette box into my blazer pocket, then watched as I walked over the lawn and into the street.

"Oh . . . thanks," I muttered.

I didn't turn around. I took a taxi home to my bedroom. I couldn't take the same long walk home that I had taken the day before. I had serious rethinking to do and little time to spare. I probably should have gone back into the art room and shared the Smiths with my friends. If Jennifer hadn't shown me that photo, I would have. As it was, I needed to be alone. I needed to focus and concentrate on whatever this feeling was that had overtaken me so completely. I couldn't do that in the company of John and Maria and Jerome and Richie, who'd accepted me as I was. What I was had been wrong. I was in possession of whatever I needed to make it right. I just had to figure out how. I knew that whatever was on that tape was more important than anything I would have learned in school that day. Or any day.

The house was empty. I ran upstairs and placed the tape on my desk.

Jennifer had written the song titles on the insert card in red ink, with little hearts dotting the *i*'s, which seemed totally incongruous to each dour title: "You've Got Everything Now" (big red heart over the *i* in *everything*), "Miserable Lie" (two hearts fighting for space over each word), "Still Ill" (more cryptic hearts).

*   *   *

how soon is never?

The tape began with Jennifer's song. The one she'd sung in my ear. "Reel Around the Fountain." But it didn't remind me of Jennifer now that I'd heard it in full. It reminded me of Sid. "It's time that the tale were told, of how you took a child and you made him old," Morrissey sang. After that came "You've Got Everything Now," "Miserable Lie," "Pretty Girls Make Graves," "The Hand That Rocks the Cradle," more recounting of some seriously fucked-up childhood. Hearing each song was like getting smacked out of a fit. Even then, the music felt timeless, as if it had always existed. I felt like the songs had been there my entire life but I couldn't hear them until that moment. Rather, I wanted to go back to various points in my young life and replace key music-related episodes with these songs. My baby-sitter humming to calm my terror during a thunderstorm when I was three. A ring-around-the-rosy session in kindergarten when I was forced to hold the hand of a girl named Crystal who told me that I reminded her of Shaun Cassidy. My first time making out with Jane. That's how familiar and comforting these songs seemed even upon first listen. I could almost predict the next melody line or lyric. I took a deep breath when it was done and felt fresh and new and relieved. I wished school was still in for the day. I wanted to quickly shed my punk rock insect regalia and return to Woodmere Academy a proud fucking wallflower. The shyness I'd been hiding seemed not only cool but also pretty sexy. Shame had become pride. These songs made loneliness, sadness, and outrage seem so cool, I wanted to become even more lonely and sad and outraged. Talk about your powerful good fortunes. Everything I hated about myself became everything I loved inside of one hour.

I rewound the tape as I stood under a long, scalding shower until my skin was pruney. I wrapped a towel around myself and walked back into my room. Stared in the closet.

Everything I owned looked strange to me now. I found a worn pair of blue jeans that Sid had purchased at the army-navy store in Lexington for me to wear while helping him assemble whirlpools. I pulled them on and went downstairs to Susie and Dick's bedroom. Looked in the closet, where Dick kept his clothes. All the suits smelled like pipe tobacco and Alfred Dunhill cologne, but the oxfords were clean. I grabbed a blue-and-white striped shirt that sort of resembled the one Morrissey was wearing in the photo Jennifer had given me and put it on. Since my growth spurt, Dick and I were pretty much the same size. I had longer arms but that was cool. Despite the determined spark in his eyes, Morrissey seemed a bit gangly. I got excited with this new transformation. I taped the *NME* photo to the still-steamy bathroom mirror and spent the hour and a half I should have been in detention carefully quiffing my hair. I took out my contact lenses and dug around my desk drawer for the old pair of specs I hadn't worn since I was twelve. They were tortoiseshell, not black, but they were sure enough geeky. They weren't perfect, but at least, I thought, I no longer looked like a silly punk. I decided that I was worthy of hearing the goddamned album again.

If you play a record long enough, you get a rhythm in your head for its sequence. You anticipate the intro of each new song before the last one even ends. The familiarity and expectation become so ingrained in your mind that when you hear a song from that record on the radio and out of context, it feels weird and wrong. By dinnertime, I had committed the Smiths' self-titled debut to such memory.

"What's he doing in there?" I could hear Dick ask from downstairs after I failed to respond to Susie's repeated dinner bell ringing. She finally walked upstairs herself and pounded and pulled on my locked door.

"Joe? Are you okay? Joe, open the door!" she called. I didn't answer. I was rewinding the tape. It clicked back and I hit play again. The lonely, dramatic beat of "Reel Around the Fountain" started again. I turned it up.

"What's he listening to?" Dick asked, joining my mother in front of my door.

"I don't know! Joe! Dinner is getting cold, and Dick and I are worried about you. Could you please open the door?"

I turned the music up.

"Joe, we're going to call the police!" Susie threatened. I could hear Dick protest.

"We're not going to call the police."

"I know, just let him think we're going to call the police."

"Joe," Dick called, playing along, albeit with less commitment, "if you don't open the door, your mother is going to call the police."

I opened the door.

"Is that my shirt?" Dick asked.

"Yeah. I borrowed it. Is that okay?"

Dick looked at Susie. She was smiling.

"I guess," he sputtered.

"Joe, you look like a person!" she laughed, and mussed the quiff I'd spent over an hour on. I recoiled and immediately checked it in the mirror. I'd put so much goo in it, it was pretty much intact . . . but I still felt violated. I was pissed.

"What do you want?"

"Dinner's ready."

"I'm not hungry."

"You have to eat dinner."

"Why?"

"I made dinner," she said sadly.

"Fine."

I followed them downstairs and we sat quietly, breaking our teeth on the vinyl-topped pasta.

"Do you want some garlic bread?"

"No, thanks. I'm going out."

"You are?"

"Yeah. I don't wanna have bad breath."

"Where are you going?"

I lied. I wasn't going anywhere. There was nowhere for me to go. But it was important that I felt like I was going out. That I was ready.

"So, is this your new look?" Susie asked, explaining to Dick what he already knew, that I was a capricious little shit when it came to fashion.

"It's not a look."

"Oh, what do you call it these days? We used to call it a look. God, I feel old. Dick, you called it a look too, didn't you?"

I got up and left the table. Went upstairs and played the record another ten times. Nobody threw a rock at my window. Nobody revved their motorcycle outside my door. I was housebound. Stuck. I thought about calling John but decided that I still didn't want to share this with him yet. I laid myself out on the floor and stared up at the ceiling, drunk on this music and wishing that I had someone with a bit more mobility at my disposal. . . .

"I just want to be tied . . . to the back of your car," Morrissey sang in a camp falsetto. I was about to turn 15. I needed a fucking car or at least someone willing to tie me to the back of theirs. I picked up the phone and made a long-distance call.

"Hello?"

"Who's this?" the voice on the other end demanded. She was drunk and seemed to be in a shitty mood.

"It's Joe."

"Joey? Is that my boyfriend?" My spirits swung from high

to low pretty quickly. She wasn't alone. "That's my li'l boy-friend Joey," she told somebody. "How are ya, hon?"

"I'm okay, Jane," I lied.

"You sound far away."

"I am far away."

"You calling me from New York City?" Jane always had the frustrating habit of referring to every part of New York State as "New York City." Albany, Buffalo . . . they all equaled New York City in her mind.

"Yeah, I'm in the city," I said, wishing I were. "Is this a bad time?"

"No, hon. Course not. I was just thinking about you." I didn't know much about women, but it was obvious she was lying. I kept the scrap of paper upon which she'd scribbled her phone number in my desk drawer, next to a pack of stale cigarettes, but I hadn't thought about her. I didn't see the point. It would only make me sad and make me feel that much more alone. But I needed to talk to her and I knew she'd be awake at such a late hour. Awake and drunk.

"You know, your daddy's been by the store," she volunteered.

"Oh yeah?" I laughed.

"Yeah, he gave me grief cause we didn't have any Chicago records." She laughed and explained to her companion, who-ever the fuck it was, that she knew both me and my daddy. I was a little relieved that it wasn't my daddy there with her. I wouldn't put it past old Sid. I wanted to hang up and if I'd had Jennifer's number, I might have. I grabbed the cassette box and looked to see if on the odd chance she had scrawled down the instructions "Call me after the content inside blows your head off. XO XO Jennifer" (heart above the *i*). Nothing doing.

"Joey, baby, when you coming back here? I miss you. Iggy misses you."

112

"I don't know," I said sadly, knowing I could never go back to Lexington, Kentucky, again.

Not when Jennifer'd been to London.

"Jane, do you know the Smiths?"

"Who?" she asked, then told her companion, "Stop it!"

"Never mind. I gotta go. I got school in the morning."

"Okay, Joey. You study hard, now. Don't make me come over there and . . . Stop it!"

"Bye, Jane."

"All right, hon!" She giggled as she got off the phone, but it wasn't for me. I felt even more lonely. Jane might have always been just a drunken punk rock girl doomed to remain behind the counter of the only punk rock record store in Lexington, Kentucky, but in my head I'd built her up to be a goddess. Hers was still the only naked female body I'd ever seen and much of my now-tedious masturbation ritual had been devoted to reviving that moment. I felt good as I hung up the phone and thought of the cigarettes and Valiums and Sid prowling the aisles looking for "25 or 6 to 4." It had only been a year, but all that felt ancient. I guess I'd called to confirm what I'd already known that afternoon. I had been forever changed.

oh, john hughes, up yours!

I did little besides play my Smiths records and eat big salads all year. Morrissey was a strict vegetarian and animal-rights activist, and I felt guilty whenever I scarfed down a hot dog or a burger, so I would make a meal out of lettuce and chickpeas and shit. I dressed like Morrissey, or at least I tried to. I kept my hair as high as my naturally wavy Jewish follicles would allow. I added bookish cardigans to my harsher punk rock T-shirts. I perfected a wounded look in my eye and would often sit in a dark room for an hour before catching the school bus so that I might appear that much more sickly. I already knew that acting sad was the fastest way to get attention. People reflexively ask "What's wrong?" And then you've got them.

Jennifer told me in passing that Oscar Wilde was Morrissey's idol and that I bore a faint resemblance to him. I found a black-and-white postcard of Wilde in a rack at the Waldenbooks on Central Avenue in Cedarhurst that summer. He wore a black velvet cape and looked very dandified and wiseassed. I liked the attitude he was radiating but secretly fretted that he was not nearly as handsome as Morrissey was. Regardless, it was enough encouragement to get me to buy his collected works, which I pored through every day. I'd sit on the lawn in my backyard, with my transistor radio playing WLIR or my Walkman blaring the Smiths' debut cassette and the compilation *Hatful of Hollow* (favorite song: "Accept Yourself," if only for the line "Every day, you must say, oh how do I feel about my shoes?"). I'd read the *Complete Works of Oscar Wilde,* write in my notebook, and nurture a serious case of Irish envy (both Morrissey and Wilde were of Irish descent). I had never read anything by choice before, save those *Creem* and *Rolling Stone* magazines. Reading had always been home-work, preparation for some quiz. I also never knew what I wanted to be before. I mean, I wanted to be a non-virgin, but really, everything had always been about what I wanted to "have." I wanted to have a normal father. I wanted to have a certain T-shirt or container of hair dye. I wanted to have sex. By mid-1985, thanks to the Smiths, I finally had something I wanted to be . . . an Irish writer.

My first stories were hardly Wildean. They were actually more like Edgar Allan Poe. Bad Poe.

I used my rough skills and easy appreciation for macabre humor (another Morrissey influence) to craft absurd tales about robots and gorillas in deep-sea-diver helmets who were trained to abduct fair maidens for a depraved mad scientist named Dr. Rude. Awful stuff, but I soon found that, like my two beloved Smiths albums, they made me feel a lot less alone in my seasonal isolation. If my bones had grown and strength-ened the previous summer with Sid and Jane and puberty, 1985 was all about expanding my head.

Sometimes I'd write long letters to Morrissey himself. Essentially, these were diary entries depicting life during a scorching Long Island summer and begging for information about cold, rainy Manchester, England. I never mailed them. I was probably embarrassed that I was acting like a goofy teeny-bopper fan. At worst, I was one. No different than my mother shrieking for the Beatles at Carnegie Hall in 1964, or the teenagers today who mindlessly scream for boy bands. At best, I was learning because I wanted to learn. And unlike those maddening days when we would sit in front of the radio waiting, there was now actual information available about the band to absorb. John and I had joined an unofficial fan club via an ad in the back of one of the *NME*s I'd borrowed from Jennifer. Every month a newsletter would come from London via airmail. I remember eagerly checking the box every day around one to see if the next dispatch had arrived. When it did, we'd devour every new bit of information. If asked, we could recite basic facts about the band like it was the Pledge of Allegiance. We knew all their birthdays. We knew that all four of them, including guitarist Johnny Marr, drummer Mike Joyce, and bass player Andy Rourke, were from Manchester. We learned that Morrissey was a onetime author and rock critic who gained a bit of infamy posting erudite and opinionated letters to the editors of the British music press. I learned that like me, Morrissey had survived his parents' divorce. We believed the legend that Marr simply showed up on the singer's doorstep, unannounced and holding a guitar, and that the creative partnership that ensued was instantly harmonic, intense. Like us, both of them were obsessed with music. We sought out Morrissey's obsessions and made them ours. We didn't require anything more than his endorsement: in addition to Wilde, he adored James Dean and the New York Dolls. John and I promptly rented Dean's 1956 film *Giant* and spent a rainy afternoon watching and trying to emulate the easy cool of Jett Rink. We ordered a copy of the Andy Warhol–produced *Flesh* from a catalog called Movies Unlimited because a still of its star, Joe Dallesandro, was the cover image of the Smiths' debut album. We knew that Morrissey designed all the album covers, which he referred to in the liner notes as "sleeves" (we knew to refer to them as "sleeves" as well). In midsummer, we learned that their second album, *Meat Is Murder,* was forthcoming. There was even talk of a major summer American tour.

While we still felt empowered by this knowledge, I couldn't help but notice that a strange thing was happening around me that year. The cultural line that separated us from the popular kids was becoming thinner and thinner. Our art room society no longer seemed very secret. Perhaps it was MTV's fault. It was now in just about every home, and the videos it rotated all day and all night had made superstars of the artists we were already familiar with. It's hard to take pride in the fact that you've been into the Cure for years when everybody can recount details of their new music video. Worse, MTV led the fucking jocks right to WLIR and soon we realized that we were no longer the only ones glued to the station. Fortunately, like R.E.M. at the time, the Smiths were staunchly anti-video. The jocks and JAPs couldn't see them on MTV, but if they'd tune in to the station to hear, say, the new Pretenders single because they saw the video, they would also be exposed to Smiths songs from the first album and *Hatful of Hollow,* which were now being played constantly. One day, when John overheard a jock humming the melody to "How Soon Is Now" in the cafeteria, he just exploded.

"Do not do that!" he screamed, shaking the guy. "They are not for you! They're ours! You fuckers already took U2!"

It was true. For the first three albums, U2 was one of our bands. We used to chant, "I wanna be an air force ranger! I wanna live a life of danger!" which was the sampled marching chant from "Seconds," *War*'s anti-militarism screed. But the

Irish quartet had just released *The Unforgettable Fire* and were soon to headline Madison Square Garden. To say John was threatened is an understatement. He was furious.

"Do you think that asshole can name one song off *October*?" he raged to his art room army. I don't mean to hang the blame entirely on MTV. John wanted Molly Ringwald's head too.

Between 1984 and '86, director John Hughes lobbed three angstsploitation classics into the multiplexes. First came *Sixteen Candles,* which essentially reduced what we'd once considered our genuine teen angst into a series of sitcom-like punch lines. *The Breakfast Club* and *Pretty in Pink* completed the trilogy. We'd fancied ourselves misunderstood James Deans. Hughes held up a mirror and showed us that in reality, we were Anthony Michael Hall. When he made *The Breakfast Club,* Hughes implied that the geeks could get along with the jocks and the princesses if only they spent a detention together. I'd spent virtually every afternoon in detention the previous year with all manner of JAPs, jocks, geeks, and stoners . . . sometimes, even the other geeks wouldn't talk to me. John's hatred of Hughes was stronger than mine. I kind of had a crush on the Ally Sheedy character, but when he put a Smiths song, "Please, Please, Please Let Me Get What I Want," on the soundtrack to *Pretty in Pink* the following year, I joined in crying out for the guy's blood. It was bad enough that certain people started calling me "Ducky."

Hughes was at his most offensive, I believe, when he inadvertently trumpeted the rewards of gross conformity. If you're familiar with *The Breakfast Club,* you'll recall that the Ally Sheedy character doesn't kiss Emilio Estevez' jock character until after Molly Ringwald gives her a makeover and gets rid of all her dandruff and black eye makeup (her most appealing affectation). If Emilio had kissed Ally as she was, all raccoon-eyed and funky, the scene would have been much more in-spiring for us geeks. Like their emotional connection was enough. I would have respected Hughes, but he was just an asshole. Popularity wasn't an evil concept. Conformity was. And really, the most subversive thing a geek can do to fuck with the high school system from the inside out is to become popular on his or her own terms. I started to see that experi-encing it seemed to be a lot better than remaining bitter and secretly dreaming of acceptance. But I wanted to enjoy it as a full-on geek. The only way to do that was to replace my anger with confidence. I'd learned, as I slowly honed my writing skills, that if I discovered and cultivated a talent, whether it was writing or a mean golf swing or a knack for telling dirty jokes, first of all, it helped me to loosen up a bit. I was happy to have something to call my own. Second, people started showing me respect for it. John, Richie, Maria, Jerome, and I, we never really tried to share with the popular kids what made us special. John was a talented artist and musician but he would always be the freak who stabbed a jock with a pencil and got suspended. Maria had a genius IQ but I doubt the popular girls were ever stimulated by her intellect. She was "the angry girl." And who knows, maybe they had more to of-fer her than a Molly-style makeover. Jerome and Richie . . . well, never mind them. I'm sure they had something. Richie was good at wielding imaginary weapons. I'm trying to make a point. We never even gave the popular kids a chance to ac-cept us either. We never even tried to fit in. We just assumed we never would . . . or could. In a way, we kept the walls be-tween us as high and wide as the jocks and JAPs did. Once you let people see the value in you, they're not so quick to disre-spect you and vice versa no matter what the fuck you're wear-ing. And if you share your talents with everyone, mass respect can grow into genuine popularity very easily. Then it's a re-ward for having guts, not for having clean hair. We were gutless and so were they. Jennifer, who was both arty and popular because she was a kick-ass actress, made me realize this, and after a while, I started to hate it.

In the spring, after contributing various pieces, I started editing the *Echo*, the school newspaper. People seemed to react positively to my writing. I'd get compliments from JAPs and jocks. Even Bert started counting me as a success story. I still ate my lunch in the art room, but not for lack of invitations to dine at a prized table in the cafeteria. There were pretty girls in the caff, girls who were now referring to me as "Joe" instead of "geek" or "weirdo." By summer, I had uninterrupted passage between my two worlds. I remained a geek but became popular by doing nothing but being a good writer, just as a jock like Mitchell was popular because he could throw a ball farther than anybody else. And I liked it. My stories began winning creative-writing awards, little blue ribbons they'd give for academic excellence. I even became more popular with the parents. Susie would Scotch-tape them to the refrigerator, oozing pride, and I even sent one to Sid, enclosed in a Father's Day card. It prompted the following long-distance telephone exchange:

"You're smart."

"Thanks, Dad."

"That's good."

"Thanks, Dad."

Jennifer and I became inseparable, and after I tapped into whatever it was I had to offer as a Wolverine, she had no problem kissing me in front of her friends (and I dressed nothing like them, thank you very much, Mr. Hughes). I would avoid catching a detention because it got in the way of us being able to hang out—and make out—after school. I assumed that was experiencing my first girlfriend. When she introduced me to her parents and older brother as "my friend Joe," I didn't give it much thought because I knew we'd soon be lying on her bed.

Jennifer had been gifted with a red Mustang on her 17th birthday. She liked to gun it. We'd pile into the thing after school, put on WLIR, and traverse from North Shore to South Shore in record time. We'd eat cheese and crackers (fancy, French) and drink cream soda, sometimes sneak some wine, while doing our homework (another novelty I'd recently embraced), then hit the sheets. Her body was skinny like mine. I wondered if I was missing something in the tit area but I didn't complain. It was intimate contact. Lips and hands and thighs. Jennifer never let me take off her panties, and so my underwear stayed on too. If the girl's stay put, you're not gonna yank down your briefs and lie there sticking up, I don't care how bad you wanna demonstrate your urgent excitement.

"How come we can't do it, Jennifer?"

"Because we can't."

"But I don't wanna be a virgin no more."

"Tough."

"Jennifer!"

"Stop whining, Joe."

"Jennnnnniferrrrr!"

Then she'd hit me. Sometimes she'd bring Morrissey into the mix.

"Morrissey wouldn't bug me to fuck him."

"Shut up."

"Would you fuck Morrissey, Joe?"

"No."

"Yes, you would, Joe. You're full of it. If Morrissey was here right now, you'd so fuck him."

"No."

"You so would."

She'd try to vex me with shit like that, but I was only really vexed by her refusal to put out all the way. I liked the fact that Morrissey was sexually ambiguous. It made it easy to view him as genuinely pure. Irreproachable. Holy. He claimed to be and sang about being celibate, but there were indeed whispers that he was gay. Certainly many of his lyrics could be construed as homoerotic, but I never really troubled myself with it. I was attracted to him the way Christians are attracted to Jesus. He was beautiful and he was my god. I couldn't imagine kissing him, but I'm sure I would have killed a carnivore for him if he required it. After all, he'd helped set me free.

our little group

If there had been a lid on our collective passion for the Smiths in the days leading up to their tour stop at New York City's Beacon Theater, it was no longer on. Only the unhappy circumstance of not being able to get tickets to see both shows of the band's two-night stand tempered our giddiness.

"How could they possibly have sold out both shows?" I'd wonder aloud in the art room. Part of me still thought of them as our discovery . . . a small band who'd happened to get on local radio. I'd never been there, but the Beacon Theater sounded like a relatively large venue.

"There can't be that many Smiths fans, can there?"

We'd long talked about driving into Manhattan but decided that the Galaxie could not contain all of us and our fidgety electricity. On the day of the show, we opted to take the Long Island Railroad into Pennyslvania Station. John, Jerome, Maria, Richie, and I boarded the train at the Woodmere station, a hundred yards from the academy campus, and immediately marveled that we were not alone. There were two chubby girls in our car, one tall and older looking, the other wide and baby-faced. It was quickly apparent that they were going our way.

"They must have got on at Lawrence or Cedarhurst," I whispered.

We didn't recognize them. They probably went to public school, but with their black clothes, geometrically cut hair, and combat boots, we knew they weren't on their way to the mall.

We stared at them and nodded in silent acknowledgment, befitting some unspoken brother- and sisterhood. It was almost sweet until the wide girl broke the silence.

"We went last night too."

"Really?" I replied.

"It was so incredible," the older girl gushed. "I can't believe it. So incredible."

"Don't tell us anything, okay? I mean, don't spoil it," I pleaded.

"Is this your first show?" the wide girl asked.

"Yeah."

"We saw them last year too."

"I bet you think you're too cool," John snapped, and walked toward the back of the car to change his seat.

"What's his problem?" The wide girl frowned.

"It's their first show," the older girl answered, and grinned like the Buddha. When we changed at Jamaica station for the connecting train into Manhattan, we made it a point to lose them. But there were more hints of what was to come as we hopped the number 1 subway line and headed uptown toward 72nd Street and Broadway. The subway car was full of even more people who looked just like us, from all over the city . . . and, judging by the accents, all over Long Island too. We meekly sat together in the car, avoiding eye contact and cringing as the fans who surrounded us sang the riff to "The

Headmaster Ritual," *Meat Is Murder*'s opening track, then went right into the bass hook for the second track, "Rusholme Ruffians."

"I can play that," John whispered proudly. "You don't see me here with my guitar, do you?"

We walked up the stairwell and out onto the concrete island on Broadway. We could literally feel that the band was close. It sounds super-corny now, but it was so exciting at the time. The Smiths were in New York City. They were within walking distance of us, housed in a dressing room two blocks away, breathing the same air we were breathing. If the Russians shot a missile at New York City, I thought, we'd all die together. There'd be no escaping it. It was the first time that the long Cold War that had plagued my preadolescent years with nightmares seemed remotely romantic. Even though seats at the Beacon were assigned, we walked quickly toward the theater, struggling to outpace the other concertgoers.

The lobby was a mad scene. The show seemed oversold. The din was intense. There were several hundred kids chattering away with wired anticipation. John and I were speechless. Maria sneered at everyone in sight. Only Richie and Jerome were all smiles. They'd never been to Manhattan. WLIR had set up a little booth inside the venue and one of the station's interns was handing out white badges emblazoned with their slogan: Dare to Be Different. Everyone who filed in made a point to grab one and uniformly pin it on their jackets and blouses and book bags or through their earlobe holes. Jerome, Richie, and I grabbed a handful of them and some bumper stickers. I made the mistake of handing one to John.

"It says dare to be different!" John scoffed, pointing out the irony. I laughed at his quick-witted observation, at my own expense, of course. He was starting to bum me out, but I decided not to make a big deal of it. My laughter seemed to loosen him up. In an effort to make him feel even more at ease, I started picking apart our fellow concertgoers.

"Look at that kid. Who the hell does he think he is?" I pointed to a skinny, blotchy-faced teenager who'd outfitted himself in full-on Morrissey drag, not realizing, of course, that I looked almost identical to him (and neither of us looked much like Morrissey).

"I think he's deaf," Jerome whispered.

"If he's deaf, why are you whispering?" Maria observed. So smart.

Indeed, he was wearing a hearing aid in his left ear. I learned a bit later that Morrissey had recently worn a similar device during an appearance on *Top of the Pops*. Not only could the blotchy kid hear me, I'd made him smile. He knew he had one-upped me.

"I'm gonna buy a T-shirt," Jerome said cheerfully as we passed the merchandise table on our way into the theater proper.

"Why? Do you want to look like everybody else here too?" John asked.

"Yes," Jerome answered, unaware that he was being attacked. "Which one should I get, John?"

John didn't answer. He kept walking and soon disappeared into the crowd. Feeling guilty, I stayed behind to help Jerome pick out the perfect tee. I soon realized that our little group was completely separated. We had lost John . . . or he had lost us. As we filed past the concession stand, we overheard some poor kid getting mercilessly berated by another Morrissey zealot for ordering a hot dog.

"What's meat?"

"Huh?" the hot-dog kid asked with his mouth full.

"Have you even heard the album?" the vegetarian militant shrieked. "Meat is murder!"

"I'm hungry!" the other one sputtered meekly, only to

have his dog seized and hurled through the air. It landed against the wall and slid down, leaving a slug trail of mustard. Things were getting serious, I thought, and pushed past all the kids in black, intent on finding an usher. Jerome, Richie, and Maria followed closely until poor Richie was grabbed and kissed on the lips by an excited blond girl and nearly had a heart attack.

"Danny!" she screamed at him. "Do you remember me?"

"No," he whimpered.

"Danny! Don't be like that!" She was drunk, maybe high too. She swayed backward, swung her purse wildly, then leaned in and pushed him. Richie was nearly in tears with fright.

"It's Lara! From Echo and the Bunnymen at the Ritz? Hello? How come you haven't called me, you fuck-face?"

"His name's not Danny," Maria corrected frostily.

"It's not?" the girl drawled, and stared Richie up and down. "Oh."

She walked away without blushing or apologizing.

"Why did you tell her I'm not Danny?" Richie asked.

"She'll give you a disease."

"So?" He'd recovered from the shock and probably kind of liked getting kissed.

Maria pushed him. We trudged ahead and soon found our seats.

"Smiths! Smiths! Smiths! Smiths!"

The lights were still on inside the venue as we all sat down. We were twelve rows from the stage. The balcony was already shaking, and the weird football chant was instigated, then abandoned, then reinstigated or altered to "Ste-ven! Ste-ven!"

"God, they even know Morrissey's full name is Steven Patrick Morrissey," I marveled. I felt pretty silly for thinking I was the only one who knew, but unlike my friend, I was kind of glad that I wasn't the only one. It was a pretty amazing discovery.

"Where's John?" I asked, looking around, anxiously. It was clear from the energy in the air that the band was close to taking the stage. We could almost feel them approaching. The lights seemed to be dimming in slow motion. Most of the seats were full and our friend had gone missing. Jerome and Richie shrugged.

"Maybe John doesn't want to sit with us anymore," Maria suspected aloud.

"Why?" I asked, even though I knew the answer. I pretended that it wasn't the case, but what else could it have been, really? He was overwhelmed with emotion. We all were. This was too much. It could only end in disaster, I thought.

And then the lights went out and the hum of the amp buzzed out of the Beacon's powerful speakers. Then a quick drumbeat . . . and then . . . the four of them.

It takes a perfect idea to inspire multitudes to check their individuality and come together as one, even for an hour and a half. The Smiths were the most perfect idea I'd ever heard. Or seen. Morrissey, in a stroke of genius that has been copied to death to this day but at the time was truly radical, wore a Smiths T-shirt. The very kind that was for sale out in the lobby. To a teenage fan, this was nothing short of a communion. I let down my guard ten seconds into the opener, "William, It Was Really Nothing," and like everyone else in the audience, I allowed myself to indulge guiltlessly in the delusion that Morrissey was singing to me alone, and more than that, I was singing to him as he danced toward the lip of the stage, then pulled himself back and blew out his voice, only to reclaim it again and again. Back in '85, it all seemed completely effortless. I turned to my left and saw boys screaming along with starstruck and possibly even sex-mad girls. I felt myself screaming along. I say "felt" because I couldn't actually distinguish the noise coming out of me from the noise filling the room. Our combined applause and sing-alongs and whistles created such a tumult that nobody could hear anything unique coming out of their own mouths. We all might as well have been Morrissey. He erased any reservation or bashfulness. Even Maria was singing. For however long this lasted, I thought, *I can do anything. I can be anyone.* I only held back by refusing to rush the stage, although I had complete empathy for the hundreds who did because they simply could not get close enough.

Live, the Smiths were more of a pure fast-and-loud rock 'n' roll band than I expected. This was no somber gathering. Even the melancholy ballad "Please, Please, Please Let Me Get What I Want" inspired total strangers to hug each other. But nobody cried. Not until the band left the stage and it was clear that they weren't coming back. They were moving on to conjure up this ecstasy in other cities. The sadness that had been effectively siphoned from my soul returned only as I led our exit toward the street and realized that some of the people floating down the aisles with me would be there . . . and that I would be back on Long Island, not getting laid. I never wanted to go home again. I was out, in Manhattan, and as revved up as I'd ever been.

"You guys don't want to take the train right away, do you?" I asked my crew, hoping they'd come away with the same level of euphoria and inspiration. "Don't you wanna go out?"

"Where?" Maria asked sensibly.

"Anywhere," I said. "It doesn't matter to me."

"Shouldn't we try to find John?" Jerome suggested.

"Yeah," I agreed. "We definitely should find John."

I was eager to see if the show had had the same effect on

him as it had on me, even though I knew that he would be way too cool to admit it aloud.

"I'll look for him down by the coat check. You guys grab him if he comes by here, okay? Either way, let's meet outside in fifteen minutes."

"Okay, Joe." Jerome nodded.

I walked toward the stairs, mingling with all the pie-eyed Smiths fans coming down to earth and realizing that they had to pee. Once upstairs, I surveyed the room but didn't see him anywhere. I walked back into the theater and peered down each balcony aisle like a police inspector. That's when I saw John with his arms around an androgynous boy. He had lank, jet-black hair nearly down to his shoulders. Bad skin and deep blue eyes.

"What are you doing?" I asked.

"Who is this?" the boy sneered. He wasn't from the Island as far as I could tell by the accent. John pulled the boy off him and, acting like nothing was out of the ordinary, asked where the rest of the gang was.

"They're downstairs, waiting for you. Worrying about you, actually. Are you . . . okay?"

"He's fine," the boy answered.

"I'm not asking you, I'm asking him," I snapped.

He ignored me and turned to John.

"Is this your boyfriend?" the boy asked him. John shook his head and indicated with his eyes that that was the wrong question to ask aloud. Suddenly, my goodwill toward all present had evaporated and I could feel myself losing my cool to confusion and a vague sense of betrayal.

"Why don't you get the fuck out of here?" I suggested to the kid.

"Why don't you make me?"

I turned to John for help, wondering if I was about to be on the wrong end of his No. 2 pencil.

"Are you gay?"

"Shut up," he laughed.

"You're gay?" I stammered. "Gay?"

"So this is what it's like in suburbia, I see," the kid said. I lost it and punched him in the gut.

It's one thing to treat me like some gay-party pooper, I thought, *but to suggest that I'm a hick!*

I connected hard and the kid grabbed his gut. Then I felt John push me backward with all his strength. I landed hard on my tailbone. Pain shot up my spine. What was happening to my euphoria? As I pulled myself up, rubbing my ass, I fantasized that Johnny Marr and Morrissey could hear the scuffle from their dressing room and decided to retake the stage for one more number that would reinstate the now dwindling bliss.

"We want to go out," I said. "We don't wanna go home."

"So don't go home," John said coldly. "I'll call you tomorrow."

"You don't wanna come?"

He didn't answer, just shook his head slowly.

"Why not?"

He gestured slightly to the boy, who was still holding his gut and grimacing. I just stared sadly . . . for too long. I should have turned and walked away, but I was still standing there staring even after he left. John was gone. I started to panic. I ran upstairs, worried that Maria, Jerome, and Richie had abandoned me to be gay as well. I don't know what I was thinking. I was still rushing from the adrenaline fix of punching someone who'd insulted me . . . and Long Island. They were still there, waiting. A little nervous.

"What happened? Where's John?" Jerome asked.

"We just missed a train. It's another hour and a half till the next one, Joe," Maria complained.

"Did you find him?" Richie inquired eagerly.

"Yeah. I found him."

how soon is never?

"Where is he?" Maria demanded.

"He found a friend. He's gone."

"Who?" she continued.

"Somebody new," I said, near tears. "Somebody gay."

"Gay?" Richie echoed, confused.

"Yeah, gay. John's gay. Come on . . . let's go." I walked toward the door, hoping they'd follow. When they did, I was relieved but didn't let on.

"John's gay?" Richie asked again. We pushed through the doors and out onto Broadway, where four or five dozen Smiths fans were still lingering in the warm night air. I didn't answer. My hand hurt from the punch. My brain hurt from what I'd seen and the shame that I was actually shocked and upset. John was long gone. I did a quick search.

"John's not gay," Maria volunteered.

"Oh yeah? Then why was he kissing another boy in the balcony?"

I was a fucking hick—that kid was right. That was the moment where, if I didn't stop being naive altogether, I made a mental note to be much more suspicious and cynical. Although it seemed to be a better way at the time, I'd love to be that naive for just one night today. I'd love to walk into a bar and ask my friends, "What are you going into the bathroom every ten minutes for, guys?" Still, as soon as I outed John to our little group, it hit me. Maybe he had just discovered that he was gay, liberated, as we all had been, by the joyous rock show. Maybe I'd interrupted a crucial moment of self-realization. Perhaps he had showed up, like we all had, not knowing what to expect, only vaguely sensing that it would change our lives.

We decided to head back to Long Island after all. As we waited for the next train, nibbling on stale pizza and drinking large Pepsis, I started to feel jealous of John. He was off discovering something because he let it happen. I was heading back to the place where I knew everyone and everything . . . most of all, where I knew myself. Nobody said a word the whole way back. Not even when we changed at Jamaica station.

I didn't see John anymore that summer. Jennifer was back in London, and I waited for her infrequent postcards and phone calls. I got a part-time job at a bagel place called Mom's and turned over my paychecks to Susie and Dick, who'd promised to safely keep them for me, tucked away in the "first-car fund." By the end of August, I'd built up a very small fortune. More than enough to cover the car insurance that they insisted I pay for on my own. By summer's end, the Smiths had released a new single, "The Boy with the Thorn in His Side." Our newsletter intimated that it was a teaser for the new studio album they were reportedly working on. I happened to be walking home from Mom's when I first heard it and had to stop in front of the cemetery, which was the midpoint landmark on my homeward path. Cemeteries used to scare the piss out of me when I was younger. The playground of my grade school, the No. 1 School on Central Avenue in Lawrence, was next to one, and whenever a kickball went over the wrought-iron fence and rolled through the land plots and tombstones, that was it. Get a new ball. But ever since discovering romantic morbidity, not only was I unafraid of the boneyard, I thought there was no better place for indulging in some seriously poetic self-pity. I walked through the gate and sat in front of a faded tombstone as the song played on my Walkman.

"Behind the hatred, there lies a murderous desire for love," Morrissey sang.

This grave hadn't been visited in forever, I thought, noticing that the name had been eroded off by weather and time. Only the date was still legible. *D. 1951.*

Thirty-four years in the ground, I thought, *and nobody cares anymore.*

I felt so lonely and wanted John or Jennifer or anybody to come and take me far away. To wherever they were.

"And when you want to live how do you start? Where do you go?"

By early 1986, Susie finally let me get my learner's permit and I drove to and from school in my first (and to this day, my only) car. A brand-new red two-door Toyota Tercel hatchback. It was a putt-putting death box, but it was *my* putt-putting death box. I pooled the remainder of my summer savings and outfitted the thing with a stereo system worthy of a sleek Italian sports car. Inside, it was so compact, I could literally make my own ears ring if I cranked it. I was proud of it. Yeah, I didn't completely buy it for myself with my saved paychecks, but I had paid for some of it, and for a lifelong spoiled brat, I didn't need much more than that to feel good about myself.

Unfortunately, I couldn't show it off. John refused to be the licensed driver who would enable me to cruise Long Island freely. My reward for outing him was total banishment from the art room. Even though she still wasn't putting out, I took solace in Jennifer's return from Europe. After play rehearsal (that year's radical Mr. Sturmer production: Arthur Miller's *Death of a Salesman,* genders reversed, *and* in quasi-Kabuki— Jennifer played Happy Loman in male drag and in a white mask), we'd stop at the diner to drink hot chocolate with whipped cream and split a plate of french fries sopped with brown gravy, then put some mileage on my new odometer just driving around, listening to LIR and watching the falling snow cover everything in sight. Jennifer had started to apply to colleges, and although the prospect of having to spend the following year without her and John (who was also graduating) terrified me, I would keep her company while she filled out applications. Sarah Lawrence and Vassar were her "safe schools" (the worthy but secondary schools you settled for if you didn't get into your first choice). She really wanted to go to Juilliard. I was pulling for her, since it was technically local. She'd stretch out on her bed and fill out form after form while I played with her long, warm twitching toes.

"Stop it, Joe, you're tickling me. I have to do this." She'd warmly giggle and flip over on her back to read the forms.

"Hey, Joe, am I a male or a female?"

"I wouldn't know, Jennifer."

Then she'd push me off the bed. Throughout our relationship, she never stopped pushing me. I took it as a bit of our preciously nonverbal communication, but deep in my heart it still felt like being pushed away. I'd gently push her back and she'd scream melodramatically.

"Joe! You're not supposed to hit a girl."

"So you *are* a female!" I'd shout, and point. She'd climb on top of me and kiss me. . . .

Then we'd not-fuck.

We'd been going out for over a year, but she still referred to me in mixed company as her "friend Joe." And with her senior prom and my junior prom approaching, I felt the pressure to formally define the relationship. Even today, in my early 30s, I can fall victim to such an insecurity-driven need to identify a naturally evolving relationship, and that impulse can ruin things forever. And this is with women I'm actually sleeping with. It's much better to just shut the fuck up and let things play out naturally. You can't arm-wrestle for the title. You're either a boyfriend or you're not. But when you're sixteen and still a virgin, with almost no experience dealing with girls . . . when you've just found out your best friend is gay and you're wondering if that makes you gay (I swear, I did), you pretty much need things clearly defined. Especially when your mother asks things like "So when am I going to meet this Jennifer? Why don't you have her over for dinner? I'll make meat loaf." And Dick pulls you into his dressing room, sits you down, and begins rooting around in his socks and underwear drawer for a three-pack of Trojans.

"I know prom is coming up, Joe, and I want to make sure that you don't do anything stupid. Do you know how to put one of these on?"

I took the rubbers and assured him that I knew how to use them. Dick was trying to be a father figure and I appreciated it. Sometimes he'd grab my school tie, undo it, and retie it, shaking his head. But I could never talk to Dick about sex. It would have been too weird, because I would assume that everything he was talking about, he was doing to my mom at night. Since I was pretty convinced that my real father couldn't even remember what Susie looked like naked any-more, what with all the drugs and clouds of bitterness, I turned to him one night via an atypical long-distance father-and-son summit.

"Dad?"

"Who's this?"

"Who else would call you Dad?"

"Joe? Are you all right?"

"I'm fine."

"Are you in trouble?"

"No, Dad, I'm fine."

"Good."

"Dad? I need to get laid."

"Oh yeah?"

"Yeah!"

"What do you want me to do?"

It was a good question, actually. What did I want him to do? I guess I wanted him to provide me with two options. The

first being a long, perfectly detailed game plan that would succeed in my removing Jennifer's panties. But I really wanted
him to light a smoke and tell me that a hooker would be
climbing through my window in twenty minutes and that I
should instruct her to bill him upon deflowering.

"You need to get laid?"

"I need to get laid!"

"How old are you?"

"I'm sixteen, Dad. You were there when I was born,
remember?"

"I'm not your father."

"Shut up. You are too. Help me. Please? I'm going a little
crazy here."

"You wanna come here?"

"I can't."

"Well, I can't come there. I got business, Joe. I'll tell you
what. You come out here this summer and we'll take care of
your problem for you."

"Really?"

"Yeah. It's not like I can mail you some pussy."

"Huh?"

"I said I can't mail you pussy."

"Dad, there's already a girl."

"What's her name?"

"What difference does it make?"

No answer. Either he was hurt that I'd shot down his attempt to make paternal small talk or he was considering my
question.

"Her name's Jennifer."

"She white?"

"Yeah, she's white."

"Good. So what's the problem?"

"She won't fuck me!"

"Did you ask her?"

"I gotta go, Dad. I'll talk to you later."

"All right. Listen . . ."

"What?"

"You come out here and we'll take care of everything for you. I don't want you looking for no pro in the city. Your dick'll fall off. You don't want your dick to fall off, do you?"

"No. I don't want my dick to fall off."

"We'll take care of it out here. It'll be clean. Fast. Easy. Boom. You're done."

"Okay, Dad. Thanks."

"Boom. You're done."

Boom. You're done. Was that what it had come down to? I'd already spent the afternoon with Jennifer and made the long drive back to Lawrence from Great Neck, but I knew I had to go back again. I pulled on my pants and boots, and after tossing through my dresser drawer, I grabbed a semi-clean Smiths T-shirt from the hamper (I knew I had to be wearing something Smithsy for this occasion). It was nearly dark out when I jumped into the Tercel and turned on the radio, which was playing "Digging Your Scene" by the Blow Monkeys. If Jennifer didn't come around, my only two options were losing my dick or "Boom, you're done." As crass as Sid's promise was, I have to admit it functioned pretty well as a safety net and gave me the nerve to head north with the intent of extending Jennifer an invite to both my prom and hers. I mulled over what I was going to say as I veered across the conduit onto the Long Island Expressway and pushed in my latest mix tape.

"I'm going to meet the one I love!" Morrissey crooned in as I cranked up the Smiths' "Shakespeare's Sister," which segued into "Bittersweet" by the Hoodoo Gurus. I turned it up and silently prayed as I pushed the Tercel to 80 (a speed at which it usually started to shake like a rocket reentering Earth's atmosphere). I could feel that my virginity was not long for the world and I really hoped it would be Jennifer, not some Kentucky hooker, who would take it off my hands . . . literally.

"Joe, what are you doing here? Did you forget something?" She answered the door herself. Her folks were already in bed, watching the late news. She was dressed for bed herself. Oversized T-shirt, underwear, thick white socks.

"How come you never call me your boyfriend?" I started without any greeting or explanation.

"Oh, God."

"Seriously, Jennifer. I have to know."

"You drove all the way back here to ask me this?"

"Yeah."

She took my hand sadly and pulled me inside.

"Let's go out back," she said, leading me across the cold tiles, through the kitchen, and into the backyard, where we sat together at her parents' large wooden picnic table.

"I need a cigarette," she said wearily. "Will you wait here?"

I nodded and she ran upstairs. I walked back into the kitchen. I could hear her explain to her parents that everything was okay. It wasn't an armed robbery, it was only Joe, her mad virgin sort of boyfriend, come looking for answers . . . and a prom date. She returned with a pack of French cigarettes. Blue packet. Very strong. She pulled one out and remarked that they were probably stale by now. Lit up and exhaled, then confirmed that they indeed were. I grabbed one anyway.

"Joe, you shouldn't smoke."

I ignored her and lit up myself, trying really hard to look as hurt and bad-assed as I felt was appropriate. In other words . . . a lot. I milked it with the Frenchie cigs. *If only it was raining,* I thought. Somewhere inside, I knew this trip would hurt me. I just knew I wouldn't come away satisfied and would probably limp away totally destroyed . . . so it felt good to have a stale European prop in my hands, especially since I'd be throwing my skinny body to the rocks below from behind the wheel of a Toyota, not James Dean's "Little Bastard," a speeding, doomed silver Porsche Spyder.

"Do you not love me, Jennifer?" I asked, trying hard to steer the mood from the light to the really heavy. I meant to say "Do you love me?" as a direct question rather than a question begging some negative confirmation. My shoulders sagged and I turned away.

"I mean . . . what about the prom?" I said, addressing the clipped topiary swans at the far end of the yard.

"Joe, I'm not going to the prom."

"What?"

"I'm not going."

"But you're a senior. Don't you have to?"

"I don't want to go."

"You don't want to go or you just don't want to go with me?" I asked, trying not to appear too needy.

She pulled me close to her and kissed me on the cheek. I started to shake.

"What?" was all I could say. I didn't know what the kiss meant, but it felt like a kiss goodbye.

"Don't make me say this, Joe. We only have a few more weeks together, and then . . . well we're gonna be separated no matter what. Can't things just stay the way they are?"

I got mad and courageous because of it. I turned to her, full eye contact, and shook my head.

"Why not?"

"Because I love you. I don't want you to go. Everyone I ever love leaves me!"

"Oh, God. You know who you sound like, don't you? You sound like Morrissey."

"So?"

"So stop it. Joe. I never made you any promises."

"Why not?" I whined again.

"Well, because . . . I have a boyfriend. That's why."

"What?"

"In London."

I got up and walked toward the topiary swans on her lawn. I wanted to mount one and fly away but couldn't remember whether or not swans could fly. This was how crazy and swirling my thoughts were. Jennifer was my girlfriend, wasn't she? Nothing made sense, so it seemed plausible that I could hop a topiary swan and fly off to Kentucky to dip my virgin wick in some hillbilly slut.

She followed me down the lawn and grabbed my arm.

"Joe, look at me."

I refused to turn around. She spoke anyway. I imagined she was talking to somebody else. I looked up at the stars.

"He knows about you."

"Oh, that's nice," I said weakly.

"He's okay with what we do . . . as long as we don't . . ."

"Fuck?"

"I guess."

"How come he knows about me and I don't know about him?"

"Well, he's . . . older, Joe. He's twenty-one."

"What's his name?"

"What difference does it make?" She shook her head in defeat and fessed up. "His name is Robin. He's a director on the West End. We've been going out for two years."

"And he doesn't mind that we . . . kiss?" I asked, wishing we'd done something a bit less innocent.

"He's mature enough to understand, I guess. He knows how much I care about you."

"Two years?" I whimpered, and started to backtrack toward the kitchen.

how soon is never?

She followed me again.

"See? This is why I couldn't tell you. I knew you'd act this way."

"How am I supposed to act?"

"Joe, I can't go to the prom with you, and I can't sleep with you. So what? I'm still here. We've still got something special."

"No, we don't. You fuck him! You don't fuck me! You fuck Robin!"

I walked faster.

"Joe, don't go!"

"Fuck you, you fucking slut!"

"Joe!"

By then, Jennifer's mother and father had descended the stairs and were staring at us in the kitchen. I didn't realize it until it was too late and I was standing right before them that they'd heard everything. They were older than Susie and Sid. Fully gray, sleepy-eyed, barefoot, and very irritated by all the noise.

"Is everything okay?" Jennifer's dad asked.

"No," I answered.

"Everything's fine," Jennifer assured them as she entered the kitchen. "Go to bed."

"We were trying to," her mother huffed. *What a bitch,* I thought, and gave her a look that said as much. It didn't go over very well.

"Can't whatever this is wait until tomorrow?" she snarled.

"Are you smoking, Jennifer?" her father asked.

I pushed past him and walked toward the front door fast, slamming it behind me, as I could feel myself about to cry.

I could hear Jennifer's muted arguing with her mother and father as I stood there on the doorstep. The fuckers wouldn't even let her follow me. They were cheating me out of my big exit, I fumed. The nerve. I walked down the driveway and stopped again, hoping Jennifer would manage to extricate herself from what looked like the beginning of a long-ass lecture. She didn't. I got into the car and waited another five minutes, revving the engine as loudly as you can in a Tercel. The front door remained closed. Finally, I threw it in reverse and peeled out of there, taking care to spread as much gravel across their newly cut grass as I could. I headed south, intent on doing something incredibly self-destructive. I didn't want a Kentucky hooker to be the only thing waiting for me at the end of the line, my best friend and now the love of my young life taken away just like that.

I'll show them both. They'll all be sorry they ever fucked with me, I thought as I cranked up "How Soon Is Now" on the mix tape and drove offensively down the Long Island Expressway. I pulled into a gas station/convenience store on Rockaway Turnpike and purchased a liter bottle of Dr Pepper, a bottle of Sominex sleeping pills, and a pack of Parliament cigarettes.

The clerk was a mullet-headed high school dropout, covered in grease and grooving on the crappy new Van Halen single, "Why Can't This Be Love." It was their first with their retarded new singer, Sammy Hagar. It didn't even sound like fucking Van Halen! *Nothing is the same anymore,* I thought as I handed him a $20 bill and waited for my change.

"Trouble sleeping?" he asked.

"No, I'm gonna kill myself."

"Oh." He nodded, breaking into a goofy smile. "Cool."

eleven

appetite for destruction

I walked back to the Tercel, realizing I'd left the keys inside and the car idling. I was out of my head. I got in and gunned it south, popping Sominex and gulping soda as I ran every red light on the way to the Atlantic Beach Bridge, secretly praying that a cop would stop me . . . stop everything.

I parked the car on the grassy island next to the bridge on-ramp and stared at the entrance to the bike path I used to take on my way to see Sid and his basehead friends. I couldn't believe things had gotten even more confusing, and reasoned that it was better to end it now, before such mind fuckery increased exponentially. It would . . . it had to, as I was clearly cursed. The sugary taste of the Sominex coating and the Dr Pepper made me gag. I waited there for a feeling of numbness to take me over. I'd floor it onto the bridge and make a hard right into the air and down into the water. By the time I broke the surface, I reasoned, I'd be endlessly asleep. I wouldn't feel it. I'd just sink to the bottom. . . . Maybe I'd come back as a Hindu or a sheepdog or a horseshoe crab, or a Sammy Hagar fan. The tape ended and self-ejected. The last thing I heard was Malibu Sue advising me to stay tuned for Thrashing Doves, Fine Young Cannibals, and the Smiths' new single, "Bigmouth Strikes Again."

When I woke up, there was pink puke all over my new cloth upholstery. LIR was playing "Ça Plane Pour Moi" by Plastic Bertrand. The battery was still alive and so was I. I vaguely remembered fighting to stay awake so that I could hear the new Smiths single and wrestling with a part of me that reasoned if I went off the bridge, I'd never be able to hear the whole album (advance buzz on the newsletter circuit was that it was their best yet). I don't know whether or not it was the Sominex or the Smiths that saved my life (maybe it was the Fine Young Cannibals). All I knew as I put the car in drive and headed for Susie's was that if I had to be alive in this world of pain, I really wanted to hear "Bigmouth Strikes Again."

What doesn't kill you only serves to give you a really bad headache. I didn't go to school the next day. And Jennifer didn't call but I remained aware each time the telephone rang. I was prepared to recount my activity after leaving her house, omitting all the sloppy, embarrassing failures and fuckups in favor of the lovesick melodrama: the traffic violations, the pills, the bridge. I didn't get the chance. She was pulling that thing that's common to high school girls (and, come to think of it, women in their 30s do this too). The whole "I'll let him heal" rationale. It's the last thing a guy wants. Really. I know we're supposed to take it on the chin and move on, maybe after a drink or an entire bottle of wussy-strength sleeping pills, but I don't care if you're the toughest motherfucker going—if a girl hurts you bad, you still want her to call and make sure you're okay. You'll heal, but you don't want her to "let" you heal. You want her to be torn up. You want her to call every fifteen minutes like a rehab nurse. Jennifer, with her European maturity, was letting me heal tough-love style and it was pissing me off.

She finally came to see me a good 48 hours, one suicide attempt, and a migraine later, as I was sitting on the bleachers listening to the new Replacements album, *Pleased to Meet Me,* on my Walkman and chain-smoking. I knew I looked bad. Sick. Sad. She pointed it out as a way to break the ice.

"Are you okay?" she asked, and sat down next to me in a friendly way I immediately found offensive. I moved away and didn't say a word.

"Can you hear me?"

She pulled my headphones off just as the opening riff to "Alex Chilton" rattled in the headphones.

"Are we like not gonna talk for the rest of the year?" she asked worriedly as she turned down the volume herself. "Cause I don't think I can handle that."

I remembered how hurt I'd been when John wrote me off completely and for a moment I contemplated doing the same thing to Jennifer, but I couldn't . . . basically, because it would mean I wouldn't get to talk to her for the rest of the year. I still cared.

"How could you do this to me?" I finally asked after what seemed like an hour of silence.

"I'm sorry, Joe. I had a long talk with Robin after you left."

"Oh yeah?"

"He said that he wouldn't mind if I took you to the prom."

"That's good of Robin."

"Will you go with me?"

"No."

"Please?"

"No."

"Why not?"

"Because . . ." I rose and threw my cigarette onto the dirt track with a flourish that I hoped would be rebellious but came off really spastic. "I wanna get laid on prom night. This is America, isn't it? I don't know what you do in London, but in America, you're supposed to get some pussy on prom night."

"Are you trying to hurt me, Joe? Are you trying to make me feel like shit?"

"Yes!"

She got up and started to walk away. I broke down and went after her, grabbed her by the shoulder hard, and pulled her around. Froze for a minute as she stared at me. Her eyes were teary.

"I'm sorry."

"Yeah," she said weakly.

"Break up with him, Jennifer," I pleaded.

"It's not that easy."

"Sure it is. He doesn't even live here. It's just one phone call. What time is it in England?"

"They're five hours ahead."

"So you can still catch him awake. Call him and get it over with."

"I love him, Joe."

"How can you love him and me at the same time?"

"I don't know." She sat down and allowed herself a small, self-deprecating chuckle. "It was easy for a while."

"If you don't break up with him, I don't think I wanna be your friend anymore."

"How can you say that? After all the time we've spent together. You think this is easy for me? I let you get to second base, Joe! I have a boyfriend . . . a serious boyfriend whom I've known for a lot longer than I've known you, and I let you kiss me and feel my boobs! That's not enough for you?"

how soon is never?

I shook my head and lit another cigarette. She grabbed one from my pack and waited for me to light it for her. After a while, I did. She sucked deeply and coughed. Laughed. I laughed too.

"Robin," I said, shaking my head. "Like Robin Zander. From Cheap Trick."

"I guess."

"Is he better-looking than me?"

"You are so vain."

"Do you have a picture of him?"

"No."

"Yes, you do. You can't lie to me. Well, I guess you can lie to me."

"Shut up."

She was happy that I seemed to be thawing a bit. After a few more smokes and some long silences, and some more insistence on my part, things got loose enough for her to reach into her wallet and show me a photo of Robin. A serious mistake. Robin was not quite as handsome as Robin Zander from Cheap Trick but he was a lot more conventionally good-looking than I was. He looked like an adult, with no traceable insecurity. Worse, he looked a bit like Morrissey, albeit fair-haired and lacking that wry glow in his eyes (okay, it was only a cracked, old snapshot, but I could just tell), but handsome enough to flip me out. I tossed the photo at her like a rotten tomato and stomped several rows up the bleachers.

"Jesus, Jennifer!"

"What? You wanted to see it!"

"Why don't you just leave me the fuck alone? Get the fuck away from me. Go to England, you fucking . . . traitor."

"Joe! You're the biggest Anglophile I know."

"That's not true!"

"You worship an Englishman! You hate anything that's not English!"

"I'm listening to the Replacements! The Replacements! They're from Minneapolis!"

"Joe . . ."

"No! Just go! Fucking go!"

She reached down and picked up the photo, which had fallen through the splintered wooden bleachers onto the lawn below. That made it worse. I walked down to her level, grabbed the photo out of her hand, and tore it up. Threw the shredded pieces into the air and ran off toward the parking lot without looking back. I cut my sixth-period philosophy class. It was obvious that I was in no shape to sit and listen to burly, bearded Mr. Edwards go on and on about the Bhagavad Gita for an hour. I got into my car and drove to Manhattan, intent on finding an advance copy of *The Queen Is Dead*. The Smiths had become the only thing I could count on. I thought they'd never let me down.

Sometimes the time at which you hear an album makes all the difference, and *The Queen Is Dead* was, at intervals, the band's bleakest and most spite-filled, self-pitying work of genius yet. The songs just destroyed me. They retained all the intelligence and wit of their previous albums, but it was clear that, just as I had grown, finding my own voice as a writer, my favorite band had grown considerably as musicians. They'd become so perfect it was almost camp. Johnny Marr was never more exciting on guitar, and Morrissey's voice seemed doubly commanding—his lyrics even funnier and more emotionally vivid than before. It was as though he had been steeping in the confidence his burgeoning pop icon status had brought him, just waiting for the opportunity to quite possibly destroy and rebuild the entire world. The brand-name Walkman might have seemed cute when Sony introduced the product to the marketplace but as I headed back to the parking garage on Broadway at Astor

Place, I wasn't porting the device, it was moving my refueled body with such a velocity that my legs ached. Simply put, this was the best music I'd ever heard, and I whispered (aloud, possibly—I couldn't hear my own voice above the full volume in my headphones) thanks to God and fate and Manchester that I hadn't driven my tiny Japanese car off the bridge. Perhaps Robin could have related to the lyrics more. Anglophile that I may have been, I didn't give a shit about the monarchy or Thatcherism but easily replaced the targets of the furious title track (the queen, the pub, the Church, the rain that flattens my hair) with every one and everything that had hurt me bad over the past decade.

"Life is very long when you're lonely!" Morrissey chanted. When you're 16, you believe your fave pop stars are psychic, don't you? They're watching you, listening to your thoughts, and singing them back to you in a language that finally makes sense. I was 16. What happened to me in the last half a year had made me feel, well . . . 30. I could not have felt lonelier. Life could not have felt longer. Well, it could have if I didn't have that album in my possession.

I popped the tape into the car stereo and as the sun began to set, I transported my new friend, my only one, to the suburbs at 65 miles per hour, slowing down and actually pulling off the parkway and stopping in the parking lot of the seedy Jade East Motel (hourly rates, I'm told) when the centerpiece ballad "I Know It's Over" came on.

"If you're so funny," Morrissey asked—himself, the listener, the world—*"then why are you on your own tonight?"*

I started to cry. Inside, even the type of people who meet for secret fucking at no-tell motels had someone. I hadn't cried in a long time. Not, at least, since I became a hairy man, not since that summer with Jane and Sid and puberty and bluegrass and punk rock. And I must have looked like a fool, alone, crying, pathetic, idling there in my shiny red compact car outside a motel while strangers touched each other on vi-brating beds that smelled like smoke and cum and vanilla an-tiseptic. Sometimes you cry so much, you start laughing at how stupid the sounds you make when you're miserable can be (this only happens when you're alone). As the song ended, segueing into the clever and morbid "Cemetry Gates," I al-lowed myself a more grateful laugh amid the persistent tears.

My heart might be broken. My best friends might be gone. I might fail philosophy and never get into college. I might even have to get another summer job, I thought, *but things are actually bet-ter than they have ever been. This is the pain of life. You are fi-nally, really alive.*

I realized that I could relate to these lyrics, I could take them and apply them to moments in my life, because I had reference points at last. I was no longer watching other peo-ple live . . . my parents, people on television. "There Is a Light That Never Goes Out," which would soon slip into rotation on WLIR, expressed this hunger for engagement perfectly. It was all about that need to *"see people and see life"* at all costs, even if a double-decker bus crashes into me or my friend or my high school sweetheart and everything is destroyed. I lived. I was there. These songs understood me. I understood them. What more can you require from a pop record? I played it every day, from beginning to end, for months. It was only when the band followed it with another singles compilation, *Louder Than Bombs,* later that year that *The Queen Is Dead* was removed from my Walkman. It didn't matter. *Louder Than Bombs* was just as brilliant. *"Sixteen, clumsy and shy, that's the story of my life,"* Morrisey sang on "Half a Person." I was 16. I was clumsy. I was shy. Morrissey was a rock star in his mid-20s. It was uncanny.

Jennifer and I rarely spoke after that day on the bleachers. She was accepted to Juilliard and I coolly congratulated her when she told me so during an awkward encounter by my locker. Then I walked away and went to calculus class to stare blankly at math problems. By the look on her face, the very last time I saw her up close, my dismissal of her dreams, her excitement, and the successful end to all those forms and essays and stamp-licks seemed to hurt her more than anything else. I delighted in that at first. It was my turn to reject. But I felt really fucking guilty for a long time after that. She was, after all, the person who had pressed the tape of the Smiths' debut into my hand. She was my first love. She had sprung me from the art room ghetto and helped me discover whatever talent I had. Still, I didn't attend her graduation ceremony and we didn't keep in touch when she moved to Manhattan, even though I was still going there regularly. Sometimes, I still wonder if we could have worked it out, if only her boyfriend had been a bit more homely. I still miss her and always look for her name in the credits of movies and television programs. I never see it.

As much as I hurt each time I saw her from across the hall, Jennifer was easier to write off than my old friends, simply because I was convinced that she'd wronged me. Sometimes, I would hear new Smiths singles like "Panic" and "Shoplifters of the World Unite" booming out of the art room when I passed it with my lunch tray and I missed sitting there, just listening in wonderment. I knew John was graduating in a matter of days and I would probably never see him again. When a *Queen Is Dead* North American tour was announced, I convinced Susie to let me use her credit card to order a ticket to the Radio City Music Hall concert over the phone, then, without her knowledge, proceeded to order tickets for John, Richie, Jerome, and Maria as well. It was to be an irresistible act of contrition, I reasoned. Even if they still hated me, I knew they loved the Smiths more. And once I got back into their inner circle, I would be charming and funny and respectful and—shit, whatever they wanted me to be. I just wanted back in. The tickets arrived in the mail the week before graduation. John was in the auditorium picking up his cap and gown when I walked into the art room and sat down. Jerome and Richie were stiff and worried but not immediately antagonistic. Maria wasn't there.

"What are you doing in here, Joe?" Richie asked.

"I just wanted to see what you guys were up to. So . . . what are you guys up to?"

"John's getting his robe and hat and stuff. We're just, um . . . we're not doing anything. Just, um . . ."

I sat down and stared at them. Only little Jerome picked up on my warm energy quickly. I smiled at him and nodded, as if to say, *It's good to see you.* He brightened. Sweet by nature, Jerome couldn't help himself. He made it pretty easy.

"Look, Joe. I got my braces off. For real. Look! They're gone!" he said, and flashed his metal-free but still somehow askew choppers. I'd been away a long time.

"I can't believe John's graduating. Do you know what he's doing after school?"

"He doesn't know yet. He said he's gonna take some time and figure it out," Jerome said.

"So he'll be around?"

"I guess."

"What are you doing here, Joe?" Richie spoke again. He was starting to get on my nerves.

"I brought these. I want you guys to come with me. All of you."

I threw two Smiths tickets onto the table. Richie and Jerome picked them up.

"Really? These are for us?" Jerome asked.

"What about John?" Richie asked, triggering my very last nerve.

how soon is never?

"I got one for John too. What are you, his fucking lawyer, Rich? Huh?"

"I don't know, Joe. I was just asking."

"Well, I'm just telling you. Stop giving me attitude," I huffed. "So, are you gonna come with me or what? I want us to do this. To try to be friends again."

"Why? Cause that popular girl dumped you? It's all over school," Richie countered. He'd gotten bold . . . or at least bold with me. I could tell he was just aping John's surliness, and kept steady.

"How the fuck would you know anyway, you fucking loser? You never leave this fucking room."

"Maria told me," he said, defeated.

I sat down next to him.

"I'm sorry, Richie. I didn't mean to call you a loser."

"That's okay, Joe."

"And she didn't dump me."

"Oh, okay, Joe. We just heard . . ."

"Here." I took out a ticket for John and gave it to Richie. "Make sure you give that to him. Don't tell him who it's from yet. Say you got it for yourselves."

"That's a good idea, Joe," Jerome said cheerfully. "It's good to see you, Joe."

"It's good to see you guys too."

I sat there for a while, nervous that John would come in and stab me with a pencil. But we managed to make conversation, and listen to the radio, and even draw pictures together. It felt great. I didn't realize how alone I'd been.

"What do you think of *Louder Than Bombs*?"

"It's so great." Jerome smiled. He was smiling a lot more with his new teeth. "Hey, have you seen *Sid and Nancy* yet?"

"Yeah. I saw it in the city. I've been going to the city a lot, you know?" I said, puffing up.

"Oh, we're gonna go see it this weekend," Jerome said. He

was too sincere to be intimidated. "It's finally playing here and not just in the city. I hear Sid kills Nancy at the end but don't tell me, okay? Cause I want to find out for myself."

"Okay." I laughed. "I won't spoil it."

"Too bad you can't come," Richie said cryptically.

"I'll see it again," I said, probably with more eagerness than I wanted.

"Yeah?" Jerome brightened even more. "Maybe you can come along."

"We have to ask John," Richie warned.

I left the art room and went to get some lunch. I felt optimistic. After final period, I returned to my car. I'd planned on going home early and spending some time with Susie and Dick. Summer was coming up fast and they were making noise about my return to Mom's Bagels or some other dreadful job. I had it in my head that if I behaved myself, maybe they would let me spend the summer just hanging out in Manhattan. If that didn't work, I decided, I'd tell them that I'd gotten a job in Manhattan and just hang out there anyway, but I decided to try the honest way first since it was clear my cultural summer "abroad" would require their economic subsidization. Anyway, I'd started complimenting her on her meat loaf and showing off each issue of the *Echo*, soliciting pride and goodwill in the dining room. But all my optimism shifted when I went to my car and saw a Smiths ticket stuck, parking-ticket-style, beneath the windshield wiper.

"Oh, man!" I screamed. "What a fucking asshole!"

I grabbed the ticket, pocketed it, and went looking for John's Galaxie so that I could kick the headlights in, but he'd already gone home after making his unsubtle statement. As I drove home, I vowed that I would take Richie and Jerome and Maria to the show with me anyway. I would even make them popular somehow. If John wasn't planning to leave Long Island to attend some university, he'd still be depending on his crew, and I was going to rob him of his only friends and give him a taste of real loneliness. I'd make him hurt like I hurt and he wouldn't be able to slum with the popular kids either. He'd be fucked. And then he'd reconsider my friendship.

It might have worked too if the Smiths had actually played their scheduled show at Radio City Music Hall as planned. But on the day of the show, Morrissey got stung by a bee. Or so it was rumored (I later found out they'd simply scrapped the dates and returned home to England). The announcement came over WLIR literally hours before the show, after all our coordination had been arranged. Richie, Jerome, and Maria were supposed to meet me in the school parking lot, where I would personally drive them into Manhattan. Shit, I was even prepared to buy them each a T-shirt and a Coke. The boys seemed apprehensive as I pulled up. I could tell their eyes were peeled for a vengeful blue Galaxie, lurking. We quickly squeezed into the Tercel (it held four but not very comfortably) and headed toward the city, only to be notified that the show was not to be by DJ Larry the Duck, who sounded as crestfallen as we were. The air went out of my lungs for a second. It didn't seem real.

How could this be happening? I thought. *It's not fair!*

There was nobody to beseech. Nobody to complain to. Nobody to give any answers except present company. . . .

"Stung by a bee?" I screamed. "A bee?"

"Maybe he's allergic to bees. Some people are allergic to bees, Joe," Richie offered.

"It's just a fucking bee!" I protested even louder, pounding on the steering wheel.

"What do we do now?" Maria, ever the pragmatist, inquired. "Go home?"

"No! We're not going home! We're going into the fucking city."

"For what?" Richie asked.

"I don't know," I shouted.

"I wanna go home," Maria whined, and got out of the car.

"Where are you going? Get back here!"

"No, Joe, I'm gonna call my mom and get a ride home."

"I'll give you a ride home."

"I don't trust you behind the wheel, Joe. You look like a crazy person."

She walked toward the Woodmere train station. I turned to Richie and Jerome in the backseat.

"What do you want to do?"

"I'll go to the city with you, Joe," Jerome volunteered.

"No, forget it. I don't want to go anymore."

I turned the car around violently and drove right across the front lawn of the academy, getting air off the curb and crashing into the wrong lane on Woodmere Boulevard. I did a U-turn and gunned down through the school zone at 40 miles per hour.

"He *is* crazy," Richie said to Jerome. "Joe, let me out!"

I didn't stop.

"Joe, I don't really care. Joe. It's just a concert, come on. You're scaring me."

"It's not just a concert!"

I didn't even turn around. I drove straight to the Woodmere docks. Straight to the water. I didn't know why. I just kept going, and if Jerome hadn't started crying, I might have never stopped. But he was sobbing like a little kid. I threw the car into park, stripping the gears and burning a layer of rubber off the tires. I turned around again.

"Oh, God. Why are you crying? I'm just mad, that's all. I wasn't gonna crash."

"I'm not crying," Jerome lied, wiping the tears from his eyes. "I just really wanted to see the Smiths. And . . . you were really . . . driving scary, Joe."

"Really scary," Richie echoed. He got out of the car and walked back toward the train station, now a much longer trip than the one Maria had had to take.

"Richie!" I called out remorsefully. "Richie, I'll give you a ride."

"That's all right, Joe."

"What are we doing here, Joe?" Jerome said, a scared quaver in his girlish voice.

"I'll show you what we're doing."

I reached into the glove compartment and pulled out all my Smiths cassettes and got out of the car.

"Joe?" Jerome called as he followed me to the water. "Joe, don't do that! Joe, I'll take 'em!"

I threw each one into the bay. The debut, *Hatful of Hollow*, *Meat Is Murder*, *The Queen Is Dead*, even the expensive double album *Louder Than Bombs*.

"Oh, God, Joe . . . why did you do that? I don't even have *Hatful of Hollow*! I would have taken it!"

"How could they do this to me? I'm never listening to that fucking band again."

"Come on, Joe, that's stupid."

"I don't care."

He grabbed my hand and tried to pull me away from the water. I must have looked like I was gonna jump in along with my cassettes. I pushed him off me and sat down on the dried seagull shit that covered the grass.

"Joe, you're sitting in poop."

I didn't answer.

"Joe, I'm sure they'll reschedule the show."

I put my head in my hands and started to cry, ashamed that

a band had this much power over my emotions. How, like a drug, they could make me happy or sad on a whim. They had more influence than a best friend. More than a girl. I sat there in the bird shit and cried. The Smiths were all I had and they'd left me too. Jerome kneeled next to me.

"A bee sting?" I must have said it five times.

"Don't cry, Joe. You'll get to see them again!"

We never did.

The Smiths went back to England. So did Jennifer, to give Robin the love she couldn't give me. John continued to wrestle with his sexual orientation miles away from me. We never spoke again. I retreated to my bedroom, where I'd spend the summer days of '86, alone, writing, reading, jerking off, and marking off the calendar until it hit September. Richie and Jerome wouldn't call me after I scared the shit out of them. Maria never called me anyway. Sid called me when he was drunk and I'd screen out his calls. I missed the Smiths more than any of them, but I could not allow myself to be disappointed again.

The first Guns N' Roses album had come out senior year, 1987, and along with *Electric* by the Cult, *Appetite for Destruction* inspired me to reembrace the angry punk behavior I'd given up in favor of sensitivity and harmony. It's a great fucking album, which I still play sometimes, but that's not why I took to it back then. It was the sound of having fun despite the hopeless decay of your surroundings . . . and I no longer had much hope. With "Welcome to the Jungle" screaming out of my already blown speakers, I entered my final year of high school with such a chip on my shoulder that most around me were convinced it would not be my final year of high school.

I'd started violating the dress code again. I showed up for class late, even English class, with unwashed, greasy hair (I'd let my quiff fall). I cursed freely. Once I even smoked a cigarette in the middle of astronomy class. As soon as detention got out, I'd suck down pot on the docks nearly every day with my new friends Bobbie and Jeffrey, a pair of zitty, wiseass sophomore juvenile delinquents. They had the pot. I had the car. We all had the bad attitude. I couldn't talk to them about anything real, but fortunately we were all too stoned to care. So I'd come home reeking and talk the jive to my horrified mother and stepfather. I'd also stopped washing my car (this irked Susie and Dick more than anything else, actually). Lazy on pot, stimulated as much at that point by bad TV and White Castle hamburgers, I even stopped going into the city. It just reminded me of my old, gone friends. Basically, after being saved, I was lost again. I'd gone from punk to enlightened New Waver to stoner . . . chubby fucking stoner too (White Castle and all). It's natural for a teenager to be chameleon-like (less natural for a 30-year-old). But you're supposed to progress, not regress. Worse, I was obliged to start seriously thinking about college . . . and I had no "safe school."

You see, for a Long Island boy, senior year was all about avoiding Nassau Community College at all costs. I'm sure it's a fine school but with every JAP and jock crossing their fingers and hoping for acceptance at a big state or Ivy League school, Nassau Community was basically a notch above prison. If you were going there in the fall, you couldn't share that information with anyone. The stigma was too much. Bert had noticed my slide and selected me as a candidate for the academy's College Guidance Program. For whatever reason, the old guy had made it his business to save me from my appetite for self-destruction. The CGP was designed to help gifted but misguided students find an appropriate school and in turn preserve the school's stellar rep for placing their grads somewhere prestigious. The CGP head was a baby-faced blond guy named Mr. Thomas, with a penchant for light cream suits that smelled more than vaguely of sweat and cigarettes. His tiny office, adjacent to the headmaster's, was covered with those cheesy college banners and pennants. His metal desk was stacked with brochures. I had to report to him once a week and just "rap." He spoke with a lisp and would never divulge just exactly where he'd attended college (I suspected Nassau Community). Thomas handed me a bunch of brochures for various liberal arts schools, Bard, Hampshire, Sarah Lawrence, Bennington, all of which might overlook my horribly unbalanced grades and standardized test scores and accept me on the basis of my writing ability alone. He advised me to start thinking about an essay.

"What should I write about?" I asked.

"What do you care about?"

"I don't know. Nothing."

"Why not?"

"Well, everything sucks."

"Nothing's important to you at all?"

"No."

Thompson got up and moved closer to me, sharing his funk and lisping in my face curiously. He wasn't angry or offended. Rather, he seemed upbeat.

"You're depressed."

"Yeah."

"But philosophical."

"I guess."

"Are you a nihilist, Joe?"

I thought about it.

"Yeah. I guess so."

I didn't know what a nihilist was. I still don't.

how soon is never?

"Well, that's great!" He smiled. "This'll be really easy."

"Huh?"

"Oh, they love that kind of stuff. Write about what it's like being a seventeen-year-old nihilist. How you've come to the conclusion that nothing means anything. But be smart and funny like your newspaper stuff. And quote some French and German philosophers. Can you do that?"

"I guess."

"I'll give you one. 'He who has a why to live can bear almost any how.' That's Nietzsche."

"What the hell does it mean?"

"It doesn't matter. Just spell his name right. I bet you'll have your pick of all four of these schools."

"Really?"

"Oh, gosh, yes!"

So I did. I wrote a page about how I didn't think anything had any meaning anymore. Love. God. Rock 'n' roll. I wrote about my suicide attempt. I wrote about being so horny and lonely and angry that it was hard to sleep or eat or do anything but listen to heavy metal and smoke weed and wear black because I was already dead (and because black was slimming). I had nothing to lose and didn't care if I impressed anyone, so I just told the truth. And I guess I tapped into whatever Mr. Thomas was after. By the spring of 1987, I was accepted to each one of those schools. And not only that . . . the hot, Hispanic, crazy-eyed admissions scout for Bennington really wanted to visit with me in person. We met in a suite at the Marriott Marquis hotel in Manhattan, and I smoked and wore sunglasses and acted like an asshole and she ate it up. Before she left, she showed me her long brown legs and gave me a copy of *Story of the Eye*, a thin, dirty book by this French guy, Georges Bataille. It was about violence and deviant sex and being a French egghead. When she bummed a cigarette and leaned in, giving me a good look at her tiny but very visible breasts beneath her black wool neckline, I knew where I was gonna end up.

"You're gonna work at Benetton?" Bobbie asked, hitting the fifth joint we'd smoked that day. Sometimes I wondered what the fuck I was doing with these idiots. No, I wondered it all the time. "On Central Avenue?"

"Not Benetton. Bennington."

"Bennigan's? In Valley Stream?"

"Bennington College. It's in Vermont, you stupid fucker."

"Oh."

"Does Pat Benatar teach there?"

I was bigger than them. I was a senior. I hit them a lot.

But we still hung out. I had nobody else. The stoners were better than the JAPs . . . and I was sick of being alone. Plus their friend Michelle, a potty-mouthed black chick from Hewlett High School, let me get to third base one night in my car. It felt bad-ass to have my middle finger inside a potty-mouthed black chick. I felt like Mick Jagger or something. I wrote a story about it and read it to Susie and Dick before dinner, and when they tried to send me to my room, I told them both to fuck off, Axl-style, got in the car, and just drove around. And around. My zits had come back, thanks to hanging out at White Castle, trying to be like another one of my new favorite bands, the Beastie Boys (who probably ate at Manhattan's finest restaurants at that point). I might have fingered a girl, but I could not have been more lost.

I was gonna stay a dirtbag. It was the only way to keep my real feelings safe and hidden. They were too much . . . too vulnerable. Sometimes, on these aimless drives, I would be tempted to go to the Wiz on Sunrise Highway and replace one of my Smiths albums, but I resisted it time and again. I even turned away from an import copy of "Girlfriend in a Coma," which was to be the lead single off their new studio album, *Strangeways, Here We Come.* The local success of *The Queen Is Dead* and *Louder Than Bombs* wised up even chain-store buyers, who were now stocking the band's records, but I didn't indulge in such conveniences. I held my grudge against that band. I cared about them too much, and it scared me. And I couldn't even admit it. Not even after they were gone. Thank God, I was pretending not to care. If I had allowed myself to remain a fan after the Radio City Music Hall debacle, I'm sure I would have sailed off that bridge after all. As it was, I indulged in self-satisfied rounds of "I knew it." I loved the Smiths. Of course they would follow Dad and Jennifer and John out the door.

Still, I was shaken. I remember where I was when I heard the news. It was around 3 P.M. and I was sitting against a brick wall just outside the gym. I was throwing cigarette butts, one after the other, at the parked cars in the school lot. Michelle and Bobbie and Jeffrey were there too. We were all wearing aviator glasses (we'd seen Axl wear them in *Rolling Stone*) and denim (theirs acid-wash, mine straight-up Levi's . . . and even if they were acid-wash, I wouldn't admit it to you now).

"I need to talk to you," Maria said somberly.

"So? Talk."

"Joe!"

"What? I'm listening."

"Fine. I just thought you might want to know the Smiths broke up today. It's all over LIR."

If you remember that pivotal scene in the movie *Grease,* it was like when John Travolta found out that Olivia Newton-John didn't go back to Australia after their summer lovin'. She enrolled at Rydell High instead. He was shaken up but he couldn't blow his crucial cool in front of the T-Birds, so he acted like a dick instead. That was me. I was a T-Bird and Maria was . . . Olivia Newton-John, I guess.

"So?"

Maria saw right through me too. Thank God I was wearing mirrored shades.

"Anyway, asshole, we're all in the art room if you wanna talk about it."

"Why would I wanna talk about it?"

She just shook her head and walked away. I sat there quiet for a while.

"She's got a nice ass," Jeffrey observed. "Too bad about that stick up . . . the stick she's got up . . . I'm so stoned."

"I'm gonna go take a piss," I announced, all tough.

"Piss on the school, man," Bobbie suggested.

"Yeah, man! Piss on the school!" Jeffrey encouraged.

"I'll be right back."

I got up and walked to the end of the lot, where the window on the art room was. Stared inside through my dark lenses . . . watched as Jerome, Richie, and Maria gathered around the stereo, looking, indeed, like they'd lost a loved one. I could hear WLIR playing "How Soon Is Now." I wanted to go inside and cry with them. I wanted to strip off my clothes right there and dig through my flesh, reach into my chest and feel around to see if I still had a heart or just two black lungs full of pot resin. Instead, I walked back to the wall and sat down next to my new friends.

"Did you piss on it?" Bobbie asked excitedly.

"Yeah," I said blankly. "I pissed on it."

twelve

too high to be shy

The Smiths newsletter itemized various theoretical reasons for the dissolution of the band. Poor business choices. Constantly shifting management. Creative differences. Personal differences. Everything but a hostile clash over someone's new hairstyle. It didn't matter to me. The Smiths' breakup destroyed me even more than my parents' divorce did. At least with that I could act out. When *Strangeways, Here We Come,* their new studio album, was released posthumously, months later, I couldn't listen to it more than once even when I was alone in my car. Not because my new friends thought it was "gay" but simply because it was just too sad. "Last Night I Dreamt That Somebody Loved Me," the album's centerpiece ballad, made me cry. Worse, there was still hope left in Morrissey's lyrics even if the band's passion and urgency had waned.

"The story is old," he sang, *"I know, but it goes on. . . ."*

Unfair as it may have been, at the time I seized on that lyric and applied it to the band. "How can he do this to me?"

I raged on and on in my bedroom. At least when John Lennon left the Beatles, he famously chanted, *"I don't believe in Beatles"* on the song "God." When Led Zeppelin or the Grateful Dead broke up it was clear they'd never be the same again because disbanding was a reaction to the death of key members (John Bonham and Jerry Garcia, respectively). These old hippies were, in their way, merciful. Their devoted fans knew they couldn't be resuscitated. The healing process could begin once the shock wore off. The Smiths, however, were in their prime. *Strangeways* was a creative peak, and the group was more popular than ever in America. It seemed plausible that the story would go on and that this was just a bend in the road. But I'd walked hopefully down too many such roads already only to find myself alone and lost. I didn't want to hope anymore. I don't know who left me with more trust issues: my mother and father or Morrissey and Johnny Marr. If part of my ability to feel true joy died when my parents divorced, the rest died with that band. I drifted into college, a vacant boy, vulnerable to any and all influences.

Sid didn't fly in for my graduation. He sent a card (my dad to this day has an infuriating habit of actually reading the generic inscriptions inside Hallmark cards, finding one that expresses his thoughts for him, appropriate to whatever occasion, then just writing the word *Sid* underneath the calligraphy). Susie and Dick took me to China Jade, the local Chinese restaurant, for a celebration dinner on the assumption that a Jew couldn't get really good Chinese up in Vermont (a logical one, but not true). As we were walking toward the parking lot, we passed the art room. I didn't look back. I wasn't defiant like Bob Dylan. I was weak and broken. Mr. Thomas was manning the exit, offering final words of wisdom to those he'd placed . . . and in some cases (like mine) basking in the success that he'd placed us anywhere at all. He glad-handed Susie and Dick, then pulled me aside and whispered, "Joe, I wanna tell you something about Bennington."

"Okay, Mr. Thomas."

His eyebrows arched sternly and his voice took on a serious gravity.

"Avoid the cocaine."

"Okay, Mr. Thomas."

It was good advice. And I heeded it respectfully. I really did. I avoided the cocaine.

It was the heroin that did me in.

At Bennington, I fell in with a bunch of would-be artists who were really just kids like me, from the suburbs of the Midwest or the Northeast or the South or places like Brussels, Belgium. Finding our identity now, as artists, not teenagers, we turned to various antecedents, looking for the right fit. For me, it was the Beat Generation writers and their offshoots like Jim Carroll and Charles Bukowski. Bad-ass characters. Of course, I didn't read any of their writing; I'm referencing their public images. My little crew of writers would pretend we were debauched urbanites in the late '50s or the early '70s as opposed to rich kids up in the mountains. We were street-tough poets with diseases instead of students at a very expensive liberal arts college. But all we had to do was look around at nature, the fucking foliage, and we were rudely reminded that there wasn't a shred of authenticity to us. I matriculated, and bohemian-ated, and fucked every willing art-girl I could find to make up for lost time, and convinced myself that my writing wasn't in fact the sum total of a barely pulled-off pose. Yeah, I finally lost my virginity to a pretty, blond dance major. But after all that build-up, I couldn't even gush cause it would have torched my cool. Charlie Parker was playing while she made me a man. Charlie Parker! I don't even like jazz . . . so there you go. I would have run off and told all my friends but . . . I didn't have friends. I had ten fellow liars who convinced themselves, and girls, that we were Henry Miller. That our $20,000-per-year dorm room was in fact a garret in Paris. By junior year at Bennington, if you haven't transferred (and most do), you're supposed to start getting really serious about all the art jive. You're supposed to be hard-core. So I worked harder on my pose. I started chasing the white wine and Brie at the poetry readings with heroin I'd pick up on the Lower East Side during fly-by-night jags down the Taconic Parkway in my Toyota Tercel. Looking back, I realize it was the '90s. Heroin was just part of the Zeitgeist chemistry, like acid was in the '60s. I was a cliché. But in my defense, I never paid attention to the calendar. I didn't want to know. It would have ruined four years of hard work.

My heavy-metal impudence (which, like punk, was never a good fit anyway) had turned to severe lethargy, which fit only when I was high on junk. So I stayed high on junk. Problem was, staying high was a commitment to the end. This was an experimental identity that was never informed by music. (Grunge? I don't think so.) It became permanent because it was informed by a drug instead. Soon, I didn't even have to wear my hair a certain way or dress a certain way, or even dress. I just needed the drug to complete the package. And the only upside to completing the package was that I didn't get horribly, violently ill. Simply, heroin made me too physically weak and spiritually lazy to cast off and look for the next cultural skin to slip into. I could have been a neo-hippie, or a pot-smoking reggae kid, or a skateboarding preppie. But I'd made my bed and I spent years nodding in it, high on junk, never seeing daylight, never feeling healthy, never calling home. I was a waste, a lump in the mattress, as people, mostly rich girls, passed in and out of my life. Each one's meaning, you know, whether I remembered her name or not, was entirely contingent on how much money they had for dope. I lost six years of my life. Four at school. Two recovering from school. Four years of my invaluable 20s in total. I don't even remember what I studied at Bennington. I don't know what I wrote for my thesis. I don't remember graduating. I still don't know where my diploma is to this day. I don't remember renting an apartment on 13th Street and Avenue A after graduation. And I don't remember what happened to my books and vintage clothes. They must have been destroyed when the water-damaged ceiling fell in.

I don't remember the ceiling falling in.

In 1992, the year after I graduated, Morrissey, two albums and a handful of singles into his solo career, released the amazing *Your Arsenal*. It was expertly produced by former David Bowie guitarist Mick Ronson (his last major project before dying of cancer, and perhaps his masterpiece . . . and that says a lot since the guy also co-produced Lou Reed's *Transformer*). It was easily the Mozzer's biggest hit, catapulting him from a large theater to an arena act in the States. Critics who'd written off Morrissey as a has-been after his relatively uninspired second album, *Kill Uncle,* publicly apologized. This was a triumph.

But if Morrissey walked into whatever room I was passed out in in 1992 (most likely the toilet at the Max Fish bar on Ludlow Street), I would have:

a. Not recognized him at all
b. Hit him up for dope money
c. Puked

That's how bad shit got. For the record, I don't blame Bennington. It would have happened if I'd gone to Bard, although, judging by the Bard students I've met, there'd be a lot more arty Polaroids of me with my eyes rolled back into my skull. I don't even blame my cokehead father and his bum genes, if you subscribe to that theory. Susie blamed Sid. At least that's the first person she called when I showed up on her doorstep one morning in January 1993 looking like I'd been buried in a ditch for six months.

"Your son is here and he's got holes in his arms!" she screamed into the phone.

It was true. I had started shooting instead of snorting heroin and that's probably what scared me into going back to Long Island and asking for help. The particular brand that I did, China Cat, I think it was called, had been blamed for several deaths on the Lower East Side, and that was mostly from people who were only snorting. I had hooked up with a clean-needle connection and spent that same weekend mainlining the shit. After reading about the overdose victims in the *Post* and matching up the little ink-stamped brand on the bags that littered my broken apartment, I decided I'd had enough. I made my way to Pennsylvania Station and with my last four dollars bought a one-way ticket back to Lawrence. I was back on the Long Island Rail Road. And for the first time in my life, it felt comforting to change at Jamaica station to the connecting Far Rockaway line. Sid must have been flush since he offered to pitch in for rehab. Dope-sick as I was, my bones scraped down to the shell and filled with what felt like fire ants suspended in shampoo, I still managed a violent argument with Susie and Dick, who wanted me to attend an outpatient program at some local youth center and move back into my old bedroom. I refused. They'd done some cursory research while I was screaming in pain and running the shower in an effort to steam the poison out of my body, and determined that an inpatient stay would be prohibitively expensive. But I already knew where I wanted to go, and like Bennington, it wasn't cheap.

"We just spent a fortune on your college education so you could become a heroin addict junkie? And now you want us to send you to rehab too?"

I nodded and doubled over in pain. I was smoking a cigarette, even though I already had one lit and burning on the ashtray that Susie and Dick kept around for cocktail parties and New Year's Eve.

"I don't even know where they have rehabs."

"I wanna go to Silver Hill!"

"Silver Hill?"

"That's where Edie Sedgwick went. Please, Mommy." I almost never said "Mommy."

"Who the fuck is Edie Sedgwick?" Susie almost never said "fuck."

"Warhol"—retch—"superstar."

"If it's too expensive, you're not going!"

"No. It's gotta be Silver Hill," I moaned. "Please? Help me."

I puked on the floor. Dick ran to get a towel. One of the dirty ones he kept around to wash his 'Vette with.

"Silver Hill!"

"All right! All right! Calm down!"

"Or Hazelden."

"What's Hazelden?"

"Rehab!"

"How do you know these places?"

"I think Marianne Faithfull went there."

Yeah. I'd done some cursory research of my own, and I decided that if I was going to commit to getting clean, I needed another archetype. I couldn't see the experience for what it was: me getting clean. It had to be me getting clean like . . . well, insert the name of any glamorous ex-junkie here, preferably one who either was a Warhol queenie or a Rolling Stones muse. After all, these were the people who moved in and filled the vacancy left by the Smiths. These were the icons who made heroin attractive to me in the first place. Twenty-four hours later, I was on a plane bound for Minnesota. A car was waiting at the airport to take me to Hazelden.

"My name is Joseph Green . . . and I'm a drug addict and an alcoholic."
"Hi, Joe."
"No last names in here, Joe."
"Joseph, actually."
"Joe Green?"
"Joseph . . . and I'm a drug—"
"Like Mean Joe Greene?"

Such was my first and only confession to the good people in "the rooms" of Hazelden. I lasted just 18 hours. I'm not supposed to talk about what goes on inside because the thing's called Narcotics Anonymous. I will say that it wasn't for me (even though I'll admit that the program saved the life of more than one friend of mine). Why didn't rehab and I click? I don't know. I guess the only time I didn't mind being friendly to strangers (there was a lot of sweaty hand-holding and hugs in there) was at a Smiths show. So yeah, I only stayed one painful night as nurses checked in on me every 15 minutes to make sure I wasn't getting high or committing suicide or reading the one book I'd brought with me, *Keith*, Victor Bockris' biography of Keith Richards. In the morning there was breakfast and a group session. And then I split. I signed myself out and headed right back to New York. I debated going to see Sid instead. I knew he'd give me a lot less grief, but I'd fucked my life up so sufficiently that I was ready to get a little straight . . . and that's just not possible around Sid.

I promised an enraged Susie and Dick that I would stay straight. They remained suspicious but I was determined to do it on my own. It was hard and ugly, and I won't chronicle the process cause this is not a drug book. I'll just say you don't see photos of Keith detoxing for a good reason. It's not perfect like "Gimme Shelter." It blows your cool like nothing else. When it was over I voluntarily entered an outpatient program, got on methadone, and even interviewed for and got my very first non-summer job. It was humble enough to impress Susie (who even suggested I apply at McDonald's, "Wherever it takes to give you some responsibility"). I started checking bags at a book-store called Shakespeare and Company on lower Broadway in Manhattan. Basically, all I had to do was hand customers a piece of numbered wood, take their bag, stick it in a cubby, then return it to them on their way out. The perfect hapless ex-junkie gig. It only got hairy when customers would lose their lit-tle piece of wood. Then you'd have to have them describe the contents of the bag as you peered into it. Actually, that was kind of fun. I didn't have my apartment anymore, so I'd crash on friends' couches, and after a paycheck, I'd spend a few nights at the Chelsea Hotel, where I'd pee in the sink because I was afraid to use the shared bathroom across the hall late at night. Like at Shakespeare and Company, inside the Chelsea I was sur-rounded by authors or the ghosts of authors. The store stocked them on its shelves, and the hotel commemorated them on brass plaques out on 23rd Street. For a time, I was happy just to be near them. I didn't have the energy to work on anything of my own. I wrote bits and pieces down on napkins or pads but I was shell-shocked . . . junk-struck. River Phoenix was dead. Kurt Cobain was dead. I was alive and clean but I considered myself a casualty. The ghost of a would-be author.

Ironically, it was Shakespeare and Company's policy of no rock 'n' roll on the in-store stereo that led me to my job writing about rock 'n' roll. We were only allowed to play jazz or classical music during our shifts, which would have been fine. I like jazz and classical music. But in the three years I worked there, the fucking place never replaced the two jazz CDs and one classical compilation it had to offer. I don't need to tell you that one of the jazz discs was *Kind of Blue,* by Miles Davis . . . a great record, of course, but it's pretty much become a jazz primer for slumming dilettantes, hasn't it? The other was an equally ubiquitous Nina Simone compilation, another brilliant artistic achievement turned coffeehouse elevator music. I forget the title of the classical CD but you get the picture. Something very important came out of the jazz and classical retail vacuum I shot and snorted myself into. I began buying and caring about music again. Maybe it was a reaction to the 10,000th time I had to sit through Miles Davis. Maybe it was being sober. It started, as all things do, with the Beatles. Since I'd lost or sold or left behind every single CD I'd ever owned, in an effort to rebuild my collection I began with the Fab Four and soon I was back in the '90s. I carried my growing collection around in a book bag, from couch to couch to the Chelsea. I'd actually look forward to new releases from Pavement or Sonic Youth. "Event records," I'd call them. The kind where you have to go to the store on the Tuesday they were released and buy them immediately. The only thing I didn't replace was my Smiths collection, which remained in my mother's attic. Heavy vinyl. Not easy to carry in every way. I was healthier, but I wasn't that healthy. The wound was no longer being soothed with junk, but it was certainly still there and red and raw.

Since I had a long, proud history of defying codes, every once in a while I'd sneak one of my new CDs onto the store stereo and enjoy a reprieve from the plastic highbrow mood music . . . until some bitch customer complained or the general manager came up from the stockroom to bust me. On the day I first befriended Don, I was playing the first Tricky album, *Maxinquaye,* and hoping that if I got busted, I could convince my boss that certain songs on that trip-hop milestone were in fact jazzy or at least less abrasive than what I'd snuck on the week before, Elastica's raucous debut, until some middle-aged lady had complained that it was giving her a migraine and that she was fixing to go around the corner to the big chain store to buy her copy of the New Age bestseller *The Celestine Prophecy* unless we took it off. My boss, a real management type who must have owned six pink oxford-cloth shirts and actually put pennies in his oxblood penny loafers, didn't notice that I was exposing innocent holiday shoppers to Tricky's blunted worldview, but Don, the buyer did. Don was a frizzy-haired, skinny guy with thick, Elvis Costello–type glasses and an impressive array of rock 'n' roll T-shirts. He was usually pretty soft-spoken and mellow, a transplanted Californian who was taking classes at the New School in the Village. He'd ascended the Shakespeare and Company ladder pretty quickly, due in no small part to his very sweet, patient nature. I liked him because he never once asked me if I was Mean Joe Greene. So when he returned to the store from his lunch break and wondered aloud who in the hell was playing Tricky on company time, I felt guilty. He stood in front of the bag check station and cocked his head like Nipper, the RCA Records mascot. I cringed.

"I'm sorry. It's mine. I'll take it off," I confessed. "But can you tell them to like invest in another fucking CD? Anything? You've got some pull, Don. They like you. You're nice."

"I don't give a shit." He smiled. "I was just wondering who had the good taste."

"You like this album, Don?"

"Yeah. It's brilliant."

"Isn't it?"

"Yeah. Bring it downstairs when you're done. The stockroom guys are playing Zappa again." With that, he informed me that his soup was getting cold and eased down the staircase to his office. I liked Don even more after that. Better still, he started bringing in his own CDs to help alter the soundtrack of our lives. Don knew that even the cocktail-hour lounge tones of Sade were preferable to Nina Simone's "My Baby Just Cares for Me" at that point. Thanks to Don, I even snuck on some old Hank Williams country music and a bit of Motown, none of which rattled any of our baby boomer clientele.

Don lived in a dorm around the corner from the store, so we both had to walk west after work. Sometimes we'd stop and have a beer at some bar and talk about writing (I was off heroin but I still liked a drink, and then another, every now and then . . . or, you know, every single day). It was on one of these post-work chats that I learned that he had been interning at the newly launched website for *Headphones* magazine. Now, this was in early 1995, and the entire world had yet to fully embrace the Internet. Don got in early and within a few months he was the big boss over there. Although at the time, checking shopping bags at a bookstore held about as much prestige.

"I get free CDs. I get into every show," Don told me.

"For free?"

"Yeah. People are really starting to realize that new media is where it's at."

"Oh yeah? New media, huh? Well, you know, I still type on a manual typewriter." I really did. I'd found one at the Salvation Army on 9th Avenue. It was perfectly useless but it looked great on my desk at the Chelsea Hotel.

"Right, with crabs crawling up your balls," he mocked.

"Yeah. Do you know any good methods of cleaning tubercular loogies out of your keyboard, by any chance?"

"Pledge."

"Really?"

"Lemon Pledge. They come right out."

Don might have worked with the management but he wasn't one of them at heart.

"So what do you write, Joe?"

"Seriously? Um . . . poems, sketches, stories. I don't know."

"Have you been published anywhere?"

"No. Have you?"

"Yeah. About fifty times."

"No shit. Why are you working in a bookstore?"

"Joe, the best thing about the Web is that you write content and within minutes it's published. And literally *hundreds* of people can read it, just like that." He gestured with his chilled bottle of Bud. "Hundreds, Joe! You know, if you have any samples of your work, you should bring them in tomorrow. I'd like to see them. We don't have much of a staff yet. The publisher is a little apprehensive about pouring too much money into Net ventures. He thinks it's just a fad."

"Isn't it?"

"No, Joe. It's really going to take off."

"That's what they said about virtual reality."

Don punched me in the arm. I guess we'd become good enough pals for him to do that.

"A boom is coming, mark my words."

"Okay, Don. I'll mark 'em." At the time, it really did sound like he was selling Amway products or something.

"Seriously, bring in your stuff. If it's any good, I'll pay you fifty bucks."

"Fifty bucks a review?"

"Yeah, and you can see it up that day. Not only that, but people will give you feedback immediately. It's like a big writing workshop."

"There's nothing romantic about it, though. Writing is supposed to be printed . . . on paper. I'm more of a coffee-stained notebook, manual typewriter kind of guy."

"Living in the Chelsea Hotel with the ghost of Dylan Thomas, right? In the future, everything will be published on the Web."

"I don't even own a computer, Don."

"Well, you can buy one after a few reviews. What do you think about Oasis?"

"I love them. Why?"

"I need five hundred words on their new one. Can you do it by Friday?"

"I don't even have the record."

"I'll give it to you."

"But it's not even out."

"It doesn't matter. We get advances."

"Can I keep it when I'm done?"

"Yeah."

"*And* the fifty bucks?"

"Yeah."

That's how it starts. "The first one's always free," the dealers say. Then you're hooked. You'll never go record shopping with your own money again. It was a Wednesday. I listened to *(What's the Story) Morning Glory?*, Oasis's second album, on Thursday night in the Chelsea. By Friday morning, I was a rock writer. A bad rock writer. I wrote things like " 'Champagne Supernova' is the gorgeous and climactic closer, with its dreamy 'We were getting high' mantric coda delivering chills of bliss that usually require said chemical assistance." Yeah, I used the phrase "mantric coda." I should have gotten out of the biz right then and there but I didn't. Six months in, I had quit Shakespeare and Company and gone to work solely for the *Headphones* website. I was drawing about $400 a week for my reviews and supplementing that with the money I'd make trading in shitty promotional discs. I could have made more if I hadn't been too fucking shy to accept an assignment to actually meet and interview a rock star in person. I couldn't, so I stuck to their

CDs in the privacy of my shitty little hotel room. I still didn't own a computer but my stays at the Chelsea became more regular and soon I transferred to a room with an actual toilet in it.

Don was right. There were people out there, and they did read your stuff and tell you that it was great or it was shit, with a velocity that became addictive. I wanted more. Soon, the website wasn't enough. See, *Headphones* was very much a high-school-like environment, and I had a strong feeling, a few months in, that I was back in the fucking art room. There was a hierarchy.

Publishers and businesspeople were the teachers.

Editors equaled jocks and cheerleaders.

Web people were the geeks.

I hadn't quit heroin to remain a 27-year-old geek. I wanted up from the minor leagues, but my aforementioned shyness made it pretty hard to talk to anyone but Don. Such ascents are pretty much built on the social lay of the place as much as your actual writing ability anyway. I would leave the dot-com cubby, not much bigger than my Chelsea garret, and stalk the editorial halls, just like the high school halls, with the hope that somebody would talk to me. For the longest time nobody did. Then one night in December, I got drunk at the company holiday party and hit it off with an assistant editor named Tom. Tom was a former drummer in an indie rock band from Minneapolis.

"I went to rehab in Minneapolis."

"You were in rehab?"

Tom only seemed like a jock from the outside. He was actually twice as geeky as I was once you broke the ice. I don't think he ever even smoked a joint in his life. The guy wore white socks, for fuck's sake. Pretty soon, it was me judging him for his rock 'n' roll credibility and not vice versa. Tom and I hit it off over a long debate on whether or not the Replacements were any good after they fired guitarist Bob Stinson. Soon the other rock writers deemed me worthy of inclusion in their ongoing discussions about how underrated Swervdriver is, whether or not Juliana Hatfield was a virgin, and who was the real talent in Dinosaur Jr., J. Mascis or Lou Barlow. For Christmas, I got my first print (as in not Web-posted) assignment. When I mailed a glossy advance copy of the January issue of *Headphones* magazine to Susie, it was almost as though I'd been absolved of all my heroin-related crimes. Again, writing had delivered me into a new world of possibility. Only it had been over a decade since I edited the school newspaper, and there was a troubling thought at the back of my mind. I worried that I had gotten there too late this time. I'd fucked around for 10 years, getting high and going to art school and selling books that other people had written. I knew that my time left as a credible rock 'n' roller was short, so I had to live fast. I decided that in order to write about rock 'n' roll at my age, I had to live, eat, sleep, and breathe rock 'n' roll. I didn't have the luxury of just listening to a record and writing my thoughts out intelligently with some kind of original insight. That was fine for the in-house geeks who'd been doing it forever. Insecure about being a late bloomer, I told myself that I was special. I was hard-core. I lived in the Chelsea Hotel. I'd been to rehab and back . . . and it hadn't even fucking worked! I was Lester Bangs. I was Nick Kent. I wore velvet jackets and scarves and chain-smoked. And the rock stars I couldn't interview earlier for my shyness? I drank them under the fucking table. I used the drugged-out years I had thrown away for all they were worth, because otherwise they would have just been wasted time. I decided that I would speed through this rarefied world and make up for lost time. And when it was over, I would go out in a blaze of glory and die on a broken couch with a drink in my hand, next to a big pile of coke on top of a razor-scored coffee table. I had too much sense to commit to this with any sincerity, so I invented a character for myself—a rock superboy who was actually an aging shy person—until pretty soon, I couldn't tell that character from the real me. Who was writing what? Who brought home that little girl? Who owes the coke dealer? Who's run out of Valium and must resort to cough syrup and prayer in order to fall asleep? Him or me? It didn't matter anyway. We were both heading for the same fate and it was neither blazing nor glorious. Like Morrissey observed so long ago, *"Life is very long when you're lonely."* It was one promise he didn't break.

And I believe that's where we first came in. Two hundred bylines into what those lucky souls outside the rock scene view as a successful career. I'd rather have them think I'm a lucky shit who can stay up till four in the morning every single night, while they have to work for the weekend like Loverboy. I'm grateful that they don't see my white walls stained yellow like my teeth and fingernails. They can't feel me shift positions in bed as I try and fail to fall asleep next to a warm body because sharing sleep seems much more intimate than the sex we just had. They can't smell the mess piled up in my kitchen because every free space stores CD boxes. They don't know that sometimes I have to wipe my ass with a sweat sock because I'm literally too fucked up and paranoid to go across the street to the deli to purchase a roll of toilet paper (and no amount of soothing Belle and Sebastian will calm my coke-wired nerves). They can't taste the sweat that pours out of me whenever I think about seeing a doctor for a routine checkup, as I'm sure he or she will tell me that I've contracted something much more dangerous than Lester Bangs disease, that fatherhood, old age, retirement, or any kind of future is out of the question, and that it would really be best if I forget the Volvo dream and just lie down on this gurney for a good long time. Forever. As long as someone, one of my hippie cousins or a young bartender new to New York City or each new *Headphones* intern, looks at me with a weird mix of respect and disgust, and is convinced that I'm lucky to do what I do at my age, then maybe I can keep faking it. The truth is I gave my life to rock 'n' roll and I don't like it anymore. The love of music is long gone but the insidious lifestyle remains.

But this is the part where I tell you about the gradual reclamation of my soul, isn't it? I admit that the soul's not nearly mine yet. There are still several payments to make but I'll begin by saying that I discovered that there was actually something there for me to reclaim one night in the spring of 1999. As usual, I was drunk in my apartment after work. Those few hours before going out, when I'm alone and fitful, are always so slow-going. By the time I'm actually supposed to go out and meet someone, I've already thought too much about how meaningless my evening will be. I'm ready to get into bed and pull up the covers. So I drink. It keeps me on the street.

I'd long since moved out of the Chelsea but my apartment still resembled a hotel room. A pile of unpacked boxes of old shit from Susie's attic provided the only indication that it was intended to be a permanent residence. I don't remember the exact date because every night in the spring of '99 seemed the same. I'm not even certain it was the spring. But one night I was definitely very drunk at Don Hill's, the charmingly grimy old rock club on Spring Street, west of Soho. I'd gone there with a few work friends, intent on getting really out of it. You see, I'd received a letter in the mail that morning along with some electronica promos, an invite to a party "in honor" of Lenny Kravitz (Lenny's attendance not yet confirmed), and an advance of the new No Doubt CD, all of which I trashed (except No Doubt, which I tossed in my To-Sell pile). The letter looked like a personal, as in non-industry, non-promotional, document. It wasn't from a collection agency either. It had an airmail stamp and a private return address but I didn't immediately recognize the name. I opened it and saw that it was handwritten on fancy stationery: Mrs. Jennifer Rosen-Todd. I looked around to see if anybody was watching because I thought I might turn red and cry. It was Jennifer. I'm sorry . . . Jennifer Rosen-Todd. At least she'd kept her name after taking Robin's in wedded bliss.

Cheers, Joe,

I don't know if you're going to get this letter but I'm going to post it anyway. I took the address off the masthead of the magazine. I was on an airplane coming home from London to attend the funeral of my uncle Samuel and I purchased a copy of Headphones *at the newsagent and I was reading this article on Nine Inch Nails. It was really funny. It reminded me of you and the stuff you used to write for the* Echo *and I looked to see if you happened to have written it and sure enough, it was you. I think I may have screamed and frightened some of my fellow passengers. I'm glad to see you're doing so well, Joe. I think about you every so often. I'll see something that reminds me of the good old days, as they say. And being back on the Island certainly brought those memories back as well.*

I'm doing fine. I've been getting steady acting work, although nothing you'd see in the States. Mostly daytime dramas like East Enders. *You'd like it, though, as I usually play the tart.*

We all live on Regents Park Road near the zoo, Robin, myself, and our two girls (Emma and Rebecca). It's not as posh as it sounds but perhaps if you're ever on assignment in the London area you could look me up and the three of us and whoever you're with could go out for a meal and catch up. I'm enclosing both my e-mail address and mobile telephone number, and I do hope you call, Joe.

Love always,
Jennifer

P.S. I have two daughters and you are a cokehead who sleeps with teenagers and you're starting to get quite fat from all the piss.

I wrote that last part myself over margaritas at the Mexican restaurant around the corner from the *Headphones* offices, where I fled to take an extended lunch break and reread the letter until my eyes started to bulge like those of Marty Feldman from the old Mel Brooks movies. I didn't go back to the office. I went home and continued to drink, this time a fifth of Cuervo while lying on my kitchen floor.

Jennifer is married. She is happy. She has grown up. Moved on. Like me, she is being paid for what she loves to do. Unlike me she can go home after playing the tart. *I am the tart,* I thought, and started to cry. *I am the tart* . . . now lying on my apartment floor, crying, holding a knife in my hands.

"The good old days," I said to myself drunkenly. I got up and wobbled toward one of the boxes, the one that housed my dusty record collection. It was taped shut. I gutted the cardboard with the knife and ripped the flaps up. I thumbed through the vinyl and tapes . . . all those beautiful album covers, faces perfectly preserved, songs ruined only by a scratch here, a deeply ingrained dust bit there.

The Head on the Door by the Cure.
Ocean Rain by Echo and the Bunnymen.
Black Celebration by Depeche Mode.
And . . . *The Queen Is Dead.* I hadn't been able to throw that

one away. I'd bought it to place on my bedroom desk. I never even played it once. I had always played the cassette in my car or on my Walkman. I treated most of the vinyl that way. They were fetish objects, and that one had been the most intense of them all. Now, they were just heads on a weather-dulled totem pole. So many beautiful songs at my fingertips. But their meaning, like everything else, had been compromised by the passing of time, leaving only silence and a fear of even touching their spines, much less putting one on my turntable. They were too good for me, too perfect even for the people who made them, now as old and ugly and lost as I am. I needed noise. Music. Beauty. Something had to fill my head or I would start screaming so loudly, I'd wake Jennifer's babies on Regents Park Road. But in my apartment, in my head, there was nothing . . . silence . . . no music, only the hum you get when you've been drinking tequila all day . . . only the disorienting noises you ignore most of the time . . . the fridge, the television . . . *This is the sound of being buried alive,* I thought, *buried alive in flash clothes.* I stripped myself naked and stood there. I called Tom and told him I was going to be very late. I finished the bottle in the shower, drinking and steaming. I reached the point where my cleansing and my poisoning were done simultaneously, rending them both pointless . . . everything pointless. I rubbed the steamed-up mirror. My hair was going gray. Rather, it was growing white. And the white hairs seemed thicker and more tenacious than the brown ones, as if to say, *This is our time on your head, my man. Ain't no stoppin' us now, we on the move.* I looked tired. Old.

"This is what thirty looks like for you," I said to myself. "This is what forty-five looks like for everyone else. Good job. Well done. Cheers!"

I walked into the bedroom, grabbed Jennifer's letter off the top of my red kitchen table, and slipped it into the sleeve of *The Queen Is Dead.* It was the only suicide pageantry that I could muster, too drunk to even write a fucking note. I reasoned that maybe someone would find it and understand. They'd spy it next to some Herb Albert and the Tijuana Brass LPs and buy it for $1.50 in a Salvation Army bin someday, five years from now. I fantasized as I stared out the window into the street. They'd read it while listening to the album I could no longer touch. Maybe they'd call or e-mail Jennifer and let her know. Maybe she'd understand . . . something. I pulled on my black trousers, black T-shirt, black leather wrist cuff, and black zip-up boots. Each article smelled old . . . like the night before . . . like cigarettes . . . like decay. I walked out the door, convinced I would never return.

"Everybody reads *Headphones* on airplanes. What's the big deal?" Tom said. He turned to Gregory, an affable free-lancer. Gregory was the kind of balding guy who shaved his head clean after the first sign of thinning, à la Moby and Michael Stipe, cause they simply can't witness the process. We sat in the booth at Don Hill's waiting on a cocktail waitress. When I was feeling especially vulnerable, I liked drinking with Gregory too because he:

a. Was older than me by at least four years
b. Hated talking about music (he was the *Headphones* video games expert)
c. Usually picked up the tab
d. Was bald

"This is my ex-girlfriend and she's married," I slurred.

"So what's the problem?" Gregory asked.

"The problem is . . . she was never my girlfriend!" I shouted. Luckily, nobody could hear me over the pumping music. It was "Genius of Love," the old Tom Tom Club dance floor smash, followed by "Rock Lobster" by the B-52's.

"You didn't tell me this was a fucking eighties night, you cock!" I mushed.

how soon is never?

"I told you it was BeavHer," Tom protested. BeavHer was the weekly Thursday night party at Don's (still is, I think). The DJ pulled out all the moldy oldies and the kids who were barely born when they were first issued danced like they were in the house party scene in the movie *Valley Girl*.

"I thought it was some kind of sex thing. Strippers. Beavers."

We got a round of very expensive Sauza shooters (Gregory was buying) and downed them as the B-52's segued into yet another painful blast from the past, "Boy" by Book of Love.

"Each one of these songs is killing me, right now!"

"Shut up, Green."

"Killing me right now!"

"This piss is killing you," Tom countered.

"Let's get another one."

After three more shots and twice as many oldies, both going straight to the head, I had to take a piss, and staggered toward the line for the bathroom, dangerously wielding my lit cigarette through the densely packed crowd of nightclubbers. The bar was low-lit and my depth perception was tequila-fied. I heard the sound of trouble first, before I saw anything—a curt, surprised, and pained "Ow!"

It wasn't coming from my mouth. I was feeling no pain. I squinted around and realized that I'd just burned a really beautiful, sleepy-eyed, slightly hunched blond girl on the top of her shoulder with my cigarette. I sobered up a bit.

"Oh, God. I'm sorry."

I instinctively grabbed her bare arm to look for a deep red mark, like some unit surgeon, but I couldn't see anything.

"Does it hurt?" I asked.

"No. It's not that bad. You just startled me," she said. She looked vaguely familiar.

"I'm really sorry. I'm fucked up. I mean, I had a bad . . . Can

I buy you a drink? Let me buy you a drink . . . not cause I'm trying to like . . . hit on you or . . ,"

"I know." She smiled. She was okay. I could have walked away guiltlessly, but . . . you know, by then, I actually *was* trying to hit on her.

"What are you drinking?" she asked.

"Tequila."

"I'll have a vodka tonic." She smiled, ending any chance of a bond over the sauce.

"Coming up. Don't go anywhere cause . . . cause I'm about to spend like ten bucks on you." A real charmer, right? But she didn't go anywhere. She was right there twenty-five minutes later when I got back from the bar. I'd forgotten to suggest that maybe she wait somewhere else besides just outside the piss-stinking toilets but she didn't complain, only thanked me for the drink sweetly. In nightclubs like this you don't say "Shall we sit down?" cause it's just too crowded and nobody can hear you over "Blue Monday" by New Order at lawsuit-worthy volume, right? You just kind of gently herd your part-ner in whatever direction you want her to go. So there I was herding this stranger. She was wearing a white '20s-style flap-per dress, white stockings, and busy white shoes, the thematic ensemble gracefully thrown away with punky jewelry . . . but it still looked carefully selected. We found a spot on the long leather bench that faced the bar.

"What's your name?"

"Grace," she said.

"I'm Joe." I didn't say my last name. She hadn't told me hers either, so there didn't seem to be a need.

"Who are you here with?" I asked, hoping the answer would be anything but "my boyfriend" or, you know, "my girlfriend."

"Some friends. How about you?"

"Same."

The DJ segued into "Turning Japanese" by the Vapors.

"Look," I said, "I don't, um . . . you know, I just want you to know that I didn't burn . . . I don't burn people with cigarettes just to start conversations with them."

She smiled again.

"I just . . . I'm glad I burned you with a cigarette. I mean, I'm glad we're talking."

"Do you want to dance?" she asked.

The last thing I'd thought about doing was dancing. It just seemed so random and ridiculous for me to be sitting there with a really nice girl after what I'd gone through earlier that day that I thought, *Why the fuck not?* I couldn't even remember the last time I'd danced.

"Are you a good dancer?" I asked.

"No." She laughed a goofy laugh and probably blushed. I couldn't tell in the low light.

"Let's dance," I said, and we did the nightclub herd toward the dance floor. I did the punk rock retard hop to the New Wave groove, which was, fortunately, right in keeping with the DJ's set. She followed along, giggling. She was a little tipsy too. The Vapors faded out. ABC faded up. Then the Police and "I Want Candy" by Bow Wow Wow.

"Does this music make you feel old?" I asked, noticing, under the brighter dance floor lights that her skin was unlined and clear.

"No." She laughed that odd, snorting laugh again.

"It makes me feel old," I said in midspaz.

"How old are you?"

"Twenty-nine."

"That's not old," she said, looking at me like I was deranged. I wanted to hug her. I would get my chance too. After peaking with "Ant Music" by Adam and the Ants, the DJ did the clear-the-floor-save-the-couples thing. Brought it down a little. And what he played should have made me run for the door. The churning, backward guitar intro to "How Soon Is Now" emanated from what seemed like every speaker in New York City. I froze for a second. She stared at me. It was one of those weird social moments where, even briefly, having fun takes on gravity. I didn't ask. I just moved in closer, prepared to back off if she didn't move in closer too. She did and soon we were slow-dancing to the Smiths, our mutual lack of coordination straightened by Mike Joyce's sure and steady beat, and for the first time in over 10 years, listening to the Smiths didn't hurt.

"You're shaking," she said.

"I'm sorry," I said, and laughed. She put her head on my shoulder and closed her eyes. For a flash I worried that somebody, Gregory or someone too cool for the room table, was watching us and sneering, but I let it go . . . I let myself not care. Morrissey sang as we swayed around the room, all my anger and fear and resentment and spite and tequila fading away as the music washed over us, saving my life all over again.

"I am human and I need to be loved. Just like everybody else does!"

In that instant, all was forgiven. The bee sting. The breakup. In five minutes, I experienced the junior and senior prom nights I'd never managed to attend, now drunk on tequila and going gray . . . at age 29. When the song ended, there didn't seem to be any point in dancing to anything else. We herded (each other, this time) over to the bench and had another drink or two, exchanged numbers, then she left with her friends and I left with mine. That moment was enough, I thought, and although I fully planned on calling her, I really didn't want to ruin it that night. It was too perfect. I would see Grace again though on magazine covers and in indie movies. Turns out she was pretty famous. To paraphrase George Michael, we never danced again.

I came on my own. And I left on my own. And I went home. But I didn't cry. And I didn't want to die. What I wanted to do . . . what I did do until the sun came up was play *The Queen Is Dead*. I removed Jennifer's letter from the sleeve. For a moment, the depression briefly returned. I fought it off by playing air guitar to Johnny Marr's nasty, snarly intro to the title track (it felt amazing, stupid as it sounds, to play air guitar again). I reread the letter and realized something that somehow hadn't registered the first 48 times I'd looked the fucking thing over. I understood the reason why she'd written it in the first place. It had fuck-all to do with my stupid Nine Inch Nails piece. She'd always been reticent. Hard to read. But that night, I had her number. Long-lost Jennifer Rosen needed me. She needed that thing. She'd lost it too, even with Regents Park Road. Even with *East Enders* and the kids and her old geezer Robin. She needed "How Soon Is Now." The whole world does sometimes. I never wrote her back but I forgave her too that night.

The tequila hangover is second only to the gin hangover in its ability to deliver cruel punishment. It'll lay you out, son. But that morning as I dressed for work, there was no lingering pain. I'd like to think it was purely the music I'd rewelcomed into my life and my ears and my soul and my apartment, but I know it was the water I guzzled (not to mention a fleeting upchuck during "Frankly Mr. Shankly") through the healing process that really helped spare my self-destructive ass. That morning, I also decided to wear the only shirt I owned that didn't smell like the smoking car of a cross-country train. It was very old and worn, and I had to stretch it a bit to fit over my slight alcoholic paunch, but I checked my vanity in favor of the raw symbolism. I got on the train with my coffee and my *New York Post* and headed into work in the Smiths T-shirt I'd purchased on St. Mark's Place in 1984. I still wasn't too keen about writing about it, but I was ready to try to love rock 'n' roll again. My rock 'n' roll.

thirteen

some girls are smaller than others

"Nice shirt."

"Thanks."

She'd been looking at it for a while and making me feel a bit self-conscious, like maybe my boozer paunch was showing a little too prominently. I waited before I spoke, and wondered if her compliment could have been genuine. I'd seen her around the office before, sometimes in the elevator, sometimes by the coffee machine. You couldn't really miss the girl. She glowed. She had the kind of physical beauty that's so severe you frequently hear the people who possess it claim that they're single because people naturally assume they must be taken. I wouldn't say she was flawless . . . it's just the way her features were put together. The broad forehead, bedroom brown eyes with a humorous glint, small nose, slightly cherubic cheeks and chin, full lips, and toothy grin comprised something lovely and very intimidating. She was petite, about five foot two, but strongly built. While I tended to lumber and slouch, she had the kind of stature that lends itself to darting through crowds. Perhaps that's the real reason we had never spoken, as I'd surely been drunk enough at office parties to hit on her just in tribute to the sheer preposterousness of any possible coupling with such a beauty. I've done it before.

I frequently checked the *Headphones* masthead to remember the names of my fellow employees and figure out why the fuck they were there (I'm terrible with names and am the loathsome type who will meet a publicist at a show and introduce a friend first in hopes that the flack will shake his or her hand and reveal her name—"I'm Jenny" or "I'm Wendy"— and then I'll jump in with "So, Wendy, how the hell've ya been?"). Wondering if her last name was vaguely Asian too (she didn't look Asian; maybe European), I checked her out on the roster once . . . or twice. She was Italian. I reasoned that maybe her parents had spent time in the Far East. Or maybe she was a fan of the dream pop band Lush, whose singer/ guitarist was named Miki Berenyi (who *was* Asian). I later found out it was indeed a nickname. Her real name was Maria. Her parents still addressed her as such. But like me, she knew rock 'n' roll in theory and was aware that Miki is, historically, a good rock name.

Miki was the new assistant to *Headphones'* new editor in chief, Bob Johnston, who had recently been promoted following a series of in-house layoffs, which were more like small coups designed to alter the magazine's entire direction. I didn't really even notice that I had a new boss, hungover as I usually was. I never read interoffice memos. Rarely answered my phone. Left my sunglasses on indoors. I had become some kind of a ghost. If I happened to scan the lineup of features in the works for a future issue, it was only to see what fresh bit of soul destruction awaited me that month. Which vacant rock star was I to interview next? I can't say why I attended the editorial meeting that day. Maybe I just followed Miki in.

She had a way of making me follow her from the start. So there I was, tense and waiting for someone to say, "Excuse me, do you work here?"

"I want this magazine to be about music again," Johnston announced in a soft but strong tone.

Music. Pretty novel for a music magazine in the late '90s. It sounded good to me.

"There are certain bands that we have to consider," he continued. "Whether we like it or not, if a band sells three million copies, we have to cover them in order to stay alive here."

Everyone nodded in respectful agreement.

"But what I would really like to see are pitches with heart. Interesting, passionate pieces. Ideas. The kind of stuff that may take longer to research and report on. And may take our readers longer to read. I don't care. Just bring me something you care about. That's the only way to avoid becoming stale." Or remaining stale, as it were. This was less a meeting than a rally, and it was working.

I decided that Johnston was an honest guy. He was physically unassuming but obviously full of that leader energy required to maintain the loyalty of his employees. After asking around, I gathered that he was a real hip-hop-head with a thing for the Beastie Boys. It also impressed me that he didn't talk or dress like a Beastie Boy. An Ivy Leaguer, he wore his khakis and oxfords with confident ease. He seemed to be a late Gen X-er, five or six years my senior, who wasn't ashamed to admit his love for Dylan and Springsteen and other icons better suited for a baby boomer. I liked that he wasn't an egghead either. He didn't use words like *meta* or *ur*. He rocked because he loved rock. He just didn't see the need to wear that like a badge.

If I ever outgrow my need to do the opposite, I thought, *I'd like to end up a bit like Johnston.* Most importantly, he didn't make me want to smoke crack and die. Plus, his assistant was hot!

There were those around the office who called her "Psycho." There were rumors that she was actually 35 years old. Some said her boyfriend was a famous punk rock singer. All this information had previously passed through my head. Everybody knew everything about everybody else there. Who was sleeping with whom. Who had a drug problem. Who wasn't pulling his or her weight. I usually tuned out most of this kibitzing, as I was preoccupied with drinking myself to death in a ditch. But given Johnston's promotion and my night slow-dancing with Grace, things seemed different. And since Miki was stepping up to me, my interest in finding out about her grew exponentially with each word that came out of those lips. They were lips, I quickly found out, that frowned a lot more than they smiled. We didn't talk much about the Smiths at first, although the old shirt was clearly an icebreaker. Honestly, I was still reluctant to bring up the band. In my decade-plus of self-imposed ignorance concerning other Smiths fans, I frequently contributed to conversations that dismissed the band's work as a bunch of whining and morose punch lines. Even as my reputation as a rock writer grew, I had no idea that the Smiths were at all influential, and certainly not so to the kind of punk rockers Miki allegedly hung out with and possibly dated. Simply put, I wanted her to think the shirt was ironic . . . like it could have been a tour shirt from Ratt's *Out of the Cellar* or ZZ Top's *Eliminator* treks (items that many a wiseass hipster picked up at an East Village boutique for just under a hundred bucks). Even more succinctly, I didn't want her to think I was a fag.

When the meeting broke up with a series of handshakes and back patting, I slid over to her and smiled.
   "You wanna smoke a cigarette?"
   "Okay."

We walked out on the fire escape and lit up. She didn't have a pack. I later learned that she never bought them. She was the kind of person who could smoke one cigarette at a party or with a co-worker on a pigeon-shit-stained fire escape, then go a month and a half without ever smoking another (they walk among us).

"This is a good cigarette," she said, sucking down one of mine.

"How do you like working with Johnston so far?" I asked without making eye contact.

"He's really nice, yeah. He's great," she said. "Great!"

I noticed a slight quaver in her voice, like her mind was moving too fast for her tongue. It's rare when you can stand next to a person and hear the gears turning, even when they say little. Rarer still when you get strange words and images that aren't coming from inside your head. Even more unusual that you assign an unconditional trust to the notion that they're coming from inside the person next to you. And still more infrequent when that doesn't freak you out or make you doubt it, but rather fills you with some kind of comfort. I wondered if she could read my mind, and maybe that's why she didn't resort to the standard Mean Joe Greene icebreaker. As I moved closer toward her, I saw images of foxes fleeing from mounted hunters, and heard words that weren't my own, like *run* and *jog* and *flight*. I didn't assume that I was making her nervous or excited. It was pretty clear that something in her brain was moving, far afield.

"Are you okay?" I asked in a fumbling attempt to put her at ease and refocus on this surprising intimacy. I finally looked into her eyes.

"Yeah," she said. I could see that she was lying. And she knew I had some kind of intuition and maybe rewarded me for it with a smile. It certainly felt like a reward to be flashed with something that pretty, anyway.

how soon is never?

She didn't answer.

"Can I tell you something?" I asked.

"Yeah."

"I think I can read your mind."

"I know," she said. "I could feel you reading my mind."

"No fucking way."

"Yeah. Stop." She laughed. "Stop!" she shouted really loudly, and made a noise like a turkey gobbling. Maybe this was why some people called her "Psycho."

"Think of a number," I said.

"Okay," she said, and stared back at me hard.

"Are you thinking of it?"

"No."

"Yes, you are." I laughed. "Okay, what's the number?"

"Thirty."

"I knew it."

"That's amazing." She laughed too. I pulled out another cigarette and offered her one. This was going to be a two-smoke hang. We finished off a full pack before we returned to our desks. We tried the mind-reading game in earnest after that first goofy attempt, a product of our mutual nervousness at such a strong connection. She read my numbers correctly twice. I read hers only once but still found it pretty remarkable. Remarkable that I was even trying to connect with anyone. That the energies around us were so encouraging. Back at our respective desks, she started instant-messaging me on my computer.

"Do you want to try words?"

"Okay."

"Think of a word."

"Okay."

"Is it *monkey*?" she typed.

"No, but that's a good one," I typed back, forgetting my word.

"Do you like monkeys, Joe?"
"Yes, I like monkeys, Miki."

Miki was obsessed with monkeys. Before I left the office, I walked over to her cubicle, just outside Johnston's spacious office. Her desk was full of photos of chimps wearing human clothes or being held by Michael Jackson. There were Monchichi monkey keychains from the '80s hanging from tacks, gold, kitschy statuettes of Hanuman, the monkey god, and excerpts from a large printout she'd dubbed "Monkeysploitation," in which she had meticulously itemized every significant appearance of a monkey or an ape in over 50 years of film and television (from *Bedtime for Bonzo* to the great "Stop the Planet of the Apes, I Wanna Get Off" episode of *The Simpsons* and way beyond).

Her brain is *too fast,* I concluded as she showed the list to me. She said that she was planning to turn it into a calendar. She was convinced that there was a huge market for such a thing.

I didn't go out drinking that night. I grabbed some promo CDs, walked down to St. Mark's Place, and traded them in for three Smiths CDs. I lay in bed in the dark and listened to them in order, from the self-titled debut through *Meat Is Murder* and *Louder Than Bombs.* Like *The Queen Is Dead,* they hadn't seemed to age one day in the dozen years since I last played them. It was 1986 all over again. In the dark, I felt young and clean. When I rolled over to go to sleep, I wondered if I could hear what Miki was thinking from a long distance. If it were any other crush, I probably would have jerked off instead of attempting telepathy with her. It wasn't a physical obsession at first. Honestly, once I got physically close to her on that fire escape, the difference in our builds alarmed me. I couldn't imagine even fitting inside her. But it was definitely love at first mind-read.

how soon is never?

The next day, I woke without the usual shuddering dread. I sang in the shower ("Just What I Needed" by the Cars). I shaved and put on freshly laundered clothes. It was the kind of stuff a boy monkey does when he's trying to impress a girl monkey. As I got off the train at 34th Street and headed east toward the office, I passed a man selling dancing monkeys on a blanket out in front of a Spanish restaurant. The monkeys wore sombreros and did the monkey twist to a hideous version of the novelty smash "The Macarena." I bought one for $15 and shoved it into my bag.

You're getting into trouble here, Green, I thought. *She's going to know you like her. You're making an ill-advised overture.*

It was an overture to the strains of "The Macarena," but I couldn't help it. I liked that I was coming perilously close to caring . . . again. About something. I heard Bob Johnston's edict in my head as I rode up in the elevator.

"Just bring me something you care about."

I kept my gift in the bag, reluctant to hand it to her right away. I worried that maybe the previous day's connection was some fluke. I'd been very wrong before. I went straight to my desk, bypassing Johnston's area and Miki's cubicle. But when I signed on to read my e-mail, I noticed a letter from her.

"Dear Joe, I have a headache," it read. "Do you have a headache?"

I didn't have a headache. I didn't write back immediately. I had work to do. There were week-old messages and phone calls to return. Months of mail to open. I'd drifted far away and coming back was going to take some time. But as I played hours and hours of catch-up and cleanup, I couldn't stop thinking about Miki's pain. I couldn't abide by the thought that she was around the corner with a pain in her head. It was a real distraction. I felt in touch with the rapid, crazy clockwork underneath her crinkled forehead, and although I still didn't know why, I knew I had to do something to try to erase it. Especially since thinking about it was giving me a headache. I threw on my leather jacket and walked to the elevator, went across the street to the Korean deli, and purchased a packet of aspirin.

You're going to look like such a sap, I warned myself. *Like a little mothering bitch boy.* But I didn't care. I had to stop her headache. Her pain had become my pain somehow.

"Hi." I said, peering over her cubicle wall.

"Hi," she said smiling. She was holding the phone to her ear and squinting.

"How's your head?"

"It hurts."

"Yeah, well, I found some aspirin on my desk . . . under some papers and stuff. Here." I handed it to her and stepped back. "I gotta get back to work."

She took it and smiled again weakly.

"Me too. I've got to arrange Bob's trip to L.A. I've been on hold with the car service. I think it's going to explode, Joe."

"Your head or the car service?"

"My head."

"Take the aspirin. I think it'll keep your head from exploding."

"Are you sure?"

"Yeah. Well, that's what it says in the commercial anyway. I got you a Coke too. From the machine. Nothing . . . no . . . trouble."

"That's so nice."

"Yeah, well . . . bye."

I walked away, returned to my desk, and locked the monkey in the drawer. I could hear the muffled noise of "The Macarena," as I'd accidentally set it going in my haste.

"Joe," Tom said as he lowered his phone and stared at my

area, which was adjacent to his video-game-box-glutted cubicle. "I think there's something doing the Macarena in your desk."

"You've never heard of Wisdom Teeth?" Tom marveled later, over a post-work beer. I needed a friend. I had monkey trouble. So even though he was past his deadline for a 750-word review of the new Sugar Ray album, Tom agreed to hear me out, provided I buy a pitcher. We sat at the large round table in the back of the Library, the bar on Avenue A that I'd started drinking in regularly as my paycheck grew more steady. The Library used to be an even more dicey place called Psycho Mongo's, where once in a while I'd cop heroin off an old lady with a crooked wig who insisted on kissing my cheek like a drunken great-aunt every time I'd swing by to score. The bar had been cleaned up and redecorated with long shelves of books, which I found comforting. I know it's weird, but just like my stint at Shakespeare and Company, I somehow felt safer surrounded by books. I felt more like a writer, even if the Library's library consisted mainly of thrift-picked classics like *Cooking with Cod* and Jamie "M*A*S*H" Farr's autobiography *Just Farr Fun*. It was extremely dark, candlelit, and reminded me of my bedroom when I was in high school. Especially since the jukebox was loaded with the Cure, Joy Division, and yeah, the Smiths. Everybody needs a third space, somebody once told me (if I recall correctly, it was a bartender at the Library). And so the Library became mine, in addition to my tiny apartment and the *Headphones* offices. The large round table in the back became *my* office . . . and on that evening a shrink's office.

"They were like the biggest hard-core band in New York City. You're from New York!"

"So?"

"I'm from Minneapolis and I have all their records."

"I'm not into punk. I stopped being into punk when I was thirteen."

"That's so . . . punk," Tom mocked, wiping foam from his stubbly chin.

"So, how long have they been going out?"

"I don't know. But I think it's pretty serious. If you've got a thing for Miki, I'd lose it if I were you. The guy was in Wisdom Teeth!"

"I don't have a thing for her," I lied.

"God, I feel like I'm in high school. This conversation. This music!" "A Night Like This" off the Cure's *Head on the Door* was playing as I pumped Tom for info like the investigative journalist I was fast remembering I was.

"How old is she? Is she really thirty-five?"

"No. Who told you that? She's our age."

"Late twenties?"

"Twenty-nine, I think."

"Why do they call her 'Psycho'?"

"Cause she's crazy. She once threw a stapler at my head."

"Really? Why?"

"You have a thing for her! Look at you."

"Is Miki her real name?"

"I don't think so. I don't know. Hey, isn't Miki the name of the lead singer of Lush?"

"Yeah. Is she the lead singer of Lush?"

"No."

I got up to play the Medieval Madness pinball machine. As I destroyed the troll-filled castle, I realized that I was in love. I hadn't thought it was possible at my age, after all I'd done to distance myself from anything so pure, but there were un-mistakable flags everywhere. I had already started to miss Miki when she wasn't around. And not just miss her, but shake and panic a little bit. If nothing else, Miki made me want to go into work every day. Not necessarily to do any work. Just to be in the same building as her.

Inspired as I was by Johnston's new direction, I still couldn't muster any real enthusiasm for pitching ideas. I was basically whipping off whatever small assignment my editors threw my way and cashing my paycheck. "Hey, Joe, how do you feel about Fatboy Slim?" met my ears this way: *Hey, Joe, how do you feel about paying your electric bill? Hey Joe, how do you feel about macaroni and cheese?* I was just filling pages, churning out content, rarely listening to any promotional CDs I was sent, or looking my interview subjects in the eye, but I had hope that my new ardor for the office would somehow translate into a professional second wind.

Miki didn't seem to be any more spirited in her climb up the *Headphones* ladder than I was. Although she had managed to rack up a considerable number of small bylines in between fielding calls for Johnston, I could tell she was more excited about the prospect of finding previously obscure bits of monkey-sploitation for her master list.

"Is there a monkey in the video for 'Monkey Gone to Heaven'? You know, the Pixies song?" she'd typed in her instant messages to me.

"I don't think there's a video for 'Monkey Gone to Heaven.' "

"But if there was, you'd think there'd be a monkey in it, right?"

"I would. An angel monkey, perhaps."

These exchanges would go on for hours as we sat at our desks. She never revealed very much about her private life. I would have volunteered every detail of mine, but some people are guarded, even when we are able to indulge in the relative anonymity of electronic communication.

"What are you up to this weekend?" I'd write.

"I don't know."

"Do you go out?"

"Sometimes."

"Do you stay in?"

"Yes. Mostly when I'm not out."

Since I was convinced that she could read my mind, I felt increasingly paranoid. Like she had started to detect this attachment, and although she did nothing to discourage it, I only focused on her lack of encouragement. I stopped hanging around her cubicle. Sometimes I'd walk by her and pretend not to see her. Like I had to deliver an important document to an editor and could not be distracted by the most beautiful girl I'd ever seen who could read my mind. It was indeed very high school. The rock-'n'-roll pose was no longer solely arresting my potential growth. It was now accompanied by an old-school-style crush. I had it bad. I even unlocked my drawer and gave her the monkey (she played "The Macarena" so much that people started to complain, and one day it mysteriously disappeared from her desk, no doubt abducted by a conspiracy of *Headphones* employees and again locked away somewhere dark and confining).

Every day after work, she'd Rollerblade away to the lead singer of Wisdom Teeth and I'd walk to the Library and try to fill up the hole she was unknowingly boring into my guts. The moment when the cleaning woman showed up to start tidying up the office made my heart sink, as it was a signifier of another day's end and another night without her. Fridays were the worst, as I knew it would be a full two and a half days before I'd see her again. After several painful weeks, I finally decided that it was time to do something about it. I couldn't taste my food anymore. I couldn't sleep. I couldn't feel the kisses of the young girls I was taking home or going home with. Like I said, I wasn't any glittering prize to begin with, but my lack of enthusiasm made me even less of a catch and soon I was going home alone. Sitting in my apartment, days away from my 30th birthday . . . playing my Smiths records, and, even more painfully, or pointedly—no, let's say *pokingly*— a song by Nirvana called "School" (it's on *Bleach*) strictly for the bridge in which Kurt screamed: "You're in high school again! You're in high school agaaiiiiiiiin!"

"Do you like me?"

I sat down next to her and said something stupid like that. She was eating curry barefoot. The latest issue was closing and sometimes the managing editor sprang for dinner for the entire staff, who stayed way into the night to make sure it shipped to the printer on time. My work for the month was already in but I stayed late. And not for the free eats either. I found her on the floor of the research department. Sat down next to her and stared at her little feet. Chipped polish. Smooth heels. Like it was with Jane, I don't need to tell you that it's cool when you see a part of a girl's body you've never seen before. Not if you're in high school, anyway. You know this.

"I mean, I know you like me but am I . . . am I your work friend or your friend friend? I mean, we talk all day long, every day, but like I don't even have your phone number. I couldn't call you in an emergency situation."

"What kind of emergency situation? Like a fire?"

"Yeah, like a fire."

"You should really call nine-one-one."

"Or . . . another disaster. You know, like . . . my life."

"Your life's a disaster?"

"Pretty much, yeah."

"So's mine."

"No, it's not."

"You don't know that," she said, her tone getting a bit less jovial. Slightly offended.

"Look, I guess I'm trying to ask you if you wanna go out. As a friend. As two friends . . . who see each other outside the office. And maybe know each other a little more . . . just more."

"You want more?" she asked.

I waited, terrified. Looked her in the eye, then down at my booted feet. Then over at her bare ones. I addressed them. Oliver fucking Twist, I was.

"Yeah. I do. I want more."

She waited a bit, then laughed warmly. I looked up. She was smiling at me sweetly.

"You want some curry, Joe?"

"No."

"It's good."

"Okay."

"I'm gonna finish it."

"All right."

"You sure you don't want any?"

"I don't want curry. I want to take you out. For a beer. Or . . . whatever you want. More curry. Anything."

"More curry!" she yelled, and threw a big piece of nan across the room.

"Or a beer."

"I have to stay late tonight."

"What about tomorrow?" I said, and hated myself for sounding pushy.

"I think I can do that."

"Great!" I was elated. I would be spared another long and torturous evening of longing—the prospect of expanding our friendship would get me through the night.

"Oh, shit," she said. I felt my legs weaken. It was that kind of "Oh, shit."

"What?" Sometimes you just say "What?" and pray for mercy.

"Nothing. I have to go to the gym after work, that's all."

Sometimes you get the mercy.

"That's okay. We can go out after that."

"But I'm gonna be all sweaty."

"I don't care," I said, desperately adding, "We're just friends." It didn't come out as cool as I'd hoped. How could it have?

"Okay, Joe. We'll go out."

"Great. Thanks. I mean . . . not thanks, but . . . I have to go. Split."

I moved toward the elevators intent on at least walking out of the fucking office in a straight line, if not a cool strut. It was then I felt another big chunk of nan hit me on the back of the head. I turned around. She was looking down like she hadn't thrown it, stifling a giggle. Holding her breath. Turning red. I shook my head. Started toward the elevator again. She beaned me one more time. I looked back. She shrugged, feigning ignorance. I picked up the bread and took a mock-defiant bite. Suddenly, I could taste food again.

"You don't work out?" she asked as she pedaled furiously on a stationary bike. After avoiding several attempts by a gregarious and extremely fit employee to interest me in a special discount membership, I'd given up on the lobby and infiltrated the members-only workout area. I sat next to Miki and violated the no-smoking rule repeatedly. Each time Miki'd scold me and worry aloud about her membership being revoked. But I'd just forget and light up again.

"No. I never worked out. Well, unless you count running from all the jocks on Long Island. That's where I grew up. Long Island."

"Really? What was that like?"

"Well, I wouldn't raise a kid there. Unless I wanted to punish him somehow. Where did you grow up?"

"Philadelphia."

"City or suburbs?"

"Suburbs."

"I won't ask what that was like, then. I'm sure they're pretty much all the same."

"Yeah. Except we had WLIR, right?"

"What?" I sputtered, and dropped my butt.

"Didn't you listen to LIR?" she huffed.

"You picked up LIR in Philadelphia?"

"Yeah. I mean, there was probably more static, but I listened to it all the time," she said proudly. "My sisters turned me on to it."

"I don't believe it."

"Are you calling me a liar?"

"What was Screamer of the Year, 1986?"

WLIR had an annual vote for the fave-rave song of the year. I'd memorized every one of them. There was no way she could have too.

"I don't remember. Gimme a hint."

"Depeche Mode."

"Oh, it was 'A Question of Lust.' Am I right?"

"Yes."

"What do I win?"

"A monkey."

She got off the bike and rubbed a towel over her bright red face. Sipped from a water bottle and grabbed my cigarette. Took a drag.

"You're a bad influence. I'm trying not to age."

"Really?"

"Yeah. This is the time to do it, when you're still young, Joe."

"How old are you, Mik?" It was the first time I called her Mik. I felt comfortable enough—after all, she was a fucking

WLIR baby, straight outta Philly. She didn't correct me either, so from then on, she was Mik.

"How old do you think I am, Joe?"

"I heard you were thirty-five," I said, mock-defending myself.

"Who said that?"

"I don't reveal my sources. I'm a journalist."

"I'm twenty-nine," she said, her light tone again becoming a bit worried and quavering. "I'm gonna be thirty in a few days and I kind of hate it. It's scary."

"No way."

"What?"

"You're a Libra?"

"Yeah. What. You are too?"

"October tenth."

"Joe." She sat down and finished her water, took another drag off my cigarette, and exhaled. "We have the same birthday."

"You were born on October tenth?" I asked incredulously.

"Yes."

"1969?"

"Uh-huh."

"Bullshit. Let me see your driver's license."

I got mine out and showed her. My photo looked haggard. I was hungover in it. She went to her gym bag and got hers out. She looked younger and even more lovely. We didn't even look like the same species, but there it was. October 10, 1969. We were both a week and a half shy of 30.

"Fuck a duck!"

"Fuck a duck," she echoed. Then waited. "Fuck it!"

"What?"

"The duck. Fuck it! Fuck the duck!"

"What duck?"

"Larry the Duck."

"This is too weird. I need a drink," I announced. "Are you gonna shower?"

She smelled her armpit.

"Do you mind waiting?" she asked. "I feel gross."

"No." I smiled, thinking that she must like me a little, since she didn't want to hang out all funky. Then reminding myself that she's a Libra and we're pretty much the vainest of all signs.

"I'll hang out," I said, stubbing my cigarette on the floor and coughing madly.

"You're smoking in a gym." She shook her head and smiled, then pulled off her clinging sweat socks and padded toward the locker room. I watched her leave. Goofy-eyed. Grateful she existed.

After she was scrubbed and smelling of soap (me smelling of smoke) we went down to the Library and spent our first "friend date" getting shit-faced. The information exchange flowed a bit more freely in the bar. Still no mention of the boyfriend. I didn't ask, content to be next to her and pretend that she didn't have one. She was a bit more forthcoming with details of her childhood.

It wasn't a happy one and she was still fucked up about it.

"But your parents were together!" I shouted at her. I didn't mean to shout but she had no divorce . . . no Sid. Her dad, apparently, was a shrink who tended to bring his work home with him and volunteered unsolicited psychoanalysis of her every move, leaving behind a very self-critical and insecure but strikingly beautiful person. It makes sense to me now. You can take potential presidents and make them feel like a piece of shit if you get to them when they're young enough.

"I bet you had a fucking pony!" I slurred.

"I didn't have a pony."

"Well, what did you have?"

"Nothing. I had the Smiths."

"Bullshit. I bet you had like a hundred million boyfriends."

"Shut up."

"Like a billion boyfriends. The Smiths . . . the Smiths are for lonely people."

"I was lonely."

"How could you look the way you do and be lonely? *I* was lonely!"

"I was lonelier," she shouted back.

"No, I was lonelier, Miki. You were not lonely."

"I was very, very lonely," she insisted.

"I was lonelier."

"No, you weren't."

"I was uglier."

"Probably, yeah." She laughed and accidentally took my whiskey instead of hers. Pounded it back. I let her. It felt sweet.

"Wait, you think I'm ugly?"

"Shut up," she said, and pushed me. I reached into my pocket and pulled out a $5 bill.

"Can you stay?" I asked, and burped loudly so as not to seem too desperate. The Library was dead except for a few barflies at the front who just sat and stared into their beers, grateful to be out of the house and among two chattering monkey idiots like us.

"I guess I can stay for one more," she said, and burped back at me, her eyes crossing.

"Okay, here. This is a test. If you really were lonely and listened to WLIR out in fucking Philadelphia—which I still don't believe, by the way—here's your chance to prove it."

"Oh yeah?" she said. She snatched away the five defiantly, then wobbled out of the booth and toward the jukebox. Turned around and flashed me her gritted teeth.

"Joe."

"What?"

"Dare to be different."

I hit the bar for another round.

She passed the test. A $5 bill at the Library gets you 18 jukebox selections. *The Queen Is Dead* has 10 songs. She pumped in a single of her own on the sly and played the thing twice. By the second "I Know It's Over" we had put away another three rounds and severely pissed off the barflies, who were no longer grateful for the exposure.

"Play some fucking Misfits!" they screamed.

"Fuck you!" we shouted back, throwing large, heavy tomes their way. "Don't disrespect the Mozzer!"

"Has the world changed or have I changed?" I muttered absently, quoting the title track's rhetorical question. Then, asking my own, "Do you wannanutha?"

"One more. But that's it," she drawled back, leaning into me affectionately.

"Okay. I'll go to the bar." I couldn't move. "I'll go to the bar . . . soon."

"Okay," she said, closing her eyes and grinning beatifically as "The Boy with the Thorn in His Side" made a second appearance on the juke. She glowed.

"Do you remember when they broke up?" I asked.

"Yes," she said, keeping her eyes closed. "It ruined everything."

"It did."

"It was like a death"—she yawned—"in the family. Morrissey and Mike and Andy and Johnny were like family, weren't they?"

I nodded. We were both silent for a long time, listening to the music.

"We're old," I said.

"I know. I don't wanna be thirty."

how soon is never?

"I don't either. I wanna be sixteen."

"I wanna be fifteen!" she said.

"Me too. Forever. I can even deal with being seventeen. I can't deal with being thirty."

"Do you think they'll ever, ever get back together?" she asked.

"No."

"Culture Club got back together this year."

"Yeah. So did Bauhaus," I offered.

"It's not the same, is it?"

"No. It was a pretty good show, but . . . no."

"The world would be such a better place if the Smiths got back together, Joe," she said, opening her eyes and looking deeply into mine. At that moment, I wanted to get the Smiths back together myself . . . for her. One giant headache-relieving aspirin in the form of a reunited band. I wanted to kill her dad. I wanted to give her the whole monkey-lovin' world.

"You know, Mik, maybe we should try to get them back together ourselves."

"What do you mean?"

"Well, look at the Beatles. It's like they never reunited, right? But like . . . why not? I mean, maybe it's cause nobody tried hard enough to persuade them. Like Lorne Michaels made a joke about it on *Saturday Night Live*, remember that?"

"Right, right. He offered them like a thousand dollars or something."

"Yeah. But who's to say that if someone really wanted it, they couldn't have tried for real? Like why shoot John Lennon, right? Why not put the gun to his head and say, 'Call Paul now'? It's always been about misguided fucking fans. There's never been a serious, intelligent campaign."

"Morrissey and Johnny Marr don't even talk anymore. And Mike the drummer sued them both for back royalties and stuff."

"Yeah, but they must miss each other. I mean, listen to

this." I pointed up at the air, which was filled with the strains of "There Is a Light That Never Goes Out." "They must!" I continued. "How could you not? They just need persuasion."

"We should do it."

"We should. We could do it as a feature. For *Headphones*."

"We could stalk them." She perked up.

"Not stalk them. We're reporters! We stalk . . . with credentials. We have access."

"We do!" She was animated now. I ran up to the bar and ordered us another round of whiskeys and a couple of large Cokes. Walked back to the booth.

"You know, Joe, that is a really, really good idea."

"Yeah." I laughed.

"I'm serious," she said. I looked into her eyes again. There was no trace of levity. She was serious.

"Do you think we could?" I said, removing the mirth from my own voice, replacing it with as much clarity as someone who's downed eight whiskeys possibly could.

"Yes. We could. Not only that, we should! Oh, we have to do it, Joe. Before it's too late. Before one of them dies or something."

"Do you really think it's possible, Mik?"

"Nobody's ever tried. You said it yourself."

"It's true. Nobody's ever tried to reunite a band before. No real fans anyway. But how do we do it?"

"We could send a telegram to Johnny from Morrissey. And vice versa. No . . . no, flowers. Gladiolas. Morrissey loves gladiolas."

"True. True. Then we could, um . . . pretend to represent the Make-A-Wish Foundation and say that this little girl is dying from cancer."

"Leprosy!" she suggested.

"Yes, leprosy, and if they don't reunite immediately, her . . . her head's gonna fall off."

"We could call the queen and have her command them. Oh no, they hate the queen. We could . . . we could . . ."

I lit a cigarette and tried to arch my eyebrows so that I appeared serious, or at least a bit sober.

"Listen, I think all we really have to do, Mik, is approach each one, you know, as journalists."

"Right, cause we *are* journalists."

"We are," I agreed. We clinked glasses. "We are."

"And get each one to agree to reunite. In writing. A contract. Do whatever it takes to get them to sign. And that's it," she said.

"We go to Morrissey last."

"Right. We say, look, Morrissey . . . look, Mozzer . . ."

"Oi, Mozza."

"We 'ave Andy, Mike, and Johnny in the other room and they're ready to fookin' play," she said, approximating a British accent with much more success than me.

"It could work," I said, filling up with a weird hope. Feeling 16.

"All we'd need is . . . lots and lots of patience and . . . money. We'd need lots of money."

"Yeah, we'd have to travel . . . far." I smiled. "Do you think Johnston would go for it?"

"Totally!" She smiled. "How could he refuse? We're gonna save the world!" She rose and kissed my cheek, then climbed over me and out of the booth. *"He's in the world!"*

"He is," I agreed.

"I have to pee."

I downed my drink. I didn't want her to leave. I was too high. Too excited. As long as the music was playing and there were alcohol and people and life, I felt like I could hold off 30.

"Are you leaving?" I called out. She turned around again.

"No," she said, "we have a lot to do, Joe." She pointed at

me sternly. "We have to save the world." She stumbled into the toilet.

They kicked us out at four. I walked her home, past Tompkins Square Park, down to Avenue C. It was only a few blocks but it took another half an hour, we were so drunk.

"Drink lots of water," I said, reverting to my bitch boy mode, echoing whatever remnants of Jewish mother love Susie had managed to send my way.

"Yes. I will." She smiled and stared at me.

"I don't know which apartment's yours so you're gonna have to figure that out."

"Okay." She laughed. I took her hand.

"Goodnight, Mik. Get some sleep, okay?"

"Okay."

"Cause tomorrow, we're going to reunite the Smiths."

"We are!"

I watched her walk up the stairs to her door and wondered if the lead singer of Wisdom Teeth was inside. And if reuniting the Smiths might somehow make him disappear into thin air. More important, I wondered where it was I lived again.

unhappy birthday

It wasn't the usual kind of pact that comes to life when you've drunk enough whiskey to forget how to get home in the city you've lived in for 10 years. It had longevity. The next morning, both Miki and I were still excited and committed to approaching Johnston with a proposal. That's not to say that we weren't aware that the project was absurd. Bands comprise individuals and in this country, as well as England, individuals decide on their own whom they want to perform music with. Certain factors, want of money being a major one, may sway them, but ultimately the decision is theirs, not those of two hungover rock journalists deathly afraid of turning 30. But we had no choice. *We were turning 30.* We'd started to hate our jobs. I had started to hate my body. I can't speak for Miki, but I had to get up 20 minutes earlier than usual each day just to pluck the gray hairs out of my head with a tweezer. I knew they would grow back, but I just couldn't look at them. They were too scary. I didn't need any other motivation for checking my rational thoughts at the door and committing myself entirely to whatever it took to turn back the clock to 1987, the final year that the Smiths played music together. But I had another. Even if I destroyed my reputation as a professional rock writer and made myself the laughing-stock of the music industry, even if I landed in prison on tres-passing or harassment charges, I would not be alone. Miki and I were now a team. In my head, that was as good as being a couple, better even. Most couples, like most successful bands, lose their passion after a few years. But ours would remain. We didn't just have chemistry . . . we had a cause. We had the passion. We would be the ones to make a difference. More im-portant, the band was just waiting for people like us to enter their lives. Or at least that's how it seemed. I did a cursory Web search that morning before our big meeting. I was trying to quickly print out some materials to support our presenta-tion to Johnston and found a two-year-old interview transcript from a July 1997 Morrissey sit-in at KROQ, L.A.'s biggest mod-ern rock station. When disc jockey Richard Blade inquired about why there hadn't been a reunion, Morrissey replied:

> There's nobody intelligent enough within the music industry to even try to get the Smiths back together. Because nobody ever did try, and there's always been temporary managers and people as acting managers for all of the Smiths. And they've never tried to get the individuals back. They've always just tried to keep everybody apart, which mystified me. I always thought that one day there would be some intelligent person who would say, "This is ridiculous! You all like each other. You all want to play music. You all want to be together. Let's get you together, and let's sort everything out." But there never has. People who represent all the individuals have always been quite spiteful, and that's just so disruptive.

"Oh, my God, Joe, he's talking about us!" Miki exclaimed when I handed her the printout.

"Isn't he? It's perfect. We should call Richard Blade."

how soon is never?

"We will."

"We should tell him it's perfect. We're perfect!"

We're perfect, I repeated in my head.

Perfect.

Johnston seemed excited to pencil us in at first. Miki usually only came to him with his memos and plane tickets. Normally, I could barely manage a gruff "Hey" when we'd pass in the halls. Now, we were responding directly to his plea for new ideas that matter. We were validating his motivational speech . . . and his authority. Miki and I sat together on his leather couch and stared at his kind face across a cold glass table littered with CDs, books, and issues of other magazines.

"Basically, we have an idea," I started.

"Good." He smiled, a little awkwardly.

It might have been good to do a little bit of prep work first, but we were too excited. So we winged it.

"Do you love the Smiths?" I started hopefully.

"Love them?" he asked, shaking his head. "They were a great band but . . ."

"They were the best band ever . . . b-but that's neither here nor there," I stammered. "Some would say the only truly immortal band of the '80s. In fact, I think Nick Kent did say actually . . . I'll have to check. I can check."

"What's the idea, guys?" Johnston asked, growing less patient with every second.

"The Smiths are broken up. No more. There have been solo albums. Ugly lawsuits. Murder. Mayhem. Well, not murder, but—"

"Right." Johnston cut me off again.

"What we want to do," Miki finally said with a confidence that must have impressed him because the whole energy of the room changed from goofy to grave, "is reunite the Smiths."

"They won't do it themselves, so we do it for them," I added.

"Show them the error of their ways," she chimed in.

"Change their destiny," I practically yelled.

"And make a lot of sad people—" Me.

"Of all ages and marketing demographics—" Her.

"Really, really happy—" Me again.

"To be sad." Her.

Suddenly, our odd telepathy kicked in and loaned itself so well to such an off-the-cuff proposal that it all seemed well rehearsed. Soon we were trading verbal riffs and finishing each other's sentences with the leanness of a power trio . . . say, the Jam or Nirvana. Nobody took an unnecessary solo. We explained to Johnston that although the band had been dead for a dozen years, their influence and popularity were greater than ever. We pointed out that the pesky Generation Y had sought them out as a band who was important to explore, much in the same way second-tier Beatlemaniacs and Stonesheads took to those groups even though we were born the year *Abbey Road* and *Let It Bleed* came out.

"You can hear the Smiths in Radiohead," I pointed out. "You can hear them in . . . in . . ."

"Hip-hop!" She picked it up . . . then dropped it. Even I found that a bit of a stretch.

"You can?" Johnston said, incredulous, swiveling in his chair. Maybe he saw our stumble as a chance to regain control of the room, or at least hear his own voice atop our buzzing harmony.

"I can," Miki insisted.

"It doesn't matter. This is so beyond the Smiths. We think of it as a much larger experiment," I offered.

"A cultural experiment," she added.

"A pop cultural experiment. We want to prove that a

Smiths reunion would change everything. Lift spirits. Stop the war."

"What war?" Johnston sighed, on the ropes.

"All war!" Miki shouted.

I wondered for a moment if Johnston was puzzling over just what strain of lunatic had been opening his mail and fielding his personal calls. It dawned on me that she was risking much more than I was at that moment.

"We have to do it now before one of them dies," she warned.

"Like John Lennon did," I said.

"Before we die," Miki offered. I stared at her, momentarily checking her head for gray hairs. Maybe she plucked too. Or dyed.

Johnston rose abruptly. He walked behind his desk and looked at something on his computer screen, then walked back to his chair and remained silent. We sat nervously.

"How do you plan on doing this? You're not going to use . . . real force, are you?"

"Define force," I said, and laughed. He didn't.

"Weapons," he said, straight-faced.

"No. We're not going to kidnap them," Miki promised.

"Unless you want us to," I added.

"No. I don't want you to."

"We haven't worked out all the details yet. We just know that not only could it be a great piece, it—it could be a great . . . thing," Miki stammered.

"We know it's going to be hard," I said. "There's a lot of bad blood there. But ideally we want to convince the band that the world would be a better place if they were still together."

"Whose world?" Johnston asked.

"Our world," I admitted. "But there must be hundreds of people who feel the same way as we do. Unlike them, though, we're in a position to do something about it. Look, we figure all we have to do is use our position at *Headphones* to get each member to agree to an individual sit-down and just persuade them somehow. We can be very persuasive."

"Oh yeah?" he said. I remember hoping he was being droll. I could tell by his tone that he really meant, *Well, then, how about persuading me to not throw you the fuck out of my office?*

"If they don't reunite, if we totally fail, you still get a feature," I boasted. "We'll document our attempts and it'll be just as readable."

He got up again. This time he paced while we squirmed. Finally, he sat down, took another lengthy pause, and cased our faces one last time to confirm that we were, in fact, deadly serious and hadn't been put up to this by one of his college buddies or an irate associate editor. We held firm.

"All right. Here's what we'll do. I'm going to tentatively assign it for the November issue. This is for the feature well, so if you're not serious, you're going to leave us with a pretty big hole to fill."

"We're totally serious," Miki promised. "We're not crazy."

"Totally not crazy."

"I want an outline and an estimated travel budget by tomorrow afternoon or I'm going to kill this quickly."

The November *Headphones* was two issues away. We would have about 45 days to accomplish our goal. It was a problem.

"That's not a problem. We'll get right on that," Miki said. "We can have it by the end of the day tomorrow."

"And I have your word there won't be any violence toward Morrissey?" Johnston asked. He wasn't smiling either.

"We won't hurt Morrissey," I said firmly.

"We'd never hurt Morrissey," Miki promised. "We love Morrissey."

"And he loves us," I added. "Well . . . he will anyway."

I offered my hand to Johnston, then wondered if that was the right thing to do. He shook it quickly. My palms were soaking. He politely ignored the dampness. Miki and I hurried toward the door, fearful that he might reconsider.

"Hey," he called out.

We both stopped dead and turned around anxiously.

"What happens if you do reunite them?" he asked.

We went out for a celebration lunch at the touristy Mexican joint around the corner. For a tiny girl, Miki could eat like a trouper. She gesticulated wildly as she polished off a pair of enchiladas the size of her arm and a big plate of rice and beans. I stuck to chips and salsa and a hair-of-the-dog margarita.

"The first thing we should do is find out their contacts," she said. "Morrissey should be easy. He probably has an entourage. Johnny must have a manager. And somebody's gotta be booking Mike and Andy into these Smiths conventions they have in Los Angeles. Do I have food in my teeth?"

She smiled. She didn't.

"They have Smiths conventions in L.A.?" I asked. "Why don't we just find out when the next one is and corner the guys there?"

"It's too late. The last one was months ago. Do you have a passport, Joe?"

"Yeah. Why?"

"Well, we're gonna have to go to England." She reached into her bag (Miki never carried a purse, only a small brown vinyl bag, which had a Paul Frank monkey illustration on it) and pulled out one of those old pens where you could switch the ink cartridges from blue to green to black to red.

"Trip . . . to . . . England," she said as she wrote. "I'll take care of the budget and travel stuff, Joe. I can do that in my sleep at this point. You try to come up with some strategies."

"Well, we could post something on the Net. On every

Smiths-related site. Or would that tip them off? It might make it hard to schedule a legitimate interview."

"No, no, no. That's a good idea. We need to win the support of the fans. We need an army. An army!"

"And an air force."

"We could do it anonymously," she offered. "We won't use a *Headphones* account. We'll just put it out there and test the waters. Okay, what else do we need? I need some more guacamole. You should eat something, Joe."

She looked around for the waiter and I realized this was our first shared meal. I could hear her chew. I became distracted by the intimacy. I started imagining how happy those enchiladas must feel to be inside her. I had it really bad.

"Joe? Joe! I need you to focus." She laughed. "This is big. We're gonna do this."

"I know."

"Now come up with some more ideas," she ordered affectionately, like some benevolent dictator, pointing her greasy finger at the salsa-smeared napkin I'd been scribbling on. "And find our waiter!"

After lunch, we tried to log on to the Internet under the assumed name "Mr. Shankly," a nod to the track "Frankly Mr. Shankly," but found it was taken. We settled for "Ms. Shankly" and posted the following message at various Smiths and Morrissey-related message boards:

Greetings, fellow Smiths fans,

Have you failed to outgrow the songs of Morrissey/Marr? Do you frequently toss gladiolas at your reflection in the mirror? Do you quiff your hair and recite Oscar Wilde in the boneyard? Are you celibate? Vegetarian? The 18th pale descendant of some old queen or other? Did your lives change for the worse when the

Smiths broke up in 1987? Would your lives change for the better if they reunited? If so, please e-mail us with moral support, any deep contacts for Morrissey, Johnny, Mike, and Andy, or suggestions that might help us with our cause: a Smiths reunion by any means necessary (except violence). It's time to make things right in the world. Let's make this happen together.

Love,

Ms. Shankly and the Vicar in a Tutu, co-chairpersons of the Committee to Reunite the Smiths

Within an hour there were e-mails in our newly set up in box from over 100 fans. That number doubled within the next hour. Within a few days, we'd heard from nearly 500 fans. Unfortunately, there were no concrete leads on how to get in touch with Morrissey and his estranged bandmates. Miki and I printed out the letters and sat over a couple of pints at the Library. We read each one aloud. I was already noticing that we'd spent the entire day together. I'd seen her eat. I'd heard her sing as she hummed along to the radio in the cab we shared downtown (she had a good voice, wasn't tone-deaf like me). I was overjoyed but decided that I really had to concentrate on preserving whatever cool I had left. I didn't want her to think I was a creep . . . or to know that I really was a creep.

"So, what are you doing for your thirtieth?" I asked. "I've got plans for mine."

"Oh, cool," she said absently, her head buried in another printout.

The date was a matter of hours away and I had no plans other than freaking the fuck out.

"Yeah, big plans."

"Me too," she replied, revealing no details. I assumed these plans involved the lead singer of Wisdom Teeth. Probably a cake. Definitely not me.

"That's cool. Maybe we can, you know, hang out after that. In our thirties."

She picked her head up and smiled a pained but still gorgeous smile.

"Can we stop talking about it?"

"Okay. Do you want another beer?"

"No, thanks. I'm gonna go home and get some sleep. I'll get up early and finish up the budget stuff."

She rose and walked toward the bar exit. I wondered for a minute whether or not I should follow her. I could have held the door and spent another 30 seconds in her presence. I opted to stay seated and give her a cool but pleasant nod of the head.

"I'll see you tomorrow, then."

"Okay, Joe. Goodnight."

She kissed my cheek. I raised my pint to my lips and closed my eyes.

The next day I arrived at the office super-early. So early that many of my co-workers gazed at me in total shock as they walked by. I'd only ever stumbled in a good 45 minutes past the suggested arrival time of 10:30 A.M. every day, then took another hour or so to ready myself to begin working. But that day, I'd already been there two hours or so and must have looked like a displaced vampire, sitting at my desk, eating a vanilla-frosted donut. At around 10:35, I looked at my buddy list in the corner of my computer screen and saw that Miki was at her desk across the office. I instant-messaged her.

"If you need me for anything, I'm sitting here eating donuts."

"Donuts!" she messaged back cheerily.

"You want one?"

"Do you have many donuts?" she replied.

I lied and after she said yes I found myself running Mean

Joe Greene–style down to the cart out on 31st Street to fetch her one.

This is not playing it cool, I scolded myself silently.

"Hey," I said, extending a chocolate, a vanilla, and a plain unfrosted one her way. "I didn't know what you took so I brought you . . . a variety of donuts."

"Did you buy a dozen?"

"No, I just found a discarded box in the trash and they seemed okay," I said, then faked a collapse and a seizure. I could hear her chuckle from behind the wall as I lay on the floor, catching my breath.

"I've decided that in my thirties, I'm going to consume nothing but coffee and donuts, Mik."

"That's a good plan."

"Yeah, that'll be my reward to myself for surviving thirty years of pain and addiction and . . . um . . . well, not addiction, but . . ." I realized that I had yet to reveal that part of my past to Miki. I already knew that she thought I was an alcoholic chain-smoker. I didn't want her to think I was gonna steal her color TV set and sell it for junk money too. Some girls might be reluctant to let you into their homes, especially the ones who live with straight-edge punks. I changed the subject to more important and impressive matters.

"I did some research this morning."

"Already?"

"Yeah, I've been here since like eight."

"Oh, my God."

"It seems Morrissey is currently without a record label."

"Shit."

"It gets worse. He doesn't have a manager either. Short of family and friends, there's absolutely nobody for us to send an interview request to."

"That sucks!" She frowned. "What do we do?"

It was time to be the man and rally our two-person army

(discounting the 500 moral supporters) in the face of our first serious obstacle.

"We hold off on that for now. Just keep going forward. I found Mike Joyce's website on the Net last night. We must have missed it. The site claims to be official and it looks well maintained. Anyway, there was a U.K. phone number, so I got in early and called England this morning. I left a message. Maybe they'll call back. I also found out that Johnny Marr is signed to Ignition Management in Manchester. That's the same one that Oasis is signed with, so they must be pretty big. I'm gonna fax over a request now."

"Wow, Joe. All this before ten A.M."

"The Smiths army. We do more to reunite the Smiths before ten A.M. than most people do all day." Reverting to crushed-out boy mode, I added, "I have an interview in an hour at the W hotel, so I won't be around till after lunch. That's how come I'm here . . . now."

"Which band are you interviewing?"

"I can't remember," I admitted.

"Well, I'll let Johnston know what we've done so far, and I'll give him the budget proposal. I worked on it last night."

She handed me a copy. It was neatly itemized. She'd found several fares to and from Manchester and factored in expense money, transportation, everything down to tape recorder batteries. She was thorough.

"Wow. This is impressive," I said.

"I want him to know we mean business. We bust balls," she said. "Joe?"

"What?"

"We bust balls!"

"We do. Nothing's going to stop us."

Nothing but total indifference, that is. Five days passed without a reply to any of our initial overtures. Still,

Johnston was equally impressed with Miki's thorough break-down (he even okayed the part about $300 for research materials, which essentially allowed us to replace each of our scratched Smiths CDs, as well as buy back issues of the *NME* and pricey U.K. music mags like Q, *Uncut,* and *Mojo*). Every day I walked into the office early and checked my voice mail and e-mail. Every day they were devoid of anything from across the sea. We seemed to be at an impasse. On Friday, we met again at the Mexican restaurant for lunch. Miki ate a four-pound burrito in three or four bites and eyed my rice and beans hungrily as we restrategized.

"Maybe we should just fly there and find them," she suggested.

"Manchester's a big city. We can't just like roll up the street shouting, 'Yo, Johnny Marr!' "

"Yeah, but these guys are heroes. Somebody must have a lead. Must know what pubs they drink in, where they do their washing."

"I'm not gonna stalk out their Laundromat," I informed her proudly. "I'm a fucking professional reporter."

"Well, maybe we should go to L.A. first and find Morrissey. At least we know where he lives."

Morrissey had permanently relocated to Los Angeles, where the Smiths enjoyed their most solid and loyal fan base. He was reportedly living in Beverly Hills in a large mansion that Clark Gable had purchased for his wife, Carole Lombard. It was gated and secure but geographically available to anyone with enough change to purchase a map to the stars' homes.

"No, we need the others first. The willingness of the others, that's our ace. We can't go to Morrissey until we've got three statements in writing or on tape."

"You're right. Well, what the hell are we gonna do?" She frowned and stared down at her empty plate. "Can you get our waiter, Joe? I'm out of food."

*   *   *

That afternoon we said goodbye. We didn't make any plans to see each other over the weekend. We didn't promise to call. We didn't mention what was going to happen. We just parted. She walked east. I walked west.

The next morning, Miki and I turned 30. I stayed home the night before, listening to the Buzzcocks' *Singles Going Steady*, pacing and chain-smoking, cursing myself for not being able to pull out some auspicious project-related activity that would have given us cause to reconvene over the weekend. I cursed myself for getting old. Of course, there was nothing short of suicide that I could do to stop it. And yet it felt so humiliating. So unglamorous. When the sun came up on Saturday morning, I stayed in bed. I decided I wouldn't get out until the day was over. I didn't budge when Susie and Dick left a message on my answering machine. Well, it was more Susie singing and Dick humming, as though his arm was being pinched.

"Happy birthday to you, happy birthday to you . . ."

Susie added, "If you're starving, we'll buy you dinner. Come out to the Island, you thirty-year-old, you!"

Long Island was the last place I wanted to be on my birthday, the last place I wanted to see ever again, but for a moment, I considered it. It was better than being alone. I decided to shower and shave and throw on some clean clothes. Nothing felt incredibly different than the day before. I felt tired, but I always felt tired. I looked the same . . . still dirty and haggard. Still young enough to get carded in a dark bar but much older than I wanted to. It was chilly but sunny, a bright, beautiful autumn afternoon in New York City. I decided to go to the zoo and maybe hit a couple of museums. I walked toward the subway at Sixth Avenue and Waverly Place. The kids were playing basketball on the fenced-in court.

how soon is never?

I lit a smoke and watched them for a while. They were moving so fast. Their eyes were raging with energy and focus. I started to panic. I pulled out another cigarette and decided I had to move. Something was following me, pressing on me, sucking out my breath. I began walking up the avenue. By 14th Street, I was running. My destination wasn't the zoo anymore. I didn't know where I was going. I just ran. It was involuntary. I just kept going. Pedestrians stared as I blurred by. In New York, there's only two reasons why someone like me runs up the street: they're chasing someone dangerous or they're being chased. By 31st Street, I needed another cigarette . . . or an iron lung. I stopped and doubled over. I could see Pennsylvania Station. A straight shot one block west. Its Seventh Avenue entrance, the one I'd gone in and out of 500 times since I first starting ditching school and coming to the city on those afternoons of discovery in the '80s, now looked like the mouth of a grave or the giant maw of some carnivorous fish, waiting to snatch me up and swallow me down.

Is that all there is? I thought. *My options are a steak on Long Island or running from an invisible demon. Why? Because it's all over now . . . it's all over now, baby blue!*

The answer came quickly and seemed irrefutable. I wondered if Miki was having a similar experience. Was she running south down Avenue B toward Chinatown? Was she being chased by that same nasty phantasm as it tried to snatch away her vitality, her relevance, her self-worth, her brown hairs? I tried to focus on reading her mind, but all I could hear were car horns and bustle. I hailed a cab.

"Take me to Avenue A, please. Second Street," I said, panting.

The cabdriver was a decrepit old man with greasy black hair. He wore a red-and-black checked flannel shirt. I noticed he was smoking a Kent King. Sid's brand.

"You can smoke," the driver said as he cut down the street toward Second Avenue and hung another left. He was listening to the Bee Gees on the oldies station, CBS-FM. "I'm smoking," he said, gesturing with his Kent.

"Thanks, man."

"You look fucked up," he said with a thick accent.

"It's my birthday," I wheezed, lighting another cigarette.

"How old?"

"Thirty."

"Oh!" He laughed. "You getting there. Right?"

"Yeah, I'm getting there." Getting where? Closer to death?

I handed him a $10 bill and used the remaining money in my wallet to get really fucked up. I drank 12 shots of whiskey with the old barflies at the Library. I had no food in my belly, so within a few hours I achieved the kind of drunk that cancels all bets. It was the kind of drunk where you could wake up in jail or in the St. Mark's Hotel next to some hooker. It was the kind of drunk where you could start crying in public. It was also the kind of drunk where you lose track of time and find yourself walking down to Avenue C and pounding on the door of the apartment that you're pretty sure your co-worker (and co-chairperson of the Committee to Reunite the Smiths) shares with her punk rock boyfriend.

"Joe?"

"I'm sorry. I'm sorry. I . . . I had to see you."

"Are you drunk?"

"No. Yes. Yes, I am. More important, I'm dying."

She was dressed nicely, in fancy black, like she'd just been from or was on her way to a really nice dinner.

"So are you," I sobbed. "We're thirty!"

I threw up my hands and nearly fell backward down her steps. She instinctively grabbed me and pulled me close to her. Most likely, she was trying to save me from a skull fracture, but I hugged her anyway. I just held her like I'd never held anyone. Not Sid when he told me he was leaving. Not Jane when I told her I was leaving. Not Jennifer when she was London-bound. Not any syringe I was lovingly sticking into a bulging, greenish vein. I hugged her with more desperation than any stage-rushing fan hugging Morrissey. With as much unself-conscious honesty and vulnerability as anybody has ever hugged anybody else with . . . ever. My knees buckled and I slid down her body until we were almost the same height. I buried my face in her neck and let loose all the tears that I'd been storing up for over 20 years. It was as if I had never cried before and I couldn't remember the last time I did. Once I started, I couldn't stop. She had no choice but to comfort me, even if she was probably on her way to Benihana or something fancy like that. I was dying. Right there. In her arms.

"Joe, you're a mess." She laughed. "Have you eaten?"

"No."

"You need some food."

"I don't wanna die. Please . . . help me."

"Come inside. You're scaring the neighbors."

She led me inside. My adrenaline kicked in at the thought of being presented to the punk rocker boyfriend, but the apartment was empty. It was small, markedly lopsided, as though the building had been founded on slick mud. The walls were hand-painted silver and gold and hung with photos. The window was open, facing out on a dirty lot and a brick wall. A raw wooden desk and a large antiquated computer sat between the entrance to a dark toilet and what I assumed was her bedroom. A fork in the road. I chose the toilet and instantly projectile-vomited a wave of bourbon whiskey.

"Oh, God, Joe." I heard her from outside. I was making a hell of a racket.

"I'm okay," I said weakly, and dunked my head in the bowl again, purging all the booze. I flushed the toilet and sat there for a while, staring back at my reflection against the water.

"I'm making you some tea," she said. "There are some left-overs here. Joe?"

She ducked into the bathroom shyly to see if I had drowned my fucked-up self in the toilet water.

"I'm fine," I said calmly. "I just . . . I'm sorry. I'm sorry, Mik. Did I ruin . . . were you going . . . were you meet-ing . . . ?" I couldn't put more than two words together, so I just smiled and said, "Um . . . happy birthday."

She shook her head.

"There's some cake and a little bit of steak. You should really eat something, Joe. You look gray."

"Birthday cake?"

"Yes. Some friends took me out."

"Boyfriends? A billion boyfriends," I muttered, and hurled into the bowl again. That last spew coupled with the urgency of the kettle whistle righted me a bit. I pulled myself up and slapped some cold water on my flushed cheeks. It felt good. I did it again.

"I'm sorry, Miki," I called. I walked back to the kitchen. She emerged from the bedroom. She'd changed into a T-shirt and a brown-and-yellow striped skirt. Stocking feet. I sat on the crooked kitchen floor, beneath the sink. I realized that al-though I was sitting cross-legged and upright, I was tilted.

"Is this floor crooked or am I still really fucked up?"

"You're really fucked up," she answered. "But the floor is tilted."

She handed me a cup of tea. I sipped it. It was peppermint. The best peppermint tea I ever had . . . not that I drank an aw-ful lot of peppermint tea.

"Thank you," I said meekly. Such a normal, comforting object had made me timid. "I'm sorry, Miki. I freaked out. I didn't want to. I thought I could hack it. I was going to go to the zoo. . . . You didn't freak out?"

She sat down next to me. "I freaked out. I didn't drink a gallon of whiskey."

"Penn Station was a fish."

"Are you reciting poetry, Joe?"

"I don't know."

I lit a cigarette without asking if it was cool to smoke. I felt polluted and rude.

"I'm sorry—can I smoke in here?"

"By the window, please."

I limped toward the window.

"Don't fall out, okay?" she requested, pulling a half-smoked joint off the desk. She lit it and inhaled deeply, extended it to me, then thought better, pulled it back, and laughed self-consciously.

"I don't smoke pot," I said. "It leads to stronger stuff. It did for me anyway. Guns N' Roses."

I looked around her gold kitchen. "Did you paint this yourself?"

"Yes. I mixed the paint too."

The silver reminded me of John's prized jars of expensive European paint.

"It's so pretty. This is a really nice place."

"Thanks."

"A nice, severely lopsided place. Did you frame all that stuff yourself too?"

"Yes."

"Did you roll that joint yourself?"

"Yes."

"So . . . you live here alone?"

"Yes."

"No . . . pets."

"None."

"No . . . lodgers?"

"That's right."

Where in heck is that boyfriend? I thought. On tour? I fantasized that the guy had embarked on an endless, late-era Bob Dylan–like tour of . . . India? I put out my smoke and thoughtfully returned the ashtray to her. She was a bit more relaxed. The weed and the fact that I'd stopped puking and crying . . . it probably helped things.

"Eat some cake," she said, gesturing to a slice of vanilla-frosted yellow cake on a pale blue ceramic plate on the kitchen counter. I reached over with my long arms and grabbed it. Swallowed some and washed it down with the tea.

"This is good cake."

She looked at me sadly.

"Joe . . ."

"Yeah?"

"Are we really gonna reunite the Smiths?"

"What do you mean? Of course we are. We have to."

"They're not calling back."

"So? We'll go fucking find them."

I patted her knee and took another bite of cake. She inhaled another toke and grew more melancholy.

"Do you really think we're dying?" she asked. Suddenly I was the cheerleader and she was morose and fucked up and primed to panic.

"No, that was just the demon alcohol talking. We're only thirty! We could be . . . forty!"

"It's so weird." She stared up at a photo of herself mounted on the wall. It must have only been two or three years old, but I saw what she saw in the frozen image. Someone younger.

"I know. I remember I was once looking through old photographs with my grandmother and grandfather. They had this house in Canarsie . . . in Brooklyn, and when my father was in town sometimes we'd drive over there and eat deli food. Knishes and shit. And just watch the Mets or the Jets and listen to Frank Sinatra records and look at old photos. She was always knitting me sweaters but after a while she stopped cause the only sweaters I would wear were all black and she was complaining that knitting all-black sweaters was a fucking bore."

Miki laughed. I finished my tea and lit another cigarette. "Anyway, these were old photos. Some of them that funky sepia tone."

"I love that," she said.

"And they were so freaked out. I mean, it seemed like a total cliché at the time, but they were really freaked out, like 'Where did the time go? It went so fast. Like where did it fucking go?' They're both dead now."

"Great."

"At the time, I didn't even wonder if I'd ever be saying that about my life. I was so young, I couldn't even imagine it. Then one day, a few weeks ago, I said it. I looked back and remembered like the first day I heard the Smiths and it seemed so long ago that it seemed like it wasn't me at all. It was somebody else. Like maybe we can't relate to who we were because we're finally growing old." I grabbed her joint and took a hit. "Which is a weird term cause old people shrink, don't they? They don't really grow."

"I never want to shrink."

"We're not gonna shrink," I promised her. "We're gonna reunite the Smiths and we're gonna be pure and beautiful and young and in love . . . with life. Not . . . you know . . . each other or anything. Just life."

She grabbed my empty cup and plate, and rose.

"Do you want more tea?" she asked.

"No, thanks. Listen, Miki, I'm sorry I ruined what's left of your birthday."

"You didn't ruin it, Joe." She took my hand and held it. She was still sad.

"Let me make it up to you. Tomorrow. We'll go out. We'll go dancing."

"Do you dance?" she asked with more than a hint of sarcasm.

"Me? I dance like a . . . yeah . . . yeah, I dance. I mean, I can dance."

"I can't picture that."

She walked into her bedroom. I stood there in the kitchen. It wasn't like she'd said "Follow me" or anything. It felt like I stood there for half an hour but it was probably more like two minutes.

"Miki, I'm gonna go."

"Goodbye, Joe."

"Don't be sad. I'll call you tomorrow and we'll go dancing," I promised, and walked to the door.

Then I realized I didn't have her home phone number.

"Um . . . what . . . where . . . how do I reach you?"

"I'm listed."

"Oh, okay. Goodnight."

"Goodnight, Joe," she said sleepily. "Happy birthday."

"Happy birthday."

I walked all the way across town. Leisurely. I didn't run. It was past midnight. Closer to three. It wasn't my birthday anymore. It wasn't Miki's. We were just 30 now. In our 30s. When I got in there was a message on the machine.

"Yeah, it's your father. How ya doin'? I'm just calling to say happy birthday. I got it right here on the calendar on the fridge. Joe's birthday. So . . . have a good day. Stay out of trouble and don't rock the fuckin' boat. All right? All right. Later." He made no mention of what birthday it was. Probably didn't know.

how soon is never?

*   *   *

The next day, I rocked the boat, baby. I tipped the boat over. But first I went to Soho to hang out with tourists and blow the rest of the birthday money Susie had tucked into a Hallmark card. Three hundred bucks. Apparently each year was worth $10, although I'm pretty sure age 15 in '84 was worth about $50 and age 25 wasn't worth shit. I woke up spared an even more vicious hangover by Miki's tea-and-cake remedy. I got dressed, threw on my sunglasses, and consumed a speedy brunch of half a bagel, five cigs, and four cups of coffee at the diner on Eighth Avenue. I read all three newspapers and felt like a normal New Yorker. Then I walked to Soho and loitered around. Went into Rocks in Your Head record store and fucked away an hour browsing the vinyl bins and later found myself in some cheesy store on Spring Street just off Broadway. The one that sells all that taxidermy and raccoon dicks and bugs trapped in amber, basically heaps of bleached bones at $500 a shin. I used to love that stuff when I was a kid, and since I'd never made it up to the zoo, I figured why not check out some dead fauna downtown? In the back of my mind, I knew I was on the prowl for a birthday present for Miki.

"Do you have any monkeys?"

"Monkey skulls?" the bespectacled, slightly creepy salesperson asked.

"No, like the whole monkey, man."

"We have a stuffed gibbon over here. Technically, it's an ape."

"How much for the ape?" I asked, checking out the handsome black-and-white beast. His expression was one of confusion. He must have been enjoying a bright, sunny day like this one, just swinging from a vine, when they poached his ass.

"That's seventeen hundred."

"Let me see the skulls."

The skulls were a bit too morbid, and given my breakdown the day before and the stoned, calm, but no less melancholy skid it had triggered in Miki, I wanted something hopeful.

"What's up with those butterflies?" I asked. "The blue one. What kind of butterfly is that?"

"A blue one," he replied, weary and already giving up on selling me anything at all.

"I'll take it. Can you put it in a box, please?"

I purchased the dead bug and walked back toward Sixth Avenue, where I stopped in a card shop and purchased a black-and-white photograph of James Dean. Scribbled lyrics from "Reel Around the Fountain" on the back: "I dreamt about you last night and I fell out of bed twice. You can pin and mount me like this. Happy birthday. Love, Joe."

It seemed cheeky enough to mask the fact that she pretty much could. I walked home and called Miki up. We decided we'd check out Fast Times at Coney Island High, the '80s night at the old nightclub on St. Mark's Place. Every Sunday some dude named Tony Quasar threw on a skinny tie and played New Wave faves all night long. Fast Times was held upstairs in a candlelit, relatively tiny addendum to the main room of the club. There were old Astroland funhouse fixtures and mirrors on the walls. A discarded go-cart that had been converted into a love seat sat in the corner, a passed-out-drunk punk snoring inside it.

"There are eighties nights everywhere now," she said as we walked through the crowd and saw a bunch of kids easily five years our junior do a spaz hop to "Never Say Never" by Romeo Void in the small, low-ceilinged dance area.

"Do you think these kids even remember when these songs came out?" I asked.

"No. It's so weird," she said. "We're being sincere and they're being ironic."

"It's almost like we should have separate dance floors."

how soon is never?

We sat down and I ordered a couple of vodka grapefruits and brought them back to the table.

She was wearing all red. I was wearing a sharkskin suit and a skinny black tie over a ripped white T-shirt. Creepers. I hid the birthday bug in a black record bag and stashed it under our booth. I didn't know where she bought her clothes. Maybe she made them herself to fit her tiny frame. I never saw anybody else wear those kinds of skirts and blouses anywhere. Not even in magazines. Romeo Void segued into "Homosapien" by Buzzcocks singer Pete Shelley.

"I love this song," she shouted. "This was my favorite song of all time when it came out."

"Do you wanna dance?" I asked. "With the kids?"

She nodded and I followed her out onto the floor and realized to my horror that I'd pretty much forgotten how. My body wouldn't move the way it used to. It was stiff. Tired. Uncoordinated. Battered by sloth and drink and drugs and cigs and sex. I tried to shake out a million and one kinks and knots as she demonstrated her considerably smoother rhythm, shakin' to the song's sinister synth pop beat. Finally I gave up and just started hopping up and down. When in doubt, pogo. "Do It Clean" by Echo and the Bunnymen, "Sign of the Times" (the Belle Stars, not Prince, which is "Sign o' the Times" anyway), "Make a Circuit with Me" by the Polecats, and some technically late-'70s cheats like "Let's Go" by the Cars and "Good Girls Don't" by the Knack came next as we worked up a real vodka sweat. She was a good dancer. Most girls can dance, but Miki had real rhythm . . . for a white girl dancing to New Wave. After an hour, we were blowing the ironic kids away. We were two 30-year-olds in serious psychic pain, but for the moment we were children again . . . without a care. We requested the Smiths and Mr. Quasar rewarded our ardor and endurance with "This Charming Man." The Generation Y kids knew it and danced

242

along, feigning Morrissey melodrama out on the floor. Around 2 A.M. Quasar grew tired of our repeated requests for more Smiths and reacted with a set of angry punk rock. It was chronologically sound—Black Flag, Bad Brains, Agent Orange, Minor Threat—but we were too drunk to thrash to it.

"You wanna get out of here?" she asked.

I nodded. We walked toward the door and I doubled back, having almost forgotten my stashed bag. I caught up with her out on the street, where we decided to take a walk. Without a particular destination, we headed up Third Avenue. Sunday nights in New York are mercifully tourist free. And most of the locals are priming themselves for the big work week, so the streets tend to be peaceful, save a homeless person or chattering club kid or two. It was a night for walking. Clear. Quiet. And we ended up a good 15 blocks uptown before we started looking around for a place to eat, drink, and pee.

"How about the Gramercy Park?"

"The hotel?" she asked.

"Yeah, they have a bar, I think."

We stopped in. The place was empty except for a couple of drunken businessmen watching a recap of the 11 o'clock news. The portly, red-haired cocktail waitress informed us that the kitchen was closed, the bar was open, but the piano player was about ready to call it a night. We sat down and ordered another round of Greyhounds . . . then another. We drank quickly, mindful of the late hour and the drying well. We toasted each other and our dismal 30 years on earth. We toasted *Headphones* magazine for giving us a chance to do something about it. We toasted our friendship. We toasted the drunken businessmen. We toasted Karen Carpenter for no reason whatsoever. And when she staggered off to the ladies' room for a second time, I reached down and grabbed the butterfly box and placed it on the table.

*   *   *

how soon is never?

Then she came back.

Then I told her I was in love with her.

Then we left the bar and got into a cab, headed back downtown.

Then we kissed.

It should have changed things. It only made me wish that I was one of the few New Yorkers with a goddamn car. Kissing the woman you're in love with in the back of a yellow cab is just cruel. It's egg-timed passion. You can hear the meter clicking. Also, it's just plain awkward for the taxi driver.

I woke up Monday morning, a good eight hours beyond that moment. I was already struggling to remember what kissing Miki was like. I pulled up old mental files of previous kisses: high school kisses, college kisses, dirty bar toilet kisses, Jane, Jennifer.

Was it anything like that? Or was it dangerous? Forbidden? Adulterous?

I've kissed girls who've had boyfriends before. It doesn't taste any different. It doesn't feel any different. Or does it? I wished I could remember. I knew it had taken place after drinks at the Gramercy Park Hotel bar and before the onset of the hangover I was nursing with an egg sandwich and a Coke from the deli. I knew her lips had been soft, a little chapped . . . but all lips are soft and a little chapped in the fall. Her breath must have tasted like vodka and cigarettes. She'd been drinking and smoking mine. Had I touched her hair? Was it fine? Had she put her arms around my waist and leaned into me with her head and shoulders and lips? Eight hours elapsed and it felt like I might as well have been watching two stupid actors act-kiss on television. But then I could have rewound. *If only I had a car*, I thought as I rolled around in bed, *a Buick*

Le Sabre or an El Camino or John's old Galaxie 500. I bet she would have stayed longer.

Morrissey was singing on the little red boom box while I shaved and prepared to go into work:

"If a double-decker bus crashes into us . . . to die by your side, well, the pleasure and the privilege is mine."

There might have been pleasure and privilege but there had been no bus. No cinematic death. Just an old, turbaned Sikh cabdriver listening to sports and weather on his radio and waiting for us to stop making out so he could drive me across town to my apartment and collect his fare. So we'd stopped. Then she was gone. Back upstairs to the punk rock boyfriend. He was probably brewing tea and snacking on something dull and vegan. I fretted.

Maybe he was aghast at her intoxicated stagger. Maybe they got into a fight. Maybe they fucked. Maybe they didn't.

What the hell am I going to wear to work?

The *Headphones* offices generally felt rather spacious but after you've been out all night drinking and kissing a co-worker, they seem to shrink down to a fucking crucible. There was no way to avoid Miki's desk as I walked through the smoked-glass front door and headed for my workspace. I figured, as I rode up in the elevator, that a cool "Hey" and the body language that suggested I'd require another cup of coffee before I could even address any situation would suffice for that morning. But as I crossed the reception area, punched in my security code, and surveyed the main floor, I didn't see the top of her head peeking out from beneath the cubicle walls.

She's late, I thought. *A good sign? Maybe she's as awkward as I am. Or maybe there was a fight and she's helping the vegan punk pack up his vegan shit.* I hustled past her area and quickly hid behind my own. Checked my e-mail. Publicist. Publicist. Porn. Publicist. More porn. Checked my messages. Publicist, publicist, publicist, collection agency, publicist, and then . . . a strange voice. Quick, clipped British accent. I got excited. Was it . . . ?

"Good morning, Mr. Green. My name is James Marsh and I handle the affairs of Mike Joyce, the former drummer for the Smiths. I'm terribly sorry I was unable to respond to your earlier messages but I was traveling out of the country. I appreciate you following up on them. I gather from your interview proposal that you're a fan, so I'm sure you're aware that Mike has also played with Sinead O'Connor as well as several other major artists, although he does not have a problem discussing the Smiths with journalists."

Each bit of information was punctuated by a cough straight out of Russian literature. Tubercular. Alarming. Infectious?

"I received your latest fax last night and I must say that your timing is excellent! I'm pleased to inform you that Mike will be traveling to New York City this very week to attend a seminar sponsored by *Modern Drummer* magazine." Cough. "As I'm sure you're well aware, it's all part of your annual CMJ festival. I'm confident that I can free him up to have a brief sit-down with you and your co-worker, Miki." Cough, cough, cough. "I must ask, is this feature being considered for a cover? If so, I will do my best to clear his very busy schedule as much as possible. Please ring my mobile when you receive this, and remember, we are five hours ahead of you here. All right, then. Cheers." Cough. Click.

I jotted down the number Marsh left and immediately called him back. The long-distance ring was as pushy and clipped as Mr. Marsh's tone. Boop. Boop. Boop. He answered abruptly.

"Hello?" Cough.

"Hello, Mr. Marsh, this is Joe Green from *Headphones* magazine, returning your call."

"Mr. Green, your timing is uncanny! I've just gotten off the phone with Mike not one minute ago."

"Wow," I replied. All I could say. "Wow." Who says "wow"? Sometimes you just do, I guess.

"We'll be in Manhattan on Wednesday. That's two days from today."

"Yes," I blurted, wishing I'd said "wow" again. "Yes, it is. That's right. I'm looking at my calendar right now." *What am I doing?* I thought. I gulped my coffee hard and hoped for some focus.

"Why don't we set something up for Wednesday night?" I asked, trying to sound professional.

Marsh chuckled.

"I realize you're very eager, Mr. Green, but I suspect Mike and I will be a little jet-lagged. How about Friday?"

"Oh, Friday's good. Friday works."

"We won't be interrupting a date, I hope?" Cough.

"No, Friday is fine," I replied. "I'm free. No plans on Friday. In New York, Friday is just like any other night of the week. In fact, it's better to stay in on Friday and go out on a Monday . . . or a Tuesday," I blabbed on, a bit too defensively.

"Excellent, then. Will we be meeting you at the office?"

"Well, we could do that, but it's a little . . . dull here on Friday nights. I know a cool bar down on Avenue A. It's between Houston and First Street. It's very easy to find."

"That wouldn't be the Library?"

"Yes. Do you know it?"

"I do. I've spent quite a few evenings there. When a well-read Englishman is in a strange city on business and he's looking for a pint and a kind word, there's no better place. Wonderful crisps." "Well-read?" I let it slide. Maybe *Cooking with Cod* is brilliantly lyrical after all. "It's settled, then. The Library on Friday night. We'll meet you there. Let's say eight o'clock sharp. I'll just make sure he gets there on time and then

I'll get out of your way. I'm rather imposing. It's best to let the three of you talk."

"Um, great!" *Is this all I can fucking say?* I worried. *Wow! Great! I went to an expensive college! I've interviewed Bowie!*

"I understand this is being considered for a cover story."

Where had he gotten that shit?

"That would be fantastic! Mike, as you must know, is one of the most respected drummers in the world."

"I know! He's amazing—"

"*Modern Drummer* is extremely excited to feature him on their cover."

"I'm sure they are."

"Well, then, Mr. Green, I look forward to meeting you and your colleague Miki." Cough!

I pondered Marsh's lungs for another second, and then the gravity of what our exchange meant hit me hard.

Four days from today, I will be sitting in the Library, a place where Miki and I have played hundreds of dollars' worth of Smiths singles on the jukebox . . . with an actual fucking Smith!

God save pushy, seriously ill Mr. Marsh, who in just over two minutes had supplied me with the most perfect post-uncomfortable-kiss icebreaker imaginable. Minutes earlier, I'd planned to spend the remainder of the workday on the fire escape, chain-smoking. As it stood, I could approach Miki not as a potential home wrecker but as the bearer of the good word that we were about to meet a genuine legend face-to-face.

Mike Joyce.

One of four.

The man who hit the first beat of the first song on the first album. The first sound the Smiths ever gave us.

It also put one on the board for our skeptical editor in chief to see. This was some much-needed validity.

*　　*　　*

I peered from behind my own cubicle toward hers and saw that she was still absent.

Maybe she's called in sick? Maybe she's left the country?

I debated calling her at home but decided to get another cup of coffee instead. I walked back through reception and into the elevator. The door opened and I stepped out into the lobby. She was standing there. Waiting for me? Bags packed? No. Just standing there.

"Hi," I said.

"Hey."

She was wearing the same red clothes from the previous night. Her hair was greasy and uncombed.

What does this mean? I'm sure not gonna ask, I thought.

"What's up?"

"I'm late," she said blankly.

"Yeah. I know."

"I didn't get much sleep."

She looked sad.

There are two words I have to say now, I coached myself silently. *I have to form them with my lips and tongue and say them. Why and not. Preferably in the form of a leading question: "Why not?"*

"That sucks," I said.

"Yeah. I feel shitty."

One word, I screamed inside. *One word now. You can do it, Joe Green, you non-football-playing asshole. "Why?" And then she'll say, "Because I dumped my boyfriend and he killed himself." And I'll hug her and take her home and feed her and play her* The Queen Is Dead *and watch her fall asleep in my arms. One word is the key to unlocking this dream state. "Why?"*

"Hungover?" I asked.

"Yeah. Do you always drink like that, Joe?"

"Yes. Every night."

She smiled, exposing her teeth.

how soon is never?

I've felt them with my tongue, I mused.

"I would have bought you a coffee but I didn't see you when I came in. I'm going for some now. You want anything?"

"Thanks anyway. I'll order from the deli."

"I have to tell you something, Mik."

She looked ashen, worried. Annoyed? Nauseated.

This can't all be from me, I thought.

"Not about . . . anything . . . you know. Not . . ." I faltered, cut myself off. "Cause I know . . . it's . . . early."

"Yeah."

Did she have to look so fucking relieved? I reasoned all the boozing must have hit her pretty hard. She couldn't weigh much more than 100 pounds. Meanwhile, I've got long, hollow arms, legs, and head and a cast-iron liver.

"In England it's not, though."

"What?"

"In England it's midafternoon . . . and . . . I've already been on the phone to Manchester!"

"What?" She brightened. All the electrolytes she lacked returned in an instant. Her hair even appeared much less funky.

"Yes, this Friday night, we are going to meet Mr. Mike Joyce."

"No!"

"Yes!"

"In person?"

"Yes. In person. At the Library!"

"A Smith!" she shouted.

"Our first. But not our last, I hope. He got our letter and he's really into talking to us."

Her wariness or self-consciousness evaporated into whatever dark place her hangover went moments ago. She approached me, beaming, and grabbed both my arms with her hands. Clenched her fingers around me.

"Oh, my God! Does he know about our plan?" she asked.

"Of course not. I think we'll have to get him piss-drunk first, don't you?"

"Yes! Very drunk!" She laughed. Pulled away. "I'm so excited!"

God, I fucking love this woman, I thought. When Miki said something goofy like "I'm so excited," it sounded totally pure and sincere. She was never burdened by that weird thing when you're young and trying to find your own, personal cool. That thing that admonished you never to allow yourself to show general excitement. I felt like I always had to be blasé about everything.

"Oh, Joe, you just won Lotto!"

"That's nice."

"Joe, your mom's dead."

"Whatever."

It's standard insecure-cool-guy behavior. Maybe my dad blames Dean or Brando. I blame Fonzie. But Miki never had the millstone of forced boy-cool. Not only was she a chick, she was also very naturally cool . . . and able to pull off an "I'm so excited" like nobody else.

"Joe, if we get Mike Joyce to agree on tape to participate in a Smiths reunion, we can take that tape to Andy Rourke . . . and take that tape to Johnny Marr . . . and take his tape to . . ."

"Morrissey."

"This is too much. I wish I didn't have to work. I wish I could start getting ready now." She laughed.

"I know. I'd quiff my hair but you can't Elvis when you're a Jew," I cracked, "you can only Dylan. I spent most of the eighties trying and I know of what I speak."

She smiled again. At me. For me.

"Mike Joyce at the Library," she said, her skin all warm and pink and glowing.

"At the Library," I echoed. And our telepathy was jump-started. I could feel her imagining the same thing I was imagining: the look on all the faces, from the mod kids to the Smiths-dissing punk barflies, when we strolled in with a real Smith. For another instant, we were like children again.

There was nothing sexual last night. Morrissey doesn't have sex. Neither do we. We are angels. Kissing, floating on clouds, playing the harp, battling gargoyles, and shit. Saving the world, I rambled in my brain.

"I'd better start opening mail and answering calls," she said, rolling her brown eyes. As she breezed into the elevator, I thought, *No matter what happens between us, if we adhere to our cause . . . if I fight to do so, our relationship will remain pure and we can only succeed.*

It will wash away all her possibly adulterous behavior . . . all my insecurity . . . all the Matchbox Twenties and the Creeds and the other shitty bands I have to smile at when I'd much rather spit in their eye. It will cure Mr. Marsh's consumption. It will reunite the Smiths. And it will unite us. If it's not love, then it's the bomb that will bring us together.

fifteen

give the drummer some

Miki was gone on a lesser assignment for most of that Friday, so I had to keep my nerves over meeting Mike Joyce to myself, as she was the only one I could allow myself to gush with. She returned around three in a perturbed state.

"Do you know," she said, "I feel a lot better about what we're doing, Joe. This job we've chosen is pretty ridiculous anyway. What we're trying to do, it's not that much of a deviation."

She was wearing jeans, a striped sleeveless blouse, and big, clunky black shoes that made her about an inch and a half taller.

"What do you mean?"

"I just had lunch with Rob Zombie. He was wearing all black leather from head to toe, with a big black beard, and he was talking about his obsession with these gruesome horror movies. Blood spurting. Dismemberment, decapitations. But when the waitress came, he was just like any other customer.

'Please.' 'Thank you.' 'Could we get a bit more syrup when you get a chance?' He ordered pancakes."

"Was it lunch with Rob Zombie or brunch with Rob Zombie? Did he order a mimosa too?"

"I don't remember. You know, he was a nice guy but all I kept thinking was, he's not a Smith."

"He's a Zombie."

"Yes." She smiled. "He's a very careful eater, Joe. Didn't get a single crumb in his big beard or on his fancy leather trousers."

"Probably had a lot of practice over the years. Speaking of trousers."

"And we were."

"Yes. Are you . . . dressing casual? This evening? For the big date with the drummer?"

"I don't know. I haven't thought about it. Have you?"

I'd been thinking about it all week. Every 10 minutes, actually. In the end, I opted for my one sort-of-good suit, the smoke-damaged sharkskin number. Once it was an expensive mod thing that loaned itself to a confident sidewalk strut. Now it was just what I grabbed when I wanted to kid myself I looked real smooth, as Joe Jackson used to sing. When I arrived at the Library, 25 minutes early, it was dead and quiet. Those happy-hour barflies never sprang for tunes, so I headed straight for the jukebox and pumped in a five. Played whatever non-Smiths Manchester bands I could find: Buzzcocks, Joy Division, New Order, Stone Roses, Happy Mondays. "I Wanna Be Adored" by the Roses came on. Eighteen tracks later, I'd run out of Mancunians, and Mike and Miki had yet to show. The bar was starting to fill up. I looked around, worried that perhaps I wouldn't recognize Joyce from his old photos. It had, after all, been nearly 15 years since I'd seen him, and even then it was from several rows back. By 8:30, the Library was jumping and there was still no sign of them.

*   *   *

As 9 P.M. drew near, a candidate for Mike Joyce arrived. He was alone. Mr. Marsh's coughing would have been a nice tip-off, but as it was, I had no idea. It wasn't like Joyce was as recognizable as Morrissey. The gentleman who might or might not have been one of my heroes looked around briefly, then sat three stools away from me at the bar. He was unassuming as he patiently waited for service. I stared at him and when I didn't get a quick nod of recognition or even a jolt of fright inside, I assumed he wasn't the one. He seemed too young and just looked too good, really. People tend to do so in low-lit bars, but I had a vision of a man in my head with gray hair and wrinkles . . . a figure from a past less than two decades old, but one that seemed centuries gone by for all my personal corruption that had transpired. It was only when he ordered a vodka cranberry in a travel-tempered British accent that I realized that he was the guy and moved closer to inspect him further. He had strong, drummer's arms, which his short-sleeved, buttoned-up black shirt exposed. Still had all his hair and teeth. Thick black eyebrows. Big ears. From less than a foot and a half away, really only a slight hint of encroaching second chin was all that distinguished him from the icon who stood next to Morrissey and Johnny Marr and Andy Rourke in front of the Salford Lads Club in photographer Steven Wright's iconic band portrait. It was time to say hello.

Where the hell was Miki? I fretted that I might have to do the deed solo. There was no chance that she would miss this, so my anger soon turned to fear that she'd been injured or something. I drew back and decided to have one more shot before I introduced myself. So there I was, two feet away from an actual Smith, but for an instant, I was much more concerned with getting the bartender's attention. Another example of the often-unspoken shame of alcohol dependency, I thought as I threw back my fifth shot and walked over to him.

"Mike?" I asked.

"Yeah. Are you Joe?" he said. "Or Miki?"

"I'm Joe." I shook his hand. The hand that played the drums on . . . well, you know.

"I'm sorry, but Miki's not here yet. By the way, she's female."

He laughed, then apologized for his tardiness with that instantly winning English politeness.

"Is Mr. Marsh here?" I asked, wondering if I should cover my mouth with a bar napkin.

"He's back at the hotel. Has a bit of a cough."

"No! Really?"

I looked out onto Avenue A, hoping to spot Miki in the back of an ambulance or a police car. "Why don't we take the back table?" I suggested. "It's a bit quieter."

He agreed and followed me to the rear of the bar. We sat down and made small talk. I told him how long I'd lived in Manhattan, how long I'd worked at *Headphones,* some of the bands I'd interviewed.

"Have you ever been to New York before?" I asked.

"Yeah. Yeah."

Obviously I knew the answer, but I couldn't even let on immediately that I knew very much about him at all, or even that on one of his trips to New York, he'd changed my life forever. Not without Miki. I was too embarrassed. Too cool. Only she could open me up . . . make me honest. Soon, Mike Joyce and I were just staring at each other, smiling courteously and shaking our empty cocktail glasses. After 15 more minutes of clumsy socializing, I excused myself and walked to the bathroom, assuring Joyce that I'd return with a fresh vodka cranberry. I paced back and forth in the tiny, filthy stall.

"This isn't gonna work. This is stupid. This is so stupid," I said aloud. I stared at my reflection in the scum-stained mirror. I splashed some water on my face and dabbed at it with a handful of rolled-up toilet paper, then pulled off the bits that stuck to my cheeks. I played with my hair, lit a cigarette, and resigned myself to failure. When I opened the door, Miki was ordering a drink at the bar . . . and blond! She'd dyed her hair platinum blond and slicked it back.

I hurried over, smiling. It was easy to opt for relief over anger at her tardiness. She was, you know . . . blond. I tapped her shoulder and she turned around and grabbed my arm.

"I'm so sorry," she said, shaking with excitement. "I decided I had to be—"

"Blond?"

"It took longer than I thought."

I stared at her hair. I hadn't thought she could possibly be more attractive to me, but I'd been wrong.

"Is Mike here?"

"Yeah. Mike's here," I answered.

"What's he like?" she whispered.

"He's really nice."

"Oh, my God," she said, shaking even more. "Oh, my God. Mike Joyce. Where is he?"

"We're in the back," I said, lighting another cigarette with my own trembling hands. "Are you ready for this?"

"I don't know," she said, trying to shrug off the nerves. "Are you?"

"I don't know."

"We should get ready," she suggested.

"Yeah," I said. I couldn't hide that I was pretty terrified to return to the table.

"We have to do this, Joe."

"I know."

She grabbed my arm again. Squeezed harder.

"Let's go," she said.

how soon is never?

"I have to bring him a drink."

"What's Mike Joyce drink?" she said.

"Mike Joyce drinks vodka and cranberry juice."

Joyce pepped up considerably when he saw Miki. She gushed her introductions to him with ease and class, as if during the short walk to the back of the dark and dirty bar, she'd reinvented herself as the charm-school-grad hostess of some uptown cocktail party. I handed Joyce his drink and he thanked me heartily. Then I took out my tape recorder and tested the vocal levels with a trembling "Testing, testing, testing." Mike asked Miki all about herself with an enthusiasm that dwarfed any he'd managed to work up for me. You couldn't really blame the guy. I was wondering how long I'd have to sit and observe this, holding the micro-recorder like a limp dick. Finally, Miki geared the conversation toward our initial objective.

"All right, should we do this now?" she asked. It was almost as though she had been waiting until the precise moment when a look in the eye of our former Smith indicated that he was fully under her spell.

"I'm ready," Joyce smiled.

Miki reached over and took the recorder from me. "So, this is Mike Joyce, former drummer for the Smiths," she said into the microphone.

"Hello," he said, grabbing the device from her.

"It's very sensitive, you don't need to pick it up," I assured him. "So, Mike, the Smiths' popularity hasn't waned at all. If anything, the energy surrounding the band is stronger than ever. Have you picked up on it at all?"

"Well, I've noticed there's been a resurgence in the U.K. of the eighties kind of music, with bands like the Human League and Culture Club and ABC getting back together and going on these package tours. But the funny thing I have found about this whole thing is that the Smiths haven't been mentioned once! Which I think is great because we didn't have anything to do with the eighties."

"So you're in a way impervious to nostalgia," I said, brimming with hope and faith that our goal was indeed something greater than generational angst and nostalgia. Miki and I smiled at each other. This was key. Something to cling to.

"Yes," he continued. "The eighties music scene was Spandau Ballet, Duran Duran, and all those kinds of bands. The Smiths had nothing to do with that. We were a real pain in their arses."

"You were never a fashion band, so you could never go out of fashion," Miki piped up.

"Right. Good!" Joyce said. "There's no fashion or musical pigeonhole to put us in. The last time we played in Boston there were fifteen thousand people in the audience, and MTV's *120 Minutes* was like 'What's this strange phenomenon?' because we were nowhere in *Billboard*. Bands like a-Ha and Tears for Fears had an album for like fourteen weeks at number one and sold forty million, and they played to like fifteen hundred or two thousand people. So it wasn't anything to do with record company hype. It was word of mouth through real people who really enjoyed what they were seeing and it wasn't something that was manufactured."

"Do you ever feel bad for the people who are upset that the band they are so love in with doesn't exist anymore?" Miki asked.

"Yes. You have to remember that Johnny left the band first and even after that we tried to hold on to it for a while before deciding that it just couldn't work without him. We did that because we loved it too. I was the one who collected all the tapes from the sound board decks, from the rehearsals, from as far back as 1982, before we got a record deal. I was a real kind of trainspotter with all that stuff. I remember playing this tape from the first rehearsal we had with the Smiths for a friend that I was living with at the time and I said, 'This band is going to be pretty big.' I said, 'We could even be as big as the Psychedelic Furs!' Of course at the time the Furs were just gods!"

"Do you have those tapes with you now?" Miki asked. "Like right now? Play 'em. Play 'em!"

Joyce laughed and finished his drink. I could tell we were working him up. He was starting to talk like a fan . . . of his own band. It was pretty weird . . . and pretty great.

"I've got stuff with instrumentals, with brass on it. Like 'Never Had No One Ever' with a trumpet on it. Oh, I've got so much weird stuff. All this stuff that's never been heard and I thought, 'Why can't we release this?' Cause it's not as though I was thinking, 'Great, I can make a fast buck here.' I'd like to bootleg it, just to get it out, cause people want to hear it. But I don't want to bootleg it, obviously, because the kind of legal problems that we had in 1996 with myself suing Morrissey and Johnny. I'm not too sure they'd take too kindly to me doin' it."

For clarity's sake here, I'll explain that throughout the band's brief career, Morrissey and Marr were apparently controlling partners in the Smiths corporation, each receiving 40 percent of the band's earnings, while Rourke and Joyce earned 10 percent apiece. This was never really contested by any outsiders since Morrissey and Marr wrote all the band's material and made the crucial decisions. And since Joyce and Rourke alleged that they were never made privy to this financial arrangement, they claimed to have no idea that they may have been considered not much more than hired sidemen throughout the band's career. Moz and Marr probably never flashed their royalty checks. Naive as it was, and most great artists are naive when it comes to monetary concerns, the rhythm section assumed everyone was making the same thing and happily continued contributing to the band's signature sound. Although disclosure might have been somewhat noble on Morrissey and Marr's part, as I see it, both sides had an argument. Morrissey and Marr certainly deserved their fortune. Morrissey was the band's face and voice, and Marr its musical engine. But to assume that the Smiths would sound anything like they do with a different rhythm section is beyond absurd (Morrissey would later intimate that such was the case, comparing Rourke and Joyce to "parts in a lawn mower"). Ringo didn't make as much as John and Paul (hence those wine cooler commercials in the '80s), but it was never because he was considered expendable. Frequently, a drummer can make or break a band, no matter how brilliant the songwriter or writers are. Look at the career of the Who after Keith Moon died in 1978 or Nirvana before Dave Grohl joined if you're still skeptical.

Rourke ultimately decided not to pursue the case against his old mates and settled for a lump sum, rumored to be in the neighborhood of 100,000 pounds. Unfortunately, an out-of-court settlement was unable to be reached with Joyce, who was seeking much more, and so the Smiths were reunited, albeit with their civil lawyers in tow, in the pews of an airless English courthouse. After heated proceedings, in which Morrissey was lambasted for his alleged "devious, truculent, and unreliable" behavior, the judge only scolded Joyce for being "unintellectual and not financially sophisticated" in his early 20s (who isn't?). Then he ordered Morrissey and Marr to pay a rumored 1,000,000 pounds to their lawn mower parts. To his credit, Marr did not contest the ruling but Morrissey fought to reverse it well into the end of the decade. Each time a court proceeding was conducted, the band was back on the front pages of every British (and some American) pop media outlet and a grim-faced Morrissey surrounded by equally un-smiling lawyers, as opposed to adoring fans, was featured. It was acrimony à go go, and a great obstacle to any potential re-union.

"So, Mike, has the dust settled on that legal bit yet?" I asked, and finished the rest of my shot.

He paused and gave my a sly look like, *Okay, we're gonna get into this, are we?*

"I don't know," he said. "Best ask them, I suppose. When I met Johnny and Morrissey, while the case was going on, we were kind of quite civil to each other and I really liked that. I mean, I kind of pushed through crowds to get to them, rather than thinking, 'Oh no, there's Johnny and Morrissey, let's go!' I'm not too sure if they felt the same but I made an effort to kind of speak to them and be with them and talk with them be-cause to me that case was only about a business aspect of the Smiths that went drastically wrong. The music side of it, to me, is more important and I don't want to lose our friendship."

"Was that the last time you've seen them?" Miki asked. "In court?"

"No. I saw Johnny only a month ago. He was picking up his children from school and I was in my car and I kind of hit the horn and I went, 'Hey, Johnny!' And he was like, 'Ah, Mike.' "

"Mike," Miki continued, "aside from the financial dealings, hypothetically, if the four of you were to plug in and play again now, could you project what it would feel like? Would it be natural? Or have ill feelings gotten in the way forever?"

"They haven't for me. I can only speak for me personally." He downed the remainder of his drink and looked around for a cocktail waitress. There was none. "Look, I'll give you an ex-ample of how natural it is. I've got a CD changer at home that plays two hundred CDs. I put it on random and it's great. So when we're loading it up, my wife said, 'We should put all the Smiths in there.' And I said, 'I don't know.' Cause I don't want to be sitting around eating dinner or whatever and we've got the CD on and it's like, 'Oh, great. A Smiths track.' So we just put *Rank,* and *Strangeways,* which is my favorite Smiths album. And it's on random and there's two hundred CDs in there and there must be what, fifteen, twenty tracks on each CD. I don't expect it, but every five bloody tracks, a Smiths track comes on! I don't know whether there's some kind of weird demon in there but it just gets the hackles on me going up when I hear it. Cause I'm just like, 'Wow! I love the Smiths.' And I love the sound. I could easily say, 'No, that was then,' but as I get older, when I do hear the Smiths it just makes me more kind of like . . . it gives me chicken skin. When I look back to when I was eighteen, nineteen, and twenty, twenty-one, when I was in the Smiths, you know, it was magic. It was quite big while it was happening but when I look back on it, the more I look back on it, the more I think just how huge it was. And not just in terms of global appeal. In terms of uniqueness."

By then all three of us were well tipsy and clinking our drinks happily. Nobody seemed to want to stop talking Smiths, so I decided to up the ante. I walked up to the bar and ordered Joyce and Miki vodka cranberries and a Jack and ginger for myself. Then I asked the bartender for another fiver and hit the jukebox while she was mixing the drinks. My selections began with "I Know It's Over," which in hindsight is just not fair. No musical foreplay. Straight to the guts with the wrenching ballad. I lightened up with "Cemetry Gates," and ultimately picked every track off *The Queen Is Dead* before I returned with refreshments. I knew it would be a little while before they'd kick in and I was intent on getting the not unsentimental Mr. Joyce sloshed and on the ropes before delivering the money question. Miki was dutifully jabbing him while I was away. As I sat down, he was pondering her latest query, which she repeated for me.

how soon is never?

"Let's just say that in a crazy, topsy-turvy world, if the Smiths came back and played again, what kind of venue would you want to play in? What size?" she asked.

Joyce looked around the bar. At first, I was wondering if he was upset that nobody recognized him.

"This big. A place this size. Actually, I'd like to play in here somewhere." He laughed and raised his drink. We toasted yet again.

"Do you think it will ever happen?" I asked. "Under any circumstances? I mean, you must have thought about it through the years."

"Yeah, I have. I don't think there's any way it will happen, though. I mean, I don't like the idea of all of us being onstage with our kids playing tambourines."

"Is it an issue of age, then? Are you too old now? Do you think it wouldn't be good anymore?"

Joyce grew a bit uncomfortable. Not only had we crossed over into pushiness, but we'd essentially trapped him in a booth and implied that he was possibly too old to rock. We were, of course, only doing so to get him going. Despite being a legend, he was not even 40.

"I don't know. I don't know," he sighed, sucking back his vodka. "I mean, it's not something I would discount happening because of my age, no."

He knocked back the rest of his drink. I ran up to the bar and brought back a fresh round. Miki was not letting up. She was pretty drunk too by that point.

"So the lawsuit has been settled, and you can still play. What's stopping you?"

Joyce grabbed his drink and slouched down in the booth. Thought about it. Took a sip.

"Ah, as far as I'm concerned . . . as far as I'm concerned . . . nothing! Absolutely nothing. All right?" he said, obviously hoping to end this line of questioning. It didn't.

"So you feel like it's not you, it's Morrissey and Marr and their own bitterness regarding the court case that's stopping a potential reunion?" she asked.

"I don't know. I can't talk about how Johnny or Morrissey or Andy feels about these things."

"But it's not your bitterness that's an issue?"

"Well, there was a lot of hardship that went on and a lot of upset between me and my family in the fight for what I believe I deserved. Some really kind of nasty things happened, you know, because of me trying to get what I thought was right." He downed another belt of his drink. He was starting to flush with anger and memories and . . . vodka. His eyes were fierce when they looked at me. Fierce and starry when they looked over at Mik. But soon . . . just starry.

"*Oh, mother I can feel the soil falling over my head!*" his old bandmate sang.

It was the opening verse of my first selection, flooding the bar with gorgeous melancholy. Joyce's entire posture changed as he recognized it. He threw his arms in the air and slid up in his seat. His eyes widened from their inebriated squint. His chest puffed out. He flashed me a glare that briefly indicted me as the culprit, then resumed letting his old music scour away, if only temporarily, any lingering memory. He began conducting with his cocktail straw and loudly praising Morrissey's vocals and Johnny's guitar work as though he wasn't the man who'd provided the gentle beat we were swaying to. Soon he was drumming on the table with his fingers. It really was surreal. Miki and I could only stare in silence. When the song ended and "Cemetry Gates" came on, Joyce flashed a "What are you two trying to do to me?" look.

"See? No matter what went on among the four of you, there's this," I said. "It's got this weird power to heal."

"Yeah, it is weird," he admitted.

"Don't you want to see if it's still there? Doesn't it just drive you crazy sometimes?" Miki said in a high-pitched drunken voice that indicated that it drove her crazy many, many times.

Mike smiled.

"You know, I'd like to play one gig somewhere, in a little club somewhere. Just for the hell of it. Not to go on tour, playing big venues around the world," he said. I checked to see if the tape was still rolling. It was.

"Not an official getting-back-together reunion tour?" she asked.

"No, just to do one gig."

"Just to blow people's minds?" she asked.

"No, just for me. I don't care about people. Or blowing their minds. I'm being very selfish. Just to play with Johnny, Andy, and Morrissey again. It would sound great. I know it would be great."

Miki and I looked at each other and smiled. We knew that we had gotten exactly what we wanted. One Smith agreeing to a reunion. Stating on tape that he would like to rejoin his old bandmates for a gig. One down!

"So, can Marsh hook us up with Andy Rourke? Since you and he are working together?"

"Yeah, probably, yeah," he answered absently.

"How about the others? Do you have phone numbers for Johnny and Morrissey?" I asked.

"I could give you the number of my solicitor, who's got the number of their solicitors," Joyce cracked.

"That's all right." I said, patting his arm. "We'll find them."

We'd done enough to further our cause for the night. It was time to celebrate, or so we thought. Miki produced a joint and asked Joyce if he wanted to smoke some. We lit up and passed the thing around in the dark corner and soon we were drunk as fuck and sky-high too. Somebody cut the juke-box and put an old punk rock videotape into the machine at the bar, which usually projected cheesy old horror and kung fu movies on a seldom-used big-screen TV that hung on the back wall just over our booth. We stared up woozily as the Ramones, Richard Hell, and Patti Smith performed. It was like being at a drive-in. Joyce, again slit-eyed, asked if we were interested in grabbing some Indian food. Miki and I agreed that that sounded like an excellent idea. Unfortunately none of us could move. I managed to trudge back to the bar for another round and to inquire as to whether they had any menus for Indian take-out. When I came back, I noticed a change in the energy at the table. Mike had started flirting a bit more aggressively with Miki, who seemed to take it in stride. But I was able to read her by then, and I could tell something was unnerving her. I tried to lighten the situation and reached into my coat pocket.

"I know this is goofy, but I brought a camera. I was wondering if we could take a picture with you, Mike."

"Okay." He smiled and grabbed his fresh drink.

"I guess we'll do this one at a time, Mik," I said. "You first." She smiled uneasily and moved in close to Mike.

"Say cheese," I slurred.

In the split second before I snapped the cheap, disposable Kodak, Mike Joyce took his famous hands and placed one on each of Miki's cheeks. Then he leaned in and inserted his tongue in her mouth. Flash. He let go of her and she stared at me and shook her head. Then I did something that I will forever be ashamed of. It was clear that we were all just too drunk and giddy and stoned and should have probably parted and gone off to bed with our happy accomplishment. But rather than suggest that, one messy moment too late, I let myself become jealous. I thought of Jennifer in high school. I thought of everyone I ever cared about betraying me. I convinced myself that while I was at the bar, Miki and Mike had kissed or conspired to do so. Of course, this wasn't the case. Miki was extremely uncomfortable, as she'd done nothing to solicit such behavior other than show herself to be an adoring fan. He might as well have snogged me if that was the case. But at the time, I opted for the typical jealous-guy route. I glared at Joyce, threw the camera across the table, downed my drink, snatched up my tape recorder, and skulked out of the bar, leaving her to be pawed against her will, telling myself it was probably what she wanted. Miki was no more a slut than Mike Joyce was an interviewee-rapist. He was a Smith, for fuck's sake. Smiths don't molest! But he was smashed. We'd made him that way. Still, as I paced back and forth on Avenue A, it seemed justified to put my new friend, a woman I told myself I loved, in possible harm's way. I don't know what happened back at the table. Miki never told me. But it couldn't have been too cool because soon she was storming right past me. She flashed me a withering look and didn't say a word. She looked completely sober too, all her booze cooked out of her system by a seething rage.

"Where are you going?" I called.

She didn't turn around. I watched her snake through the street traffic and for a second I thought about following her, but decided against it. I knew even then that I'd sold her out. I was ashamed but decided that it would be better to let her cool off before begging her forgiveness. I figured it was easier to face Joyce, who was probably realizing he'd messed up. I walked back into the bar. Joyce wasn't at the table. He was in the toilet. I sat at the bar and ordered one for the road. He walked up to me and sat down at the vacant stool.

"Do you want another?" I asked coldly.

"Sure," he said. I ordered him a final vodka cranberry and stared straight ahead at the plastic Halloween skeleton mounted on the bar's back mirror. It had been there since the previous Halloween, and probably the Halloween before that. Like the '80s, it was about to come back into style.

"So," Joyce eventually said, "you and Miki, er . . ."

"Listen, man, you're my hero, but if you say another word about it, I'm gonna fucking deck you right here."

I turned back to my drink. The bartender brought him his. And we sat there in the Library. Me and the Smith. Drinking in silence, long after we should have stopped. The fleeting euphoria had turned into pain once again.

Is it always gonna be this way with this fucking band? I thought.

sixteen

you're about as easy as a nuclear war

We didn't speak over the weekend. Mike Joyce flew home to Manchester. I crawled home to sleep it off, and Miki did whatever was necessary to erase the memories of being kissed by two mad drunks who weren't her boyfriend within one week. That Sunday, I felt polluted and decided to take the train out to the Island. It's always a weird feeling, getting off at the Lawrence station and walking the same three blocks to my childhood home . . . the same three blocks I walked to junior high school every day. Weirder still that I was doing it as a 30-year-old man. Long Island is always there. And with the exception of an influx of Hasidic Jews, it hadn't changed very much in the 12 years since I'd left. A shop closing here, a shop opening there. In short, as dreary and ghost-filled as it was to me, my hometown remained a constant and therefore great comfort in moments when Manhattan life became dirty. I didn't like going back, but I was glad that it was there when I absolutely had to. And, to my discredit, these return journeys seldom had anything to do with Jewish holidays, family get-togethers, weddings, or funerals. Everything to do with drying the fuck out. I hadn't seen Susie and Dick since saying good-bye to my 20s and so I decided to take them up on their offer to buy me a nice steak. It was raining and chilly as I walked up the driveway in my leather jacket and torn jeans. Soaking wet, I was greatly relieved that I'd made it all the way to my mother's door without being stopped by a police cruiser (this had happened more than once and in itself was a comfort more than a bother—*Thank God they're concerned about people who look like me trolling their streets,* I'd say to myself with a smile after showing the officer my old driver's license, which still had Susie's address on it, and convincing him that I wasn't there to steal color television sets or slit some old lady's throat). I kissed Susie and shook Dick's hand. They stared at my unshaven, wasted, and worn appearance with concern. I looked older. They appeared exactly the same. Clean living, you know.

"It seems like you haven't slept in a while, Joseph," Susie said, but I could tell she was worried that I'd had a relapse. That I was back on smack. "Do you wanna take a nap before we eat?"

"No, maybe just a shower, Mom," I said, smiling, trying to conjure up a ruddy, healthy hue just by grinning really hard. It didn't work. I lied instead. I was tired of worrying my mother. "I have no hot water in my building. They're fixing the boiler."

Susie bought it, largely because she wanted to. I flashed her a look of recognition, indicating it was okay to feel relieved, and then smiled again.

"I should shave too."

"That's probably a good idea," Dick agreed. He cheerfully offered the use of his razor and a clean blade. I hiked up the carpeted stairs toward my old room, which Dick had long since converted into his private study. Spy novels, pipe racks, a big-screen television, and a pile of *New York Times*es littered the floor. I opened the closet. My old clothes were still there, dangling from white plastic hangers. I bypassed the green-and-black leopard-print shirt that I bought at Unique Clothing Warehouse in 1985 and grabbed a clean white oxford button-down and a skinny black tie with orange polka dots on it. I walked to the bathroom closet and pulled out a large, fluffy pink terry-cloth towel, then went into the bathroom to draw a hot bath. I shaved and sank into the boiling heat and felt my muscles being soothed and strengthened. Stared up at the ceiling and drifted off.

Susie banged on the door nearly an hour later.

"Joe?"

I woke startled and for a second wondered where I was. After realizing I was home, I wondered what year it was. Only a quick glance at my 30-year-old alcoholic paunch reminded me that I was not, in fact, a child anymore. That I didn't live here anymore. And that I should probably finish up bathing here.

"I'm all right, Mom."

"You've been in there a long time."

"I fell asleep."

"Joe, are you sure you're okay?"

I got out of the tub and wrapped the towel around me. Rubbed a clear spot on the steamed-up mirror and stared at my thinning, graying hair and the deepening line that had started to bisect my forehead and snake around my eyes.

"Yes, Mom, I'm fine."

An hour later, we were sitting at a large, round table at the old Al Steiner's steak place, one town over. It faced the Cedarhurst train station and taxi stand. Just another railroad stop. Al's was the kind of old-school joint with a big fiberglass cow mounted over the awning outside. Thick-necked, leathery waiters. Inside you were obliged to drink scotch and carve big slabs of red meat. Morrissey would gag.

"You're trying to do what?" Susie asked as she picked at her chopped salad.

"Reuniting the Smiths," I said, sipping a large ginger ale. I didn't drink in front of them anymore and as far as they were concerned, I was dead dry.

"The Smiths broke up?" Dick asked, trying to sound hip, even concerned.

"Yeah, like twelve years ago, Dick."

"Nobody told me." He smiled and raised his martini. "I didn't get the memo."

"It's an experiment," I said proudly. "I even met the drummer two nights ago."

"Your job is like a fantasy," Susie enthused. "Isn't it like a fantasy? Everybody says it's like a fantasy."

"Sometimes," I allowed. "Lately it's been a bit of a nightmare."

"No, it's a fantasy!" she maintained.

"Okay, Mom. It's a fantasy."

"If you met one of the Smiths when you were sixteen, Joe, you'd have gone crazy. You would have been dancing on air. I remember what you were like. Everything was Morrissey this, Morrissey that."

After dinner, the crusty old waiters brought out a birthday cake with 31 candles (one for good luck) and Susie and Dick sang to me. It was sweet. On the train back to the city, I stared at the towns whizzing by—Hewlett, Gibson, Valley Stream, Locust Manor—and felt a bit young again. A bit clean. I'd gotten my fix of suburbia and subsequently a bit of much-needed cleansing. That night I made Miki an I'm-an-asshole mix tape. It wasn't too Smiths-heavy. And I took care not to lard it with hidden-message songs (sometimes the Ramones' "I Wanna Be Your Boyfriend" can be misinterpreted, you know . . . and "I Don't Care About You, Fuck You" by Fear is sometimes just a good song, not necessarily a big, bitter kiss-off). This time, though, I was especially concerned with keeping things sweet and upbeat. I put "This Will Be Our Year" by the Zombies, the most optimistic love song in recorded pop history, as the intro to side B, but took care to label that side "Sappy Side" on the cassette card (first side was "Penitent Side"). It's what a shy teenager would do, which was fine with me. Perfect, even.

"I just want to say that I'm sorry. I realize what I did was stupid and childish and totally, completely disrespectful of you and your virtue as a woman and as a friend, and I made you a tape and there's a . . . a . . . what?"

She was just staring at me. Even after I handed her the mix tape first thing Monday morning. She just took it without looking at the listings on the insert card. She placed it on her desk next to all the monkeys. I couldn't figure out if any of this was working. I knew it was necessary, but I was taken aback by her lack of reaction. Mix tapes usually pack a lot of power. Better than flowers. This was graceful groveling that you can dance to.

"Let's just forget about it," Miki suggested.

She looked tired. Maybe because it was Monday morning. Maybe because she hadn't gone home to Philadelphia and eaten a steak. She rapped her pencil on the edge of her desk. The phone rang. She ignored it. She stared back at me sadly.

"Okay," I agreed, and grew quiet. Turned to walk to my desk. Stopped. Turned back. "Does this mean you're not mad at me? Because I can tell you why you should be mad at me. I mean, I can tell you that I'm aware of what I did . . . and what I didn't do. And if you're really not mad, that's great, but I had a much longer apology planned."

"You're making my life difficult, Joe."

"Why?"

"You know I have a boyfriend, right?" she said flatly.

"Um . . . ," I said. "Yeah. I think."

I pulled out a cigarette. My hands were shaking.

"I don't want to talk about this here," she said, and rose to approach me. We walked toward the fire escape. I lit up. She took a drag. It was another chilly day. I pulled up my collar and hunched over, leaning on the iron railing, staring down into the empty, litter-filled alley. Doing anything not to look into her eyes.

"Joe?" she said. I kept my head down. "Joe, look at me."

"Okay," I said, still training my vision on the papers and cups and millions of discarded cigarette butts below.

"You asked Tom about me. You know I have a boyfriend."

"I did not," I said. I was looking at her now. Looking at her and lying. "We were just talking and . . . you know, I was curious. That's all. Why did . . . how did . . . did he tell you anything?"

"Yes." She smiled. "I can't read his mind. Only yours."

"I don't want to take you away from your boyfriend, Miki," I said. This was not easy. I was saying things just because I knew I should, not cause that's how I was feeling. It cheats both parties. It's an odious quality.

"Are you sure?" she asked, searching me. I tried to imagine some kind of thought-protecting lead skullcap to keep her from reading the truth.

"No. Of course I want to take you away from him," I said. "How can I do that?"

She smiled in appreciation of the honesty. It was a good call on my part. I smiled back.

"What happened between us was . . . it was . . . what was it, exactly?" I asked.

"I was just kissing you goodnight," she said with a dead-animal flatness to her voice.

Just kissing me goodnight, open mouth, with sort of tongue . . . for almost two full minutes, I thought. *What the hell?* "Oh. Okay." I lit another cigarette and sucked in the smoke deject-edly. Returned my burned-out eyes to the garbage below. I knew I wasn't crazy. I was drunk but I was there. "So it didn't mean anything. Fine. What now?" I asked with a beaten-little-boy whimper.

"Well, I'm really, really pissed off at you."

"I know."

"And I was obviously not into Mike's behavior either. But I thought about everything that happened over the weekend."

"Me too. While I was making you the mix . . . never mind."

"I realized that we got what we wanted. And then I got ex-cited again. The end, getting him to say on tape that he would play drums for a reunion, that meant everything. The kiss . . . it didn't mean anything. To me *or* him, probably."

I wondered if the same went for my kiss. I didn't bring it up. But I wondered . . . a lot.

"Do you understand, Joe?" she asked.

"Yes," I whispered.

"Do you feel the same way?"

"Yes," I said, barely audible.

"So no matter what happens, we're not going to give up, right? No matter how hard things get."

"No," I said, nearly in tears. She touched me on the shoul-der. I pulled away.

"Joe! I love being with you. I want to be your friend. I want to do this. We need to do this. But you're gonna ruin every-thing if you don't accept what I have to offer you. Which is a lot, trust me."

"Fine," I said, recalling Jennifer's ghost and convincing myself I was fucking cursed. I walked back to my desk and sat down. Left her on the fire escape. I passed Johnston as I crossed the office, away from Miki's cubicle. He was lingering outside his door, thumbing through his large pile of promo CDs and probably wondering where the hell his assistant had gone. Why his voice-mail box was jammed with unanswered calls.

"Hey," he said. "How's the cause?"

"We got the drummer," I said blankly. "We're closing in on the bass player."

"So Mike Joyce is in?"

"Yes."

Johnston laughed.

"Amazing." He said. "Do you want this INXS box set?"

I wondered if this was some kind of gesture of friendship or a small reward. I knew it would be impolite to refuse it, but I couldn't work up any fake enthusiasm (no disrespect to INXS, who have a couple of really great songs, you know).

Happily, our first real lead regarding getting through to Morrissey, who at the time was coming up on two full years without granting a major interview, arrived just in time to table all the kissing drama and put us back on course. It came from an anonymous tip e-mailed to us by someone named Our Frank (cribbed, as most things Moz-related are, from one of his obscure song titles from the *Kill Uncle* album). I was randomly checking Ms. Shankly's in box when I came across it and, in keeping with the way things had been going, nearly deleted it without opening it.

"Hello there," it read. "I don't know if you people are crazy or what, but I too would love it if the Smiths got back together, even just for one show. I know Morrissey would rather eat a giant plate of pork chops than take the stage with his former band but I think it would be good for him, so I'm writing you with some information that you might find helpful." I read on excitedly. Our Frank was hinting that he may have been a part of the star's retinue . . . a mole, keen to steer the reluctant star toward us.

"It hasn't been announced yet," he continued, "but I can tell you that Morrissey will tour this year. He has already hired a tour manager and currently that is the only way to reach him with any media requests. His name is Harry." The snitch went on, leaving the rep's cell phone number, and concluding his secret message with the suggestion, "You may or may not have read that Morrissey has developed a real fondness for pasta. If you approach him bearing gifts, you might have a better shot at accomplishing your mission."

Our mission? Pasta? Was this a crank? We'd received a few bogus letters already. One 16-year-old Londoner claimed to be "Steven's girlfriend" and compared herself to Lolita and him to Claire Quilty (from that famous book by Nabokov, you know).

"Harry?" Miki instant-messaged after I forwarded her the e-mail.

"Pasta?" I added.

"This is great!" she typed.

"What do we do?" I responded.

We decided to call Harry and pretend that we were agents interested in booking a Morrissey show in New York City. From Miki's desk, we dialed the number. A gruff-sounding man with a deep voice and apparently a very short temper picked up.

"Yeah?" he asked.

"Is this Harry?" Miki said. I listened from the adjacent desk.

"Yeah. Who's this?"

"My name is Polly Twinkle."

"Who?"

Miki flashed me a wink and stepped up her guise confidently. I had to bite my hand to avoid breaking into mad

278

laughter. Like I said, her brain worked fast. Twinkle was the name of the obscure '60s chanteuse who had recorded the original version of "Golden Lights" (which the Smiths covered, allegedly to Johnny's chagrin, as a B-side).

"That's Polly Twinkle. I'm an entertainment booker and promoter in Manhattan. Polly Twinkle!"

"What do you want?"

"I am very interested in booking Morrissey into the world-famous Madison Square Garden arena for his upcoming tour. Would that be something of interest?"

"Polly Twinkle?" he asked again.

"That's right. Would that be something of interest?"

There was a long pause. Miki, sensing she was losing him, sharply bargained down.

"We are a very reputable agency, I assure you. If you could provide me with an office address, I could overnight you information about our firm."

"Yeah, all right." Harry finally agreed and hung up. Miki and I stared at each other in a panic.

She quickly hit redial.

"Yeah?"

"Yes, hello, Harry. It's Polly Twinkle again. You hung up before you gave me the mailing address."

"You don't have it?"

"No."

"How did you get this number?"

Miki stared at me.

"From Adam," she answered.

"Adam?"

"That's right. Adam."

There was another long, unnerving silence. Then he finally gave her the address as well as an office number.

"Never call this line again," he spat before hanging up again.

how soon is never?

"What an asshole," I said.

"I know!"

"Who's Adam?"

"That I don't know."

Adam. Harry apparently knew him. And didn't like him much.

After work, Miki and I took the subway downtown and found ourselves in the fresh pasta section of Balducci's, the famous West Village grocery. Unsurprisingly, such folly made it much easier for us to hang out together in the aftermath of our Sunday kiss and whatever the fuck happened with Mike Joyce. It was hard to bring up serious issues when you're selecting the perfect pasta and sauce to gift a reclusive rock star. Sausage and prosciutto were out, of course. We finally selected an array of expensive pastas, both eggless and classic.

"Do you think he's a vegan or just a vegetarian?" I asked.

"Probably just a vegetarian," she said.

"So cheese isn't murder."

"I don't think so." She laughed.

We threw in a couple of packages of cheese-filled ravioli because we loved the guy. The sauces looked so delicious and hearty inside their glass containers, we didn't need to sample them. We didn't know what the fuck we were doing but it was nice to be breezy and stupid again. Breezy and stupid and 30. Plus as ridiculous as it seemed, we really believed we were feeding Morrissey.

Why not? We'd already met one Smith and fed him plenty of cheap cocktails (and quite nearly force-fed him his own teeth). Pasta felt a lot more pure and innocent, and it reminded us of the tales of Morrissey's abstaining from the post-success reveries the other three indulged in both on tour and in the studio. It made sense. Joyce drank with us. Morrissey would eat our sauces. While Miki arranged for the gift package to be shipped, I walked a few paces up Sixth Avenue to a tacky gift shop and picked out a black-and-white card with two tabby kittens on it. Bad journalist that I was, I also had to purchase a pen.

Dear Morrissey,

There's a persistent rumor going around that claims that you have become very fond of pasta. We believe this is the finest pasta available, and hope that it brings you as much pleasure as your music has brought us through the years. We know that's not possible. It's only pasta. Pasta didn't help us get through high school in one piece. You did. But please accept this sincere gift anyway. Oh, and please, please, please allow us to interview you for Headphones *magazine soon. Just say the word and we'll be there . . . with more sauce. We look forward to hearing from you very soon. We're not mentally ill, by the way.*

Sincerely,
Miki and Joe

We left the *Headphones* address and our phone and e-mail addresses at the bottom of the card, sealed it, and tucked it in with the pasta.

"Do you think he'll eat it?" I asked as I walked her east. For a moment I wondered if maybe I should just continue west and get out of her hair, but she didn't seem to mind.

"Of course he'll eat it," she replied. "He loves pasta!"

"Maybe he'll have a food taster sample it first."

"Harry!" she said.

As we came up on Third Avenue and St. Mark's Place, I turned back. I didn't want to leave her, but I knew it wouldn't be cool to walk her to her door. I was kind of hoping she'd mention the mix tape I made her, but I'd given up and was too proud to ask about it. Too concerned about looking like a psycho too.

"I think I'm gonna head back," I said.

"Okay."

"What are you up to tonight?"

"I'm going to a party," she said. "It's not a big deal, just a couple of friends at that bar the Stinger. Do you know it?"

I knew it but never drank there. Sure, it was easy for an envious Jew to feel like an Irish writer inside, but they only served beer and wine, and I was strictly a spirits kind of guy. They didn't have a jukebox either. Why on earth anyone would drink there was lost on me.

"You can come if you want," she invited.

"Yeah, maybe. I'll see."

"Okay, Joe," she said, and stared at me. The strain had returned. We'd reached a point where shaking hands was too stiff and a kiss on the cheek was too awkward. Our casual goodbyes had become formal.

I sat in my apartment for hours, chain-smoking and wondering whether or not to take Miki up on her halfhearted offer to attend the party at the Stinger. I didn't have any other plans that night. I got up from my bed and found my cool black suit with skinny lapels and three buttons. I was looking for an occasion to wear it out, so the outfit kind of decided for me. If nothing else, I could drink Cokes and listen to shitty piped-in Irish music (they didn't even play the Pogues or nothin') and stare at old Mik while looking very, very mod. It wasn't much but it was a Monday. I pulled on the suit and headed back east to the bar, not expecting an awful lot. When you're walking the streets of Manhattan in a new (or rather, new vintage) suit, you tend to bounce and strut. The city seems full of possibility when you're dressed better than you usually are. If you've got some nice new shoes too, forget it. Why I didn't go shopping every single day, I don't know. It was like Prozac, and cumulatively less expensive than boozing. As I headed into the bar, I made a promise to myself to consider it. At least purchase a new skinny tie or a vest each day. That wouldn't break me. And when I was really low on cash, I could thrift-pick like I used to on Long Island. As soon as I sat at the bar and looked around for a familiar face, I knew just why Miki had invited me down. It didn't seem too strange at the time, or maybe I was just not picking up on the fact that this was a test. If indeed I was okay with the fact that she had a boyfriend, it was time to walk the walk, since the guy was there—and pretty soon up in my face. She was sitting next to him, chatting happily with a bunch of people I didn't know: a completely bald dude with a friendly air, a cool-looking Asian chick (yes, a real Asian), a fearsome big bouncer-looking guy, and him. The punk rock ghost made flesh. He answered to Floyd. Wore a white crew-neck T-shirt and Dickies. Black boots. Nerdy Timex wristwatch. Short brown hair. Handsome features. Very clean. Couldn't be more of a different animal than me if he'd had a set of dog titties or a curly pig's tail. Culturally, this was a different species and I picked up on that tense energy instantaneously. So did they. As I scanned the bar for anything strong and alcoholic that I could substitute for a few shots of whiskey, I heard my name called. It was Miki. I turned around and all four of them were looking my way. I didn't have any liquid courage. Nothing to fortify me . . . but I looked good and I decided that I would meet this challenge if it killed me. I smiled broadly and shot them a genial "Hey." Miki smiled back and waved me over. I sat down and was introduced.

"Joe Green?" the bald dude asked. "Like Mean Joe Greene?" The Asian chick cracked a thin smile.

how soon is never?

"Yep," I said, shooting him a wide shit-eater. "Like Mean Joe Greene."

I turned to Miki and gave her one of the same, as if to say, *Is this the only kind of hell you're gonna show me? Cause I've seen worse, darling.*

"This is Suki," Miki said, gesturing toward the Asian chick, who didn't extend her hand or say hi, only lengthened her snarky grin a little bit for me. "This is Carl." The bald guy nodded his head.

"Hi, Suki. Hi, Carl. I'm Joe Green. Like Mean Joe Greene."

"And this is Floyd."

I turned to the boyfriend and extended my hand.

"Hey, Floyd."

He shook my hand firmly and nodded. We stared at each other for an uncomfortable minute or two. I imagined Miki watching us too. I imagined the entire bar watching us, actually. And the cops cruising 5th Street outside. And God.

Someone had to break. "Well, this is great Irish folk music. Listen, gang, I'm going to go up to the bar and get a glass of beer or wine. Can I get anyone anything?" I finally asked.

"I'll take a glass of red," Miki said, and handed me a $10 bill.

"I'll have another pint," the bald dude said. The Asian chick, of course, said nothing. Floyd apparently didn't drink. He asked for a glass of water. I walked to the bar and put in the order.

After a few minutes, Floyd joined me.

"Hey, Floyd."

"I'll help you carry that," he said.

"That's all right, man. I got it."

"So you and Miki are pretty close," he stated.

"Well . . . yeah."

He stared at me.

"She told me you're really close. She talks about you all the time, actually."

"Oh, well. That's cool," I said, trying to hide any trace of elation at hearing such an ego-boosting thing. He looked me over, then moved closer, up in my face. I didn't really know what was about to go down, but I knew it was something I'd have to roll with. I backed away slightly. He got closer.

"You're going to England together soon," he said. I could smell his breath. He didn't smoke either.

"That's right."

"Gonna reunite the Smiths," he said flatly.

"We're gonna try, Floyd," I said, and pulled back again. Again, he bridged the gap.

"I wanted to ask you something, Joe."

I felt my muscles stiffen and readied myself for some kind of assault, whether verbal or physical. I was bigger than Floyd by about 20 pounds and three or four inches. His proportions were more physically tuned to Miki's. But he was obviously fit and I knew that it would be a fair fight despite my size.

"Shoot, Floyd."

"You know that tape you made her?"

Oh, shit, I thought. *What the fuck did I put on that tape?* I tried to remember "Sappy Side." Was it gonna land me in the ICU? I had been a little drunk when I made it. No, I'd been very drunk. And, like I said, as much as I'd tried to censor any meaningful songs, I was sure that something had gotten past me. Was it the Zombies after all? And why had she played it for him?

And we're gonna fucking brawl. My thoughts dashed around my brain. *And worst of all, I'll fail her test.*

I took a pull off my beer and gripped the neck of the bottle just in case I had to swing it. I looked back at Miki, who was watching us with growing concern.

"What's that song that goes 'neh neh neh neh neh neh'? The guitar. It's very New Wave, but it's got a great riff. Do you know the one I'm talking about?"

I swallowed hard.

"What's the lyric, Floyd?" I asked.

"Shit. I don't remember the chorus. The guitar is like—"

"Neh neh neh neh."

"Yeah," he said. "Fucking amazing riff. It's like 'Get me outta here!' Something like that."

I felt relief. It was a fairly innocuous track. "Private Life," the old Oingo Boingo New Wave semi-hit. From "Penitent Side." Straight-up filler. I didn't even know why I'd included it. I guess I'd wanted to secretly let her know I was lonely . . . even though she already knew I was lonely. But somehow it had caught Floyd's mind on a snag.

"That's Oingo Boingo, Floyd," I said.

"Oingo Boingo!" He smiled. "It was driving me crazy."

"I'm sorry, Floyd."

"What album is that on?"

"I have it on a greatest-hits compilation called *Skeletons in the Closet*."

"Someone should cover that song. I should cover that song." He smiled and grabbed the bald dude's pint and his water.

"You should, Floyd. Nobody'd see it coming."

"Thanks."

We shook hands. He even left me Miki's wine to bring back myself. I was glad Floyd and I didn't have to fight. He seemed like a nice enough guy, even though I couldn't figure out what the hell he was doing with Miki. He didn't seem to know shit about New Wave and she was a New Waver if I've ever met one (and I've met hundreds). Convinced I'd passed her test, I finished my beer and got the fuck out of there. I left the jigs and the fucking ales behind and hightailed it over to the Library and drank five bourbon whiskeys and listened to the Cure like a normal person. I never confronted her to ask whether or not it was a test at all. Maybe it wasn't. Miki only seemed calculating when it came to deceiving employees of former Smiths. Whatever it was, just a shit shoot on a boring Monday night, it wasn't easy.

seventeen

one million pounds

To fly by her side was such a heavenly way to die. I was sitting next to Miki in the aisle seat of a Manchester International Airport–bound British Airways jet out of New York City, and I was terrified. Thanks to the wheeling, dealing, and coughing of Mr. Marsh (whom we now regarded as the liaison nonpareil to all manner of Mancunian former rock stars), we were on our way to roll tape on Mr. Andy Rourke, the player of "the bass guitar," as he was credited on the inner sleeve of the Smiths albums. Also one of four. And second to agree to sit down with us, albeit on his turf. Miki was merely excited and eager to meet her second ex-Smith and transform him into a future Smith. Happy to get out of New York. Glad to keep moving in our quest after hearing nothing so much as a long-distance burp from Morrissey or his cantankerous flack Harry after our pasta overture. I shared all these sentiments, but midtransit, utter dread was mine alone. I should mention that since I'd kicked heroin and turned 30, I'd rediscovered dread. I'd started obsessing over all those things that failed to put the fear of untimely, arbitrary death in me, shit like flying . . . or crossing the street. When you're really high, on the nod, technically—and don't hold me to this, I'm just repeating what a drug counselor once told me—you're the closest to death that you've ever been. He claimed that you don't even start nodding, really, till your lungs malfunction. Then your heart rate and breathing slow down to a dangerous rhythm, and you're in that odd place between life and death. I can't count how many times I've been in that state and never feared the Reaper. Or for that matter, how many times I copped drugs in mugger- and axe-murderer-filled streets without regard for keeping my hide from getting slit and splayed. Keeping my guts from spilling out between Avenues C and D. Coke and Dope. Smack-free and out of my 20s, whenever I read about an infant being carried off by a bear (it happens), I'm convinced that the same fate is awaiting me. All the seldom-pondered dangers of the planet rush my thoughts and create a web of dread that probably should be neutralized with prescription medication. Every time I board a plane, I stare down at the final step between the walkway and the jet entrance and wonder if that small gap will prove to be the barrier between life and death. I wonder, *Will this plane be the one that will break apart at 37,000 feet and never get to LAX or Heathrow?* Or in this case, Manchester International. But with Miki sleeping next to me, a copy of the new issue of *The Face* in her lap atop the torn black sweater she was using as a blanket, I didn't care as much. I wasn't afraid. I knew that there was no real chance of us dying together because that would just be too fucking romantic, like "There Is a Light That Never Goes Out," the Smiths song I was paraphrasing in my head on a loop. If you can't get any Valium, the next best thing is to fly with a pretty girl. She'd taken some pills. I just ordered round after round of cheap airline champagne and watched her doze. She didn't look peaceful when she slept. She looked sad. The girl actually frowned in her sleep. Miki had dyed her hair jet-black and grown it out a bit in the days between being kissed by Mike Joyce and receiving a second phone call from Mr. Marsh, which prompted our final booking and boarding of this flight. Who knows if Miki colored it for the occasion or to achieve something that might ward off blonde-transfixed, drunken kissing bandits. Or maybe she'd just gotten bored. She never explained. Never even fished for compliments or critiques. She was the most confident insecure person I'd ever met.

We were to check into the Princess Hotel in the heart of the city's business district, sleep off the jet lag, and meet Andy Rourke the following day at some Chinese restaurant on Faulkner Street. We were given sixty minutes of his time, so both of us were determined to make it count. It was a long way to travel for a one-hour audience. We still hadn't heard back from Johnny Marr's people, so the two-birds-with-one-stone was out as far as we knew. Whenever I questioned our journey, I reminded myself that we were en route to meet the very man who played the warm and languid bass melody on "Heaven Knows I'm Miserable Now." Not to mention the sly rhythms of "Rubber Ring," which conveyed the track's empathetic wink and nod to any and all listeners as directly as Morrissey's vocals and lyrics . . . without, of course, the benefit of fucking lyrics. I should also mention that the giddy bass jump of "This Charming Man" still makes me feel like I'm pulling up my jacket collar and braving the chilly city streets in search of tremulous romance, or at least a wet kiss and some shared body heat against a brick wall.

We landed in Manchester in the middle of the night and picked up our luggage. I learned another important detail about Miki that day. Whereas I always made a point to travel light, Miki brought everything she owned with her. I packed a suit, some clean socks and underwear, a notebook, some CDs, a toothbrush, and a razor. She cleaned out her closet. Maybe it was a girl thing. I offered to carry some of her bags as we drowsily made our way through customs, where we listed ourselves as journalists and indicated that we would be there a minimum of two days. Very professional. Very legit. A taxi was waiting for us out in the street, and the red-faced old driver loaded our bags into the trunk. The air was a good 10 degrees colder than it had been back home, and wet with mist, so I pulled the plaid scarf from my travel bag and wrapped it around my neck. Lit up a cigarette in the back of the shiny black car and stared out the window as we sped toward the city at an alarming rate. Miki drifted back to sleep and leaned against my side, frowning again. I wanted to watch the scenery but only watched her instead. In that peaceful, transported state, with my ears still clogged from the altitude shift and my sense of time all screwy and jet-lagged, all I really wanted to do was sleep a few hours, then get up and be ready to rock. I almost didn't want to allow myself a sense of excitement till I'd had a shower and some Z's. But, despite the weird relief of not being dead, and the temporary but lovely sensation of having Miki sleep next to me as we cruised through the odd traffic and turned down Portland Street toward the Princess, I thought, *I want to go out and take Manchester, England, into my pores.* Travel-delirious, drowsy, but sentimental, I thought of all the songs. *I want to go to the humdrum towns. The pub that wrecks your body. The Holy Name Church that just wants my money, wherein the Vicar in a Tutu surely dwells. The fair. The moors. The iron bridges. The cemetry gates (sic). Back to the old house, wherever it was. I don't want to sleep. I want to physically enter this dimension where their songs fold and unfold infinitely. Surely it must be here. I want to walk lightly through the geography of the Smiths as though I were the star of the music videos they had such distaste for.*

how soon is never?

And I wanted Miki to take my hand and join me. During our journey to the core of what made this band magical, we would become the fifth and sixth members of the Smiths and share a previously unknown understanding of the sights, smells, chills, spills, chips, and ales that inspired their words and melodies. We would see the gears and instruments that harnessed their chemistry and converted everything into energy so vital to the both of us. Fuck if I didn't have some strain of post-punk Jerusalem syndrome. That night, however, Miki and I were destined to share something a bit more terrestrial.

It wasn't until we checked in that I learned that Miki and I would be occupying the same room. Apparently, a standard room was much less expensive as opposed to a small suite. Grim as the converted Victorian mansion appeared from the outside, the interior was posh and the rooms were not cheap. For economy's sake, Miki had incorrectly assumed that I was mature enough to handle such an arrangement. There were two beds, of course, but it was still pretty awkward. I'd seen her eat, heard her sing, kissed her, even seen her sleep, but we'd never spent the night in the same place before. I didn't know what she wore to bed.

Did she sleepwalk?

Did she snore sometimes?

I snored. Plus I was pretty sure my feet stank after that long flight. Fortunately, unlike most bed-sit-sized London hotels I'd demolished on *Headphone*'s tab, the accommodations at the Princess were fairly spacious. Fax machine. Stereo. Fake bowl of fruit on a small table. Large desk. Shower I could fit in without crouching (I'm convinced all of England's showers are designed primarily to accommodate stunted baby boomers who were rationed nourishment as children). I dropped my bags in the corner and stretched out on top of the rough navy blue bedspread. The room felt airless and cold.

"I'm going to take a shower," she said weakly. She took off her shoes and padded barefoot into the toilet, carrying her nightclothes and a toiletries bag. I lit another cigarette and rose to open the window. I wondered if maybe I shouldn't smoke in the room. Maybe that would gross her out. After a minute or two, I heard the sound of the shower spray. I found the minibar and poured myself a tiny shot of Jameson's. Belted it down while trying not to picture her wet and naked, just a few feet away. If she came out wrapped in a towel, I might have to jump out the window. I cursed Floyd and then cursed myself and poured another $16 shot of booze. I was feeling a buzz when she opened the door and walked out dressed in a large T-shirt. I tried not to look, but I could make out red panties underneath. I was still fully dressed. Drinking. Smoking. Wired. Horny. Entirely wrong. I quickly stubbed out my cigarette and searched for something to say.

"How was it? The shower? Was it . . ."

She pulled off her bedspread and inserted her half-naked body between the sheets. Pulled them up and shivered.

"Could you close the window, Joe?" she asked.

I jumped up and shut the window, then stood in the middle of the room. She turned off the light and rolled over on her side. I just stood there in the darkness, unable to move. I couldn't figure out what to do with my body. In an effort to keep from responding in any undue way to our business-like close proximity, it had taken upon itself to shut down completely. She spent the night sleeping, frowning, dreaming . . . I chain-smoked Camels in the toilet and cleaned out most of the minibar. When I stumbled out at five in the morning, reeking of cigarettes and booze and improbable sweat, I noticed she'd pushed away the covers in her sleep. The panties were red indeed. I got into bed wishing somebody would just drop the bomb cause it wasn't love that was bringing us together. I stared at the ceiling, spinning a little from the whiskey and trying not to glance to my right at her mind-scrambling ass. It was like falling asleep on a raft floating in a shark tank. Not very easy, man. Not very easy. But the booze took over and soon I was snoring away, or so Miki told me. She had ordered coffee and pastries from room service and was stretched on her stomach on the carpeted floor, in jeans and a green sweater. She was reading a day-old copy of the *Manchester Evening News,* bare toes twitching in the air.

"Joe, you snore like . . . I don't even know what." She laughed. "Like ten men snoring."

"Oh, fuck. I'm sorry." I blushed.

"I put a pillow over your face and you didn't stop," she said without looking up.

"Really?"

"Then I sat on it."

"Really?" My blush deepened. I was redder than those panties.

She turned to me and smiled.

"No, but I thought about it. It was awful. How are you ever gonna get married?"

I rose out of bed and went straight for the hangover-mitigating pot of coffee, not realizing that I was still fully dressed. And by fully dressed, I mean leather jacket, shoes . . . everything.

"Is that what you always wear to bed?" she asked.

"Yeah. In case there's a fire and I have to leave really quickly. It's safer that way," I joked, in an attempt to shrug off the horrible embarrassment. "I guess I must have just passed out. I couldn't sleep."

"Really? Why not?"

"What time is it?" I asked, ignoring her question while sipping the bitter black sludge that passed for coffee in these parts.

"New York time or Manchester time?" she asked.

294

"Manchester time."

"It's nearly nine. Four A.M. in New York."

"Shit. I'm going to take a shower," I said.

"I'm going to call the concierge and double-check Mr. Marsh's directions."

I grabbed my black crew-neck sweater and black jeans and hustled my dirty ass into the john to freshen up. I pulled off my clothes and despite my efforts to ease the tension, the same stupid notion hit me. There I was, naked, only a few feet away from her. And I would never see her naked. And she would never see me naked. And the world could collapse in on itself and leave us trapped in there with nothing but minibar pretzels and a cold pot of coffee to sustain us, and we'd still never see each other naked. Looking down at my little paunch, I was almost relieved. I had developed my father's body. From the neck down, I was Sid. But I still wanted to see her naked and would have exposed all my Sid-ness if some kind of physical union required it. I threw on my jeans and shaved off my stubble. Mussed up my hair, pulled on my sweater, and walked out of the toilet to find the socks I'd forgotten, confident that my feet were now powder fresh and unoffensive.

"Why do people break out on airplanes?" I said by way of informing her that I knew I had a zit on my chin.

"I think it's the tension," she answered. "Everyone's braced for disaster. It's murder on the complexion. That's why I took a shower last night." I pondered what she said. In a perfect world, we would have showered together. Instead I got a hangover and a zit.

Manchester by day was not the gray, murky industrial town I'd imagined, having listened to so many Smiths and Joy Division songs. The fall air was cold and oppressive, but the sun was wide and bright, and the sky was cloudless and almost ocean blue. Of course, we had yet to venture out of the business center, but there were cinemas and galleries and newsagents where I'd pictured a homogeneous industrial landscape of factories and slaughterhouses. I handed some coins to an alarmingly young beggar we passed as we walked down Princess Street toward Faulkner Street (according to our crudely drawn map). Maybe we were just overjoyed to be there. Maybe I was just a bourgeois, Anglophile former JAP but even this bearded, New Agey panhandler seemed saturated with gloomy, Dickensian charm. We gamboled on, neglecting the taxis and trams in favor of walking the streets the Smiths walked together. In the distance we noticed a large gothic-looking convention-center-type building.

"I wonder if that's the old Hacienda?" I said aloud, thrilled at the possibility of just being near the legendary Factory Records–owned nightclub where Joy Division and New Order and the Smiths and all manner of our beloved WLIR mainstays had played nearly two decades ago.

In New York, I'd frequently stood in front of the Korean deli that used to be Max's Kansas City in the early '70s and imagined Debbie Harry of Blondie waiting tables inside, the Velvet Underground performing onstage, and Andy Warhol holding court in the back room, where Candy was everybody's darlin'. Once, on assignment in Los Angeles, I stood drunk in an alley on Cherokee, off Hollywood Boulevard, and stared through an iron gate into the basement entrance that used to be the illegal Masque club, attempting to hear the ghostly wail of the Germs' Darby Crash in the soily wind. I was fully addicted to the ghosts of pop culture and Manchester was full of them.

"That's not the old Hacienda, is it?"

"I don't know."

"I think it used to be the Hacienda."

"How do you know?"

"I don't know."

"It's not the Hacienda."

"Excuse me, sir, is that building the Hacienda?" I asked a speed-walking gent in a trench coat as he passed. I felt like a tourist, but I was damn happy to feel like a fucking tourist after spending the last half decade a terminally jaded New Yorker.

"That's the town hall," the pedestrian answered gruffly, and continued on his way.

"Oh, well, at least we don't look like tourists, do we?" I asked Miki sheepishly.

We later found out that we were nowhere near the Hacienda site, which is now an unrecognizable block of condominiums in the making, fitted with ugly scaffolding.

We kept moving and gaping at everything those around us passed without noticing. A cat darting around a corner. The electronic beep of the crosswalk wiring. It was all so strange. So English. So out-of-time and refreshing. Even the cigarettes tasted better.

"There's Chinatown," she exclaimed.

"How do you know?"

"That's the arch Marsh mentioned. It's a Chinese arch, Joe."

Miki was a confident navigator. I was reminded of that first day when John guided me down St. Mark's Place. It was comforting. It's always better to adventure as a team. Lewis and Clark, Starsky and Hutch, and all. We walked in and shook off the cold in the shadow of tacky gold dragons, festooned with red ribbons. We hardly blended in so well with the crowd of somberly dressed locals eating their business lunches. If we looked like tourists, we were also very obviously the only potential Smiths fans in the place. I took comfort in the fact that Andy, unlike Mike, would easily recognize us upon arrival but it wasn't necessary. Miki was with me this time and she recognized him before he even walked in. She pointed beyond the glass storefront and mouthed a single word.

"Smith."

He was wearing baggy, olive-green trousers. Boots and a baggy khaki jumper top. His hair was light brown, shaggy, and in need of a trim. He wore sunglasses and didn't take them off once indoors, even as he peered around the dimly lit space in search of two strangers.

"Andy?" Miki asked.

"Is that Miki?"

"Hi!" She greeted him as though he were an old friend. In a way, he was. He laughed and shook her hand vigorously. Barely acknowledged me. It may have taken Joyce several rounds of cocktails to expose his prurient interests in my partner, but Rourke was flirting from the start. It made me wish we were reuniting some long-split gay act like Bronski Beat or the fucking Village People. All my heroes wanted to shag her!

"I'm Joe," I said with a boldness that usually required alcohol.

"Hello, mate," he said warmly. I couldn't see his eyes, but I could feel him sizing me up, wondering if I was Miki's boyfriend. I reminded myself that the hand that I just shook not only longed to touch Miki's flesh but had held the holy bass guitar. Rourke bobbed his head to the easy-listening elevator music funk that was being piped into the restaurant. We sat down and ordered drinks, munched on noodles, and began, as we had in New York, with some small talk.

"So how are you?" Miki asked, as though it had only been a few days since she'd last caught up with him.

"I'm fine."

"What have you been up to?"

"Mike and I are busy working on a new project. We've more or less finished an album. It needs producing and mixing. Hopefully we'll do some gigs in the spring. All over the world."

"What's the music sound like?" I asked.

"Well . . . it's sort of Manchester meets Asian." His accent, like Joyce's, was not indecipherable. The product of years of touring, no doubt.

"Do you mind if we roll tape now?" I asked politely.

"Go ahead." He said it with the casual air of a man who's given 10,000 interviews on the subject of his old band.

"So you're based in Manchester primarily?" I asked.

"Yeah. How do you like it here?" He addressed Miki, despite the question being mine.

"We love it," she said. He laughed like it was the funniest thing he'd ever heard.

"So when you're walking down the street, do you run into kids who accost you and want to hear about the Smiths and the old days?" I asked.

"Cause we're those kids," Miki confessed. He chuckled again.

At least he's getting warmed up, I reasoned to myself, straining to contain my jealousy.

"No, it's cool. I do a bit of DJing now and again. I hang around sometimes afterward, signing autographs and stuff."

"Where do you DJ?" Miki asked.

"I used to work at this place called the Sad Cafe. I did some recently in Newcastle. And I've just come back from Belfast."

"What do you spin?"

"A lot of indie stuff. Stones. Beatles too. A mix of stuff."

"A soup!" Miki said. Another guffaw from the bass guitarist.

"From what I've read, it seems to be a close-knit community

here among musicians," Miki pointed out. "Do you have any relationship or rapport with Johnny Marr?" she said, seizing the moment to segue gracefully. "He lives here too, right?"

"I don't, unfortunately, no. It's been a bit strained since the court case. That was the last time I saw him and Morrissey."

"Seeing them under those circumstances must have been strange," I said.

"Yeah. It was a bit bizarre," he admitted.

"What if you saw them out and about in Manchester? What would that be like?" Miki asked.

I checked the red light on the recorder to make sure it was still rolling.

"Would you be able to just go to a pub and talk?" I followed up.

He stiffened a bit. Clearly he was uncomfortable. Fortunately, our waiter came and took our order, which eased the tension a bit. We switched to something less hypothetical, in an effort to keep the mood friendly.

"When was the last time you saw them?"

"Um, the last time I saw Johnny was at an Echo and the Bunnymen gig in Manchester about two and a half years ago. My daughter spotted him and she said, 'Dad, I think that's Johnny Marr.' And I looked around and he started running in the other direction. He didn't feel comfortable, obviously. I just saw the back of his head. It was about six months after the court case."

"No!" Miki shouted—so loudly that several patrons stared over at us.

"He was ducking you?" I asked.

"I don't know." I didn't get a laugh.

"Do you think you might have a chance to hang out? Someday?"

"I'm sure we'll probably get together sometime in the near future. Johnny and I have a lot of mutual friends in the music business. Every time they work with Johnny, they mention me and vice versa, and when I work with them, they say Johnny's asked about me."

"When you think about the court case now, are you at peace with it?" I continued.

"Well, you just have to get on with your life. You can't be bitter all your life. It will eat you up."

I stopped probing. His comment tripped me up a bit, to be honest. I started to wonder how much of me had been eaten up by bitterness already. How much damage had I done to myself? Would we ever succeed in this vain endeavor to make things light again? I felt suddenly exhausted and poured myself some tea. Miki seemed to pick up on my waning energy and labored to revive me by steering the conversation to that very cause. Like I said, she was a good navigator.

"It's almost a new century. It's a perfect time to start over clean," she noted, leading him along.

She barely had to make an effort. He was close behind. Hit her with another grin.

"That's it, yeah."

"So, let's talk a bit about the music," she continued. "One thing Mike shared with us is his fondness and pride for the old songs, despite everything else."

"Yeah," he answered. "Absolutely. I still listen to them too. They stand the test of time. It's something that I'm proud of and a lot of people still want to come up and talk to me about it, which is nice."

"Purely from a musical standpoint, do you ever think, when you listen to those songs, 'What if we got back together for even one show or a tiny mini tour?' "

"No."

"Will you think about it now?" she asked. He took a moment, looked around the room at the supping businessmen, then shrugged.

"It'd be interesting, yeah," he finally answered passively, then added with a bit more bite, "If the price was right, I'm sure I'd do it."

"Well, you must have had offers," I inquired.

"People don't really come to me with offers. They'd have to go to Morrissey or Johnny, wouldn't they? Without them two it wouldn't be a show, really."

"But without all four, people would think it's just for the money," Miki pointed out. "You're all still living and making music."

"It might be interesting," he said again, this time a bit more slowly, as though he was growing fonder of the idea.

"I read somewhere that the Police were just offered two million to reunite for one show," Miki said.

" 'Roxanne' would be a hundred grand. 'King of Pain' would be another hundred grand," I quipped. Nobody laughed.

"So you would be open to it if the other guys were?" Miki pushed. I noticed her glance toward the red light of the tape recorder.

"Yeah . . . if the price was right. Sure."

"So if there was enough money on the table you'd partici- pate?" I asked.

"Yeah."

"Would you do it in private for free just to see what would happen?" Miki inquired suspiciously.

"Um . . ." The guy clearly wanted to get something for his genius bass playing. And who could blame him after what he'd been though? Once she was satisfied that his participation would be conditional, she lightened things yet again.

"Or maybe for lunch? How about a gig for lunch?" she joked. He smiled.

"A little matinee?" he asked.

"Yeah. We'll buy this lunch, you just be a Smith again." I said.

"All right. It's a deal!" he joked. This time he looked at me, and I know it's goofy but I felt honored, flattered, blessed . . . like a pretty girl.

"No, seriously, if the price was right, you would play?" I asked, holding the tape recorder toward his lips.

"Yeah."

I stared at Miki. We had it. Half the band on tape, stating that, under reasonable conditions, they would not sit out a reunion.

I smiled at her.

She smiled at me.

Andy Rourke smiled at her.

"So, out of curiosity, if it did happen, what would you like to play? I mean, what songs?"

"I'd like to do a bit of everything. A sprinkling from each album and then maybe some new songs, that might be nice. But if I was getting a million pounds for it, I wouldn't be fussing really. Gimme the bass! I'll play it!"

Andy and Miki exchanged phone numbers, and we parted warmly after a particularly disgusting meal. His conditional assent provided us with even more focus and determination. By midafternoon, we'd turned our dim hotel room into some kind of production office for a holiday telethon. We'd passed a flower shop on the way back and splurged on a few cheap sprays to liven up the room. To be honest, I didn't really know a gladiola from a daisy but Miki insisted they were close enough. They were white anyway. Then some tape at the newsagent so we could tape the unfolded inner sleeve of the Smiths' debut to the wall. It was the centerpiece of a makeshift shrine that at once made the space seem warmer and lived in. We'd put red X's over the individual portrait of Mike, and left those of Morrissey and J.M. (as Marr is referred to) and Andy untouched. We lit a few candles, hit play on the mini CD player we'd lugged across the Atlantic, ordered up some egg-and-mayonnaise sandwiches and a pot of tea, and as "Reel Around the Fountain" filled the room, we went to work. Later that night, after a quick Web search of concert promoters, I opted to call Silversound, California's largest such firm. After a few tries, I was finally connected to a very enthusiastic executive named Peter Harnett, who happened to be a huge Smiths fan but assured me that he was speaking hypothetically as I battered him with questions.

"So you'd be interested in working a Smiths reunion tour?"

"That would be a dream tour. A dream tour." He laughed.

"What kind of houses would you expect? I mean, where would they play?"

"I would feel comfortable booking them into arenas, definitely," he said. "Maybe even a couple of stadium dates in L.A."

"How much would something like that net each member?"

"I couldn't give you a figure. Let's just say a lot of money."

"One million pounds each? I guess that's almost two million dollars or so, no?"

"Oh, easily. Easily."

I lowered the phone and picked up the red pen. I winked at Miki and walked over to the shrine and crossed off Andy. As far as we were concerned, he was in.

eighteen

like the young
bob dylan

By the second sundown in Manchester, New York City seemed even farther than an ocean away. I couldn't even remember what the inside of my apartment looked like anymore and I was grateful. It's always an amazing feeling that usually overtakes a traveler 48 hours or so into his trip: temporary amnesia. In addition to the rote details of the bed you sleep in, the streets you walk, the shops you pass, the bars you drink in, you also lose track of the fears and tics and dread they inspire. For me, the drugs and young girls and illness seemed like ancient history. Even my complexion grew a bit pink as my system adapted to an environment that was still so new, it tricked me into feeling clean. It was a store-bought, or rather travel-agency-purchased, cleansing but it felt real. Not cheap. And it would endure at least for a while, since I knew that as soon as I arrived back in New York, that city too would seem brand-new . . . temporarily. It usually took another two days for all the old demons to resume their positions. But we weren't troubled by that as we hopped about the room like tea-wired monkeys. In our minds, we'd already accomplished half our goal.

We wanted to go out to celebrate but decided to stay local as our cell phones were useless and we believed word from Johnny Marr's management was imminent. We'd placed three calls to them already, requesting an interview, and each time, they were unfailingly polite and promised to ring us back with a time and a place. Plus the local air, full of centuries of soot, had damaged Miki's contact lenses. Amazingly, she'd brought only one pair amid all her portable clutter, so she had to linger blindly as they soaked. I hadn't known that, like me, she was very nearly sightless without them. It made me love her even more as I pictured us both in our old age, bumping into door jambs, hand in hand, Mr. and Mrs. Magoo. I romanticized the fact that those deep, soulful brown eyes were essentially useless. Remove her corrective implements and I could be Floyd, or Morrissey, or anybody. A disc, thinner than a dime, slipped onto the eye, was the only thing that allowed her to visually differentiate between me and somebody she already loved. As she felt her way into the bathroom, I ordered vodka cocktails from room service, then stalked down the Princess's halls in search of an ice machine. When I returned, unsuccessfully, I could hear her laughing and talking from outside the door. I wondered if it was Floyd on the other line. I couldn't really begrudge her for staying in touch with her own boyfriend while we were away but I did anyway, imagining it was an intrusion on "our time." And in a way, I reasoned, it was. I was happily transplanted, if only for the next day and a half, and didn't want to be reminded that there was a place called New York, filled with people called Floyd. The room service arrived and for a moment, we both lingered outside the room, until I became uncomfortable and let him in. She ignored us as I signed the check and began mixing us some drinks. She just chattered away, squinting like Popeye and smiling like a schoolgirl.

"How are your eyes?" I asked as I handed her the cocktail. She fumbled around for it and finally grabbed the cold glass.

"That good, huh?" I joked.

"That was Andy," she said, sitting on the bed, sipping the booze in an attempt to anesthetize her ocular discomfort.

"Really?"

"Yeah."

"What does he want? His million pounds? We don't have it yet."

"He wanted to know how long I was staying." She laughed.

"Why?" I asked, trying not to appear too pissed off.

I sucked down a cold belt of vodka to soothe the burning jealousy that was welling again in my chest. I wondered if even the famously celibate Morrissey was destined to hit on Miki once we cornered him. It took three hand-mixed, strong vodka cocktails to douse my rage, and soon Miki and I were giddy and drunk. She was stretched out, staring at the ceiling. I moved over to her bed and sat down next to her. I looked at the clock. It was eight P.M. No call from Johnny.

"What should we do?" I asked. "Are you tired?"

"No." She laughed.

"Do you want to go out?"

"No," she said again.

"Do you want to go to sleep?"

She shook her head. I tried to read her mind but my head had started to spin. I stretched out in an identical position next to her. She didn't seem to mind. There we were, lying on the same bed in a small Manchester hotel room, drunk as punks.

What should I do next? I thought. *If I try to kiss her, what will happen? Will she hit me? Will she kiss me back? If I don't kiss her, one day I'll be old and sick and I'll certainly regret it. Is this a moment?*

The phone rang again. She picked it up.

"Hi!" she slurred. "Uh-huh . . . Uh-huh . . . no way! Oh, my God!"

"Is it Johnny's people?"

She ignored me and talked for ten minutes. Long enough to kill the moment that was probably never a moment. I still don't know. But at least I was spared being a kiss-coward. She probably would have hit me anyway. I determined that it was Andy Rourke once again. Apparently they were comparing upset stomachs from our shared Chinese lunch. If only I were a former Smith, I would be spared the unending torture of forced cool. I could call her every two hours and not worry about being subtle. But I was a stupid writer who couldn't even kiss her during a "moment" and every shred of bitterness at not being born a rock performer, like Mike and Andy, like Floyd, wove itself into some kind of bile-filled and alcohol-soaked tumor that I couldn't keep inside for it would surely eat up my guts. When she hung up and laughed to herself, I just spat it out.

"You're making me hate the Smiths' rhythm section!" I screamed.

"What?"

"God, why don't you just fuck them all?" I screamed. "Spare us all this trouble. Just . . . just say you won't put out until they book Madison Square Garden. They obviously just want you. Give 'em what they want and they'll give us what we want and—"

She threw the phone at my head.

It just missed. She didn't say a word, just glared at me.

"I'm sorry," I said. "I didn't mean it."

"Fuck you, Joe."

She seethed. She returned to the bathroom and didn't come out. Not even when the carefully replaced phone rang with the news we had been waiting for all night long.

"Miki?" I knocked on the door. "Miki, I just got off the phone with Johnny's people. Miki? Will you please answer me? Miki, he's agreed to meet us tomorrow. Miki, are you alive? If you're alive just say 'Yes.' Okay? Just so I know you're alive. Please say 'Yes.' Or just bang on something."

I felt like Susie must have felt, knocking on my teenage bedroom door years ago.

"Miki, come on! Open the fucking door! Please? I didn't mean it! Come on! We're gonna meet Johnny Marr! Johnny Marr!"

After another hour, I gave up, got into bed, and turned over on my side in the dark. I couldn't sleep. I was still fitfully shifting positions when I heard her open the door. I didn't turn over as I listened to her undress. I shut my eyes tight and wished I were dead. Then something happened that made me glad I could still feel. That's the problem with blankly wishing for death. It makes you forget that there are surprises in life . . . or more accurately, that pretty girls sometimes exist just to surprise sad boys back to life. I felt her weight at the end of my bed. She was sitting down next to me.

Am I dreaming? I wondered. I didn't turn over. She placed her hand on my tight shoulder and whispered my name.

"Joe," she said again.

"What?" I answered sadly.

"We have two Smiths."

"I know." I turned over and stared at her. She was wearing an old T-shirt and probably some panties underneath. Her legs were short but shapely. A couple of bruises here and there.

"And Johnny Marr?"

"Tomorrow."

"It's exciting."

"I know."

"We can't fall apart now." She smiled.

"It's really hard. It's hard to be so close to you."

"I know," she said. "What can I do? Do you want me to smash my face till I'm hideously ugly?"

"No." I laughed. There was an answer. It was simple but I couldn't say it. It was very easy to crassly and cruelly and drunkenly suggest that Miki fuck aging rock stars to get us what we wanted. It was impossible to ask her honestly to give me what I wanted, because what I wanted from her was increasingly resembling what we wanted from the Smiths. I didn't want her to just fuck me. I didn't even want her to love me. I wanted her to save me. She offered nothing of the kind. Only volunteered, in jest, to smash her face in for me. To disfigure herself. What she didn't know was that even such a rash act would have been pointless. I would have loved her anyway.

The river was polluted and black as it reflected our tired faces in the harsh morning sunlight. We had ventured there in preparation for our meeting with Johnny. I guess we hoped to fortify our energies with such dreary visions, culled from Morrissey's lyrics. I imagined that this was the river that he sang of in "This Night Has Opened My Eyes," the "river the color of lead." But it was darker than lead. It was a river the color of space. Of death. Of nothingness.

"I want to drown myself," I said as we smoked and watched the motionless slate of water.

"Do you want to get breakfast first?"

"Sure."

We chain-smoked as soon as we got off the musty bus that took us from the business district and made our way through the less congested streets where Manchester's main university lay. We were to meet Johnny nearby for tea at a place called the Crescent, one of the many student-filled pubs that dotted the weather-worn and crooked streets, but we had two full hours to kill and knew exactly what we needed to do. "Excuse me," Miki asked a friendly-looking male student type dressed in a maroon scarf and brown leather coat. He was the first pedestrian we encountered as we reached the district, and like any male type in general, he was magnetically pulled to Miki as she smiled.

"Could you please direct us to the Salford Lads Club?" she asked sweetly.

"Smiths fans, are ya?" He smiled knowingly.

"Yes. Are you?" she confessed. I watched him look her over flirtatiously.

"They're all right. Bit before my time."

I wanted to punch him in his young, fresh face but held on to whatever strands of cool I had left. He directed us down West Crown Avenue and told us to hang a left on Coronation Street. We hurried down the path he put us on until we saw its famous arched windows and all the breath left our lungs.

"Oh, my God. That's it," she said. I was speechless. Our quest was once again holy. Pure. Just beholding the site where the four of them had stood thirteen years earlier, posing for that legendary promotional photo for *The Queen Is Dead,* washed away all the ugly, vodka-soaked residue and we were again 16. We desperately looked around for a passerby who would snap our photo together but we were alone. The corner was deserted.

"Help! Someone! Help!" Miki shouted.

After twenty minutes, we decided that there was no way to shoot us together. No way to remotely approximate the Smiths, with their solidarity and youth and beauty and gang confidence. So I shot her and then she shot me grinning madly before the arched doorway. We agreed to see it as a disappointment, not an omen. That's how clean and newly optimistic the very touch of the building made us feel.

The Crescent was a dilapidated but charming pub. A warm fire burned in the charred fireplace. Two aged tabby cats crawled the tiled floor. A few students chatted loudly in the booth by the window under the glowing bulbs of the old Victorian fixtures. A kind-faced old man sat with his pipe and tweed cap and his pint of bitter in the corner, reading the paper. We grabbed two threadbare chairs in the front room and stared at each other.

"I think I need a pint," I said. "I'm nervous."

"Me too."

I walked over to the brass-railed bar and ordered a couple of pints. It's always weird buying booze in England and not tipping, but at that moment, I felt even more awkward than usual. I wanted everything to be absolutely perfect. No disrespect to Mike Joyce or Andy Rourke, but the excitement we felt over the imminent arrival of Johnny Marr was fucking ridiculous. This wasn't just one of four, but rather one of two, really. The man who wrote the music. Second only to Morrissey, who wrote and sang the lyrics, and in some eyes superior. This was godhead. This was almost too much. I noticed my hands shaking as I delivered the pints to our little table and for once it wasn't for want of the drink. Miki's tiny hands were trembling too as she grabbed her pint and we cheered each other with vibrating glasses.

The first thing I noticed about Johnny Marr, other than the fact that he was Johnny fucking Marr crossing the pub and about to sit down next to us and share a pint and a conversation, was that he looked so young. Younger even than Mike and Andy. He was already a living legend, with four immortal albums and over a dozen classic singles already affecting a second generation. And he was only 36. Morrissey had recently turned 40. He had started to show little signs of his age. Widening temples. Thickening build. But Marr, with his thick black shag and unlined face, dark paisley shirt, silver bracelet, and olive drab anorak, looked like he could have been a member of Oasis. He looked as if he could have been one of us. A friend. Alone, with none of the minders, press flacks, and assorted flunkies usually circling someone of his stature.

"Is that Joe?" he asked, standing before us.

"Yeah. Hey, Johnny! How are you?" I asked, rising and extending my hand. "This is Miki."

"Hello, Miki," Johnny said, and offered his hand in a manner that was devoid of any lasciviousness whatsoever. If he had been my hero before, he was my god right then. Better, my mate. He pulled out a pack of cigarettes and I jammed my hands into my coat to find my lighter.

I'm lighting Johnny Marr's cigarette! I thought as he inhaled and thanked me. I remembered how his guitar playing had given me shivers when I listened to the first album in my bedroom on Long Island. Fifteen years later, I was giving him a light. One of the pub cats evidently picked up on the scent of a rock legend and slowly padded its way over to us and began rubbing itself against Johnny's leg and purring loudly. Even the cats adored him. He picked it up and for a moment reminded me of Bob Dylan on the cover of *Bringing It All Back Home*. I had to catch my breath. With Andy, we started the conversation with questions about what music they were currently working on. It was a point of politeness and respect. With Johnny, we were actually interested, even if it flew in the face of our purpose. We happily chatted about his new band, the Healers, for a long while, and downed several pints before either of us felt it appropriate to raise the subject of the Smiths.

*   *   *

"Can we talk a bit about your old band?" I asked.

"Electronic?" he joked, referencing his very good but significantly less earth-shaking early '90s project with Bernard Sumner, the lead singer of New Order.

"No!" Miki laughed. Johnny sipped his tea and nodded happily, as if to say, *Yes, you can mention the S-word.* Clearly, like the other three, he could conduct an interview about the Smiths in his sleep. The way an old baseball hero can reflexively recount his perfect game or a pennant-winning homer. It probably wasn't his favorite thing to do, but he was game.

"What do you make of this crazy mythology that's grown up around the band since the breakup?" I asked.

His manner loosened a bit and he got into it.

"I'm astounded by it."

"Why?"

"Because I've lived a life and made records and been living for the last twelve years and I think that a lot of the people who perpetrate the legacy of the Smiths are probably people who didn't actually see us," he said, raising his voice slightly.

"Some of them were seven years old when you were around," Miki noted. "We hate them."

"It's so very sweet and everything but there are other groups out there who deserve that kind of attention, groups you can actually go out and see. I find it really, really weird. Although we were pretty good." He laughed.

"Yeah, so I hear," she quipped.

"There are reports that Morrissey is getting ready to go on tour again. What do you think of him playing Smiths songs in concert?" I said by way of introducing the subject of his old partner.

"That's fine. He co-wrote them. He wrote the words. It's not something that I'd do because I'm more into what's going on in the present in my life, really. He must have his reasons.

I haven't got a problem with it at all. It's a funny one cause there seems to be this mini industry built up around the break-up of the Smiths. The post-Smiths saga has basically taken on a life of its own and is being constantly fueled by whoever, and I wonder whose interest it's in, really."

"Have you not seen him since the band split?" I asked, wondering whether or not there had been any unpublicized meetings à la John Lennon and Paul McCartney in the mid-'70s.

"I've seen him a couple of times, yeah," Marr confirmed.

"Really?" Miki exclaimed.

"Yeah," he said casually.

"Did you get along?" I wondered.

"Yeah, of course we did. That's why we got together. I sort of felt like the relationship had been hijacked by the media and thousands of strangers and they can do with it what they like but at the time when we got back together as friends, I wanted to have some kind of resolution in private that was real. And it was very pleasant. So it was all very nice." He poured himself a fresh cup of tea and smiled amusedly at our astonished glances. Both of us spaced out at the same time, imagining the two songwriters sharing a secret pint of ale in some local dining room. Hugging when they parted and reinserting themselves conspiratorially into myth.

"So you're on good terms? Cause popular opinion is that you're not."

"Yeah," he repeated.

"Wow," Miki said.

"We got together a couple of times. It was kind of weird, though." Responding to the look of utter shock on both our faces, no doubt, he added, "Our relationship is so intense and when the band split it was kind of ugly but that's pretty much the same for every band who ever split up cause it's like a family, like a marriage. Times changing . . . you have to move on. But all the Smiths, I don't hold any weird feelings toward any of them. We all went through so much together."

"Has there ever been any talk of playing once more together?" Miki asked.

"There's been talk not among the group but there's been a couple of offers come my way. Just promoters fishing around. Silly sums of money. But I'm really not interested in it in the slightest. It seems like getting together with a bunch of friends you used to hang out with when you were fourteen. For what reason, you know? Maybe to make a lot of money but . . ."

"So are you saying it's not possible to be musically or creatively inspired by them at this point? Have you ever written a song and said, 'It would be great if Morrissey could contribute lyrics to this'?" It was the right way to approach him, I told myself. As an artist.

"No. No, I haven't. I don't mean to be disparaging at all but I'm caught up in doing what I'm doing right now."

I pressed on, protected by the angle of my approach. We would speak of creativity exclusively. When dealing with what may have been the greatest songwriting partnership since Lennon and McCartney, focusing on the art was the way to go. What other way could there be? He'd already bypassed the issue of money without so much as blowing on his tea.

"If you did, would you get him on the phone?" I asked. He took a pause.

"I don't think I'd ever write that kind of song anymore, Joe. It was a moment in time."

"Well, what if the opposite happened? What if he called you in the middle of the night and said, 'I have this song and I need your help'? Would you hear him out?" I asked. I was starting to feel proud of myself. This was the most professional unprofessional, immature, self-serving interview any-one had ever conducted.

"I doubt it," he said. Then, clearly reacting to the droop in both Miki's and my lips, maybe a faint tear in the eyes, he added, "Because I don't really have enough time to see the people in my life now that I want to see. There's quite a few friends . . . mostly musicians that I find it difficult to keep in contact with. I'd love to see them but I don't have the time so the idea of taking time away from where my life's at now to revisit something that ended twelve years ago seems a little bit absurd to me. I guess that it's different for me than it is for the outside world and sometimes it's hard for people to un-derstand that."

"Well, I think people are blinded by the hope that you'll somehow reunite." (Yeah, "people.")

"Look," he continued, "I'm still obsessed with music on a twenty-four-hour-a-day basis and everything else in my life runs concurrent or secondary to it. Therefore even though it was a band I formed, it's an old band to me . . . and old music, however great it was. I was sorely disappointed when the Velvet Underground re-formed."

"And the Sex Pistols?" Miki asked.

"Yeah, although I suspect there was more to it for the Pistols. Good luck to them but . . . I'll tell you what it is to me. When bands re-form it just smacks of show biz to me. If you want to re-form to resolve relationships, just do it in private and keep it out of the public eye. Keep it real. I'm into keep-ing it real. I'd be more interested in a reunion in private."

"So you'd reunite if it were unpublicized?" I asked, looking again at the red light, recording it all, readying a case to pre-sent at the feet of the Mozzer. He took another sip of tea.

"That would be much more interesting to me and much more real. Something I wouldn't spray all over the media or turn into a record opportunity or some kind of Vegas show biz."

He gently shooed the love-struck cat away and glanced briefly toward the door. I could tell we were starting to bug him and felt terrible. But we had to press on. We had him on tape expressing interest in a reunion . . . in private, for fuck's sake. Johnny Marr!

"You could get together in an underground bunker," I offered. He didn't laugh. He looked into my eyes. I had to look away. I pretended I was searching for the men's room or something. He turned to Miki.

"I'm really proud that we made records that still stand up and I think the reason for it is that there was one hundred percent emotion there," he offered. "It was our lives. We were living it. Our lives came out in the music and I sometimes think that people think that I'm dismissive of the Smiths and I'm not. I'm fiercely proud of it and I won't have anyone put the Smiths down, but it was so long ago."

"Do you keep in contact with Mike and Andy?" she asked, leading.

"Not intentionally." He laughed.

He excused himself and walked to the men's room. I shut off the tape.

"Did he agree?" I asked her.

"I think so," she said.

"I don't care where they play, do you?"

"No."

"I mean, I don't even care if I'm there, just to know that they did would be enough, right?"

"No."

"Right." I lit another cigarette and stared at the closed men's room door. "Miki," I whispered.

"What?"

"That's Johnny Marr in there."

"I know!"

"This is so weird."

"I love him!" she said. For once I understood. I was free of jealousy.

"I do too," I said. "He's so cool."

"We have to stay focused," she said.

"Okay," I agreed, and went to fetch a new round. I asked the bartender for another pot of tea as well and returned to the table. Marr came out of the bathroom and returned to his seat. Thanked me for the tea but didn't touch it. His body language suggested he wasn't planning on staying very long.

"So, where were we? Nineteen sixty-five," he cracked.

"We were talking about you getting back together with the Smiths and playing a show," Miki said, smiling. *Well, it was focus,* I thought.

"Oh, is that what's happening?" He laughed.

"Yeah," I joked, "you're late! Everybody else is there."

We pulled on our coats and followed him toward the exit. His body language suggested that he was perhaps a little worried that we were going to continue to trail him forever. A light rain had started to fall. He pulled the hood of his coat over his head and seemed to hide from us. I raised the subject of the Healers again. It was important for me to leave him on a happy note. He was, after all, our new best friend.

"So will you be touring when the album's done?"

"Yeah, I really miss playing live."

"And when they scream for Smiths songs? Will you kick them?" Miki joked.

"Oh, they won't. I'll have two snipers there. That's why the new band's so big."

A black taxi noticed us and stopped on the corner.

"You want to grab this?" Johnny asked politely. Or perhaps he was dropping a hint.

"Yeah," I said, wiping the rain from my brow. The last thing we wanted was to leave his presence. Like, ever. We sadly got into the cab and thanked him for the interview. Expressed eagerness to see the Healers if and when they came to the States.

"All right, Joe, Miki. Take care." He smiled.

"Thanks, Johnny." I smiled.

"Thanks, Johnny." Miki beamed.

Johnny Marr!

nineteen

we look to los angeles

Miki and I were pretty full of ourselves as we prepared to check out of the Princess and fly back to New York City with three out of four Smiths on tape expressing in their own varied ways that a gun to the head wasn't entirely necessary to conjure up a glorious reunion.

Andy wanted some well-deserved money.

Mike wanted proof that the band could again be brilliant and brotherly.

Johnny, it seemed, might do it just to see what it would sound like . . . brilliant or crap. Maybe. We decided that even his reluctant admission of curiosity was close enough, especially since it was extracted during an 11th-hour cold interview. We were confident that we had enough on tape to sway Morrissey once we got him alone in a room and played him our excerpts. After all, he'd said it himself: "There's nobody intelligent enough within the music industry to even try to get the Smiths back together."

*   *   *

Despite Bob Johnston's suspicions, we had not been feckless industry types. We were intelligent. We were succeeding! So for a time, at least, the unsavory incidents of the previous evening were tabled in favor of back patting and good cheer.

"We did it," I crowed as I downed my nerve-bracing pint of Guinness in the chilly Marble Arch pub. We'd gone there to wait out the three hours between checkout time and our departure flight.

"It's done, Mik!"

We clinked our heavy glasses and grinned at each other.

"Johnny's the hard one, man. He was the first one to fucking leave!" I reminded her.

"I know!" she marveled.

"Morrissey will be a snap. Everything will be easy from here out."

Miki and I triumphantly entered Bob Johnston's office on that first Monday morning back in New York to report our great progress. I kept my shades on throughout the meeting. Too cool for the room. His direct subordinate, Miki, had to be a bit more respectful, but she was no less self-satisfied than I was.

Amazingly, Johnston seemed lighthearted and happy to see our safe return. "Tell me something good." He leaned back regally in his swivel chair. "What do you have for me besides receipts?"

"Well, we got Andy and Johnny, man," I bragged. "On tape!"

"Really?"

"Yeah. Conditionally," I continued. "Johnny might consider playing if it was just a jam in private. In like a basement or something. Andy would do it for, um . . . a million pounds."

"We have it all on tape," Miki reiterated.

"We looked them in the eyes, man." What the hell was I saying?

And I wasn't even drunk.

"So do you think someone's going to pay Andy Rourke a million pounds to play in a basement?" Johnston asked with a mixture of impatience and amusement.

He had a point.

"Um, probably not, but you never know. We'll figure out the logistics later," I promised. "The point is, we've got three. We just need Morrissey."

"And you don't have anything set up with him, right?"

"We would have by now but he has no representation. The guy has no manager. No label. Just some miscreant named Harry," I complained.

"Who's probably eating our pasta right now," Miki said worriedly.

"Eating your what?" Now Johnston was completely impatient.

"We were thinking about just going to Los Angeles," I quickly put in.

"You want me to send you to Los Angeles with no leads? For how long?"

"We should be able to find him pretty quickly. We know where he lives."

"So you're just going to knock on Morrissey's door?" Johnston probed.

"Yeah." I shrugged. "We're just gonna knock on his door. Fans do it all the time. He's very accessible. You know, despite the fact that there's pretty much no way to contact him."

Johnston didn't seem to take too much issue with bankrolling this flimsy plan. After all, he had yet to see our Manchester room service bill.

*   *   *

how soon is never?

We left his office and returned to our desks. I can't speak for Miki but my workstation felt queer and alien. It was weird being back in the office. In the short time we'd been on the road, Miki and I had become much more than co-workers. Our time together felt more like hanging out. We were friends, intimates, confidants. But within the context of the office, we were still just fellow *Headphones* employees. I couldn't very well spend every minute by her desk. People would talk. But I'd crossed a line out there and I didn't want to go back to the way it had been. It only took 10 minutes, alone at my desk, for me to realize that every moment on the other side of the office was destined to be marked by painful longing and false decorum.

I was overjoyed when she appeared again an hour and a half later and announced that she'd booked us into a pair of bungalows at the Sunset Marquis. The lush, sprawling Marquis, long a legendary rock star haven, was rumored to be Morrissey's favorite hotel in the Los Angeles area. Surely, if we were ensconced in a bungalow, which is essentially a small apartment (although much larger than either of our own), Morrissey would know that we really weren't just a couple of kooks, right? All we had to do in return was agree to mention the establishment in our piece. A small bit of corruption but what the fuck. It beat the Hyatt on Sunset, where I'd previously stayed when on assignment in L.A. Miki could really hustle when she wanted to.

I was deflated almost immediately, however, when she told me that it was four full days until we were scheduled to depart. It seemed entirely too long a wait to resume what we'd started building outside these confines. I watched her return to her desk again with a sadness I was sure would consume and possibly kill me inside of one day, forget four. I was deprived of the giddiness all New Yorkers feel when they return home from traveling. I could only feel shortness of breath and more dread.

Since Miki didn't invite me to come home with her or even stay out with her during those few times I saw her at the office, I spent the next three nights drinking alone and resisting the urge to call her and beg for help. When you know there's something better out there that's beyond your reach, one lonely stint at a bar can really start the self-pity machine madly rolling. Soon, I couldn't even remember Manchester. I tried to imagine how she related everything to Floyd, then felt angry that he was more privy to our experiences than I was. My memories were clouded by whiskey and heartache. Whatever he experienced vicariously through his girlfriend was fresh and nourishing. I was jealous of him. I resented her for what I considered abandonment. I hated myself for being the kind of person someone can abandon. And, worst of all, I couldn't listen to the Smiths without feeling sad in all the wrong ways. Whenever a track off *The Queen Is Dead* came on over the Library's speakers, I'd flinch and gulp my drink hard. If two came on in a row, I'd leave for another bar, or just head home to mark off another day on my wall calendar, then crawl into bed and repeat her name in a way that made me wonder if I was some kind of psycho. Withdrawing from heroin wasn't so cruel by comparison. It got so bad, I called the only person I knew who had survived a painful separation and remained sort of sane.

"Who are you going to see?" It was late and Sid was groggy.

"Morrissey, Dad. Morrissey."

"Van Morrison?"

"No, Morrissey. From the Smiths?"

"That band?"

"Yeah, that band."

"You still listen to them?" he marveled in a voice that probably wouldn't have changed if he were investigating why I still wet the bed or played with dolls.

"Yeah, I still listen to them. But it's work. I'm on assignment for *Headphones*."

"Oh, that reminds me. I was gonna call you. Listen. This is very important. Are you listening?"

"Yeah."

"I need you to send me the one with Eminems on the cover. You got that one?"

"Eminem."

"Whatever. Just send it."

"You like Eminem?"

"I don't even know who the fuck that is. But this girl in my building is nuts about him. I told her you're friends with him. She does her laundry in these tight little shorts, man."

"I don't know Eminem. I didn't even write that piece, Dad."

"Just send it and I'll wire you some money."

"I don't need money," I shouted. Then thought twice. "All right, send me the money. But I'm actually calling cause I need some advice."

"Oh yeah?"

Sid seemed pleased. It had been a long time since I'd turned to him for anything other than money for drugs, much less guidance.

"What do you do when you're with someone, like a girl, right? And when you start out, it's cool cause you both want the same thing. And then something happens and what you want isn't the same as what she wants anymore."

"That happens."

"Do you tell her?"

"Yeah."

"But what if you know that when you tell her, she's probably not gonna want to be with you at all? Do you risk it or do you pretend nothing's changed?"

"You tell her the truth," he said without hesitation. "Honesty is the best policy. It's not my policy but it's the best policy."

"But I can't be without this girl, Dad. I'll fucking die. I swear I'll fucking die."

"Listen to you. You're a grown man now. You're twenty-eight years old!"

"I'm thirty, Dad."

"I don't care. You know what you sound like? You sound like a fucking teenager."

"I feel like a teenager. That's the problem, man. I don't wanna be one anymore. I did but . . . everything's different now."

"You gotta tell her the truth. Sometimes in life, you gotta take a gamble, boy."

I lit another smoke and watched its trail float across my empty, dark, cold apartment. The place felt like an 8-by-10 prison cell. A box. I worried that this was where I would spend some kind of life sentence if Miki rejected me.

"Hey?" Sid said. "Are you still there?"

"Yeah. Sorry."

"You know why they call it gambling, son?"

"Why, Dad?"

Sid paused, as though he'd been waiting his entire life for a chance to be profound.

"Cause it's a gamble."

The Sunset Marquis had set aside two gorgeous bungalows for us. They were essentially mini one-story houses off to the side of the main grounds. I helped Miki into her room and we both gasped. We weren't accustomed to such luxuries when on assignment. Sunken Jacuzzi, big-screen TV, full media center with fax machine and computer. Huge bedroom. Couch. Kitchen . . . not a kitchenette but a full kitchen. It was insane. I'd dated rich girls who had inferior pads off Gramercy Park. And the whole place stank of fresh flowers. Sure enough, my bungalow was just as crazy.

"We can never leave," I said, setting my bag down on the floor and feeling instantly ragged and poor. "We have to find out a way to stay here forever."

"I know," she agreed. "I'm going to get cleaned up and take a quick nap. We should meet in a few hours and go find Morrissey."

She said it in a way that made it seem easy, despite the fact that we had no appointment and were searching cold in a city of millions. Like, *Let me freshen up and then we'll go win the lottery.* She was so high on the improbability of our luxurious surroundings that she probably believed anything could happen. I said a weak, forlorn goodbye as she left to settle into her own bungalow, then walked into the toilet to run a bath. As I sank into the hot water, I felt the urge to wank but I was sick of jerking off. Sick of doing anything alone. I got out of the soak and wrapped my pruney body in a plush Sunset Marquis robe. Sat down in front of the big-screen TV and flipped around the channels, looking for porn or music videos or any kind of temporary distraction. I pulled on my pants, found my last clean pair of socks, lit a cigarette, and rang Miki's room. Got no answer. I paced for a while then pulled on my dirty T-shirt and boots, grabbed my leather jacket, and decided to check out the hotel's bar. It was cocktail hour and the sun had started setting, not that I ever really needed an excuse to hit a bar. I ordered a double Jack Daniel's, charged it to the room, and sat down beneath a framed portrait of Keith Richards (I had my pick of iconic black-and-white photos of rock stars, as they were hung on every free inch of wall space). The place was full of a scattering of goofball tourists so I felt pretty rock 'n' roll by comparison. Jane's Addiction's *Ritual de lo Habitual* was playing on the bar stereo as I knocked back the booze. That particular album will always remind me of getting incredibly high on smack. It was one of our Bennington smack sound-track records, the *Sergeant Pepper* of modern junkie albums.

I was too caught up in bad memories of copping and puk-ing and copping again to notice the really hot blonde checking me out. She didn't even look old enough to drink but she was the kind of striking southern California rock-'n'-roll type they let into places like this because people with money come to places like this looking for them. Twenty-five years ago, her type would have had a beach tan but in the post-post-post-rock era New York City cool had long informed Los Angeles, and she had evolved (or devolved) appropriately. She was wearing a black sleeveless dress and heels. No stockings. Pale. She sat down at my table without asking, which striking blond southern California rock-'n'-roll-type young girls are also per-mitted to do out there. Or anywhere.

"Hi," she said. I could tell she was a little fucked up on something.

"Hello."

"Are you in a band?"

"Yes. I am in a band."

"I knew it. You're in that band, right? The one that's stay-ing here? What are you called again?"

"We're called Joy Division," I answered. It was the first band that came into my head. And yeah, it was a test. If she knew who they were, I was out of luck. If not, this little girl was fair game.

"Right." She retched slightly, then batted her eyes to erase that memory from my mind. It worked.

"I'm the lead singer. Ian Curtis."

"Right! I love you guys."

"Thanks. That means a lot, cause, you know, we do it all for the fans. Are you staying at the hotel?" I asked.

"No, are you?"

Well, no, because I hung myself in 1980, I thought. Instead, I muttered, "Yeah. We leave tomorrow for . . . Cleveland, but I've got a bungalow out back."

"Wow."

"You want a drink? What are you drinking?"

"White wine."

I walked up to the bar and ordered a white wine. *There's no way this girl is that fucked up on white wine,* I thought. I walked back and pulled down my sunglasses. Checked out her pupils.

"Whatever you're on, do you have any more of it?" I asked.

She sipped her drink and nodded.

"Why don't we go back to my bungalow and get fucked up?" I suggested, embracing the Sunset Strip sleaziness of the whole thing. "I'll play you our new song."

"Okay, Ian." She smiled. I was waiting for her to say something like, *But my three girlfriends have to come and we like to get it on first before we have any cock.* That's how weird and improbable it was, but no more or less improbable than me inviting her back to a fucking *bungalow* in the first place if you think about it.

"What's your name?" I asked as I led her through the garden toward my temporary lodging.

"Cherry." She hiccuped.

"What's your real name?"

"Cherry. I love your apartment," she said absently as I gave her the tour. "I mean, your bungalow."

"Thanks. The record company takes pretty good care of us when it comes to shit like this cause they know we're very big in Japan."

"Where's the rest of the band?"

Again, if Miki had ever expressed any interest in being my girlfriend, I might have confessed, *Well, Cherry, we've been broken up for nineteen years. They're called New Order now.* Instead, I blurted out, "Sound check."

"So we're all alone, Ian?"

"Yeah."

"Is the door locked?"

"Yeah," I answered.

"Are you sure? Check it again."

I checked the door and confirmed that it was indeed locked. Cherry sat down on the couch, reached into her purse, pulled out a bag, and dumped out a sand-castle-sized mound of coke on the jewel box of my *Meat Is Murder* CD. Cut out an earthworm-like line and horked it up her button nose. Looked around the room, confused.

"Let's fuck," she said. "For old times' sake."

"But we just met, Cherry. How can we fuck for old times' sake?" I protested as I sat down next to her and did an equally ridiculous amount of drugs in one snort.

"Never mind," I said as I came up for air.

We took off our clothes and got into bed and we started having sex. But both of us were way too high. Cherry's body was ridiculous. The kind of shit you see on late-night cable. It seemed airbrushed. I was touching her thighs and her ass and her tits but I couldn't really feel any of them. Cherry was about as physically perfect and willing as it gets, but even though an hour before my only other option had been jacking off in the tub, I didn't want her.

She wasn't Miki.

I felt sick. It was probably the coke and the shock of abrupt sex with a stranger but I needed to rise and steady myself, as I literally and figuratively felt spineless. I hated myself for being unable to fully commit to one shade or another. Light or dark. Love or lust. Life or death. It was too complicated and with the gun-to-the-head rush of a wallop of coke, it was terrifying. I couldn't pursue Miki and our dream of reuniting the Smiths with a clean conscience anymore. There was no purity in my search for purity. But I couldn't tell her why for fear of losing her as a constant companion and winding up with nothing. To use a crude analogy, I was convinced that I had to straddle purgatory because admitting to myself that there was no heaven to be found even in a glorious Smiths reunion would relegate me forever to some hipster hell full of booze and coke and writing about bad bands and fucking little girls who've never heard of Joy Division. To use an art school analogy (and I did take one sculpture class at Bennington . . . I think), it was symbolized right there on the fucking fancy table. A perfect Smiths CD larded with really good pink West Coast cocaine. To use no analogies at all and just be truthful, lying to myself about Miki and me going back to teenage heaven was preferable than remaining where I was. Or doing another line. But I needed another line.

" 'I was happy in the haze of a drunken hour, but heaven knows I'm miserable now.' " I sang a Smiths refrain as Cherry pumped up and down on my useless Ian Curtis dead dick.

"Mmmm, Ian," she moaned. "Sing me a song."

I grabbed her waist gently and pulled her off me. Got up and lit a cigarette.

"I'm sorry, Cherry. I can't do this."

"Why not?"

"I feel dirty."

I walked over to the living room. Did another line. She padded after me, naked, sweating, and twitchy. Refueled herself too.

"How about I just suck your cock?"

I considered it for a bit.

"All right."

We walked over to the bed and Cherry blew me.

"I wanna suck your cock," she said between inhales.

"You *are* sucking my cock."

I finished my smoke and stared out at the swimming pool through the crack in the drapes.

I have thirty-nine dollars in my checking account and I'm being blown by a shit-hot blonde in a thousand-dollar-a-night bungalow. And I can't feel anything, I worried. *Purgatory.*

There was a knock at the door.

"Shit." Cherry spat me out and wrapped the bedsheet around her. "Don't open it."

"It's okay," I calmed her, and stared through the peephole. "I know her. She's cool. She's not a cop. She's a rock journalist. But put that shit away."

Cherry squirreled the CD and the bag away in one of the kitchen cabinets.

"Is it your girlfriend?" she asked.

"No," I answered sadly.

I pulled on my pants. Cherry yanked on her dress. Finally I opened the door and Miki walked in. She had purple hair.

"Hey, Mik," I said, using my left hand to light the cigarette clenched in my teeth while I held a burning cigarette in my right.

"Your hair is purple," Cherry said by way of a friendly opening line.

"Mik, this is Cherry."

Miki and Cherry shook icy hands and traded equally chilly looks.

"We have work to do, Joe," Miki reminded me sternly.

"Why is she calling you Joe, Ian?" Cherry inquired. I looked at her, then back at Miki, who was also curious to hear my explanation.

"I should go," Cherry suggested.

"Yeah, that's probably not a bad idea, Cherry," I agreed. She waited awkwardly. For a minute I couldn't figure out why the hell she was lingering there.

"I need my stuff, Ian."

how soon is never?

"Oh, right." I stared at Miki just to confirm that I was already in the shitter. I could have sworn I saw her nod in affirmation. I walked to the cabinet and handed Cherry the CD.

"Thanks for everything," I said politely.

"You can have what's on the thingy," she said, and placed the jewel box on the table. Pocketed the bag. Kissed my cheek and headed for the door.

"It was nice meeting you," she told Miki. Miki didn't acknowledge her.

"Okay. I'm ready," I assured her. "Let's find Morrissey."

"Are you?" she asked skeptically.

"Yes, please. Let's do it. Come on!"

I tried to muster whatever enthusiasm I could. I didn't want Miki to know that really, I couldn't give a shit. I just wanted her there, with her purple hair. I didn't want her to leave me alone and high.

"Yeah. Totally. Let's— Let's go find the motherfucker," I stuttered.

She walked over to the table, picked up the CD, and sneered with disgust.

"*Meat Is Murder?*"

I shrugged. She was offended.

"Nice, Joe," she said. "Where are the car keys? You're not driving."

Miki and I walked down Alta Loma to the lobby. She didn't say a word as the valet brought the car around . . . as we drove to Beverly Hills. I just stared out the window like a dog and tried not to shake. I couldn't look her in the eye.

"Your hair looks nice," I said. "Really, really nice. Where'd you get the dye? Did you, um . . . buy it?"

"You know, this is not the way to get me to like you, Joe," she finally said. "You should never, never do cocaine."

334

"Wait, is it okay for me to try to get you to like me? I mean, you just said . . ."

I could barely think, but it occurred to me that she was revealing something. I couldn't see it for the Bowie-in-'76-style snowstorm in my brain, but in her anger, I was convinced, she'd let something show.

"You look blue, Joe," Miki said as we drove toward Morrissey's house, not knowing exactly what we'd do when we got there, but again, just going . . . to go. "You should eat something."

"I'm not hungry."

"If you don't eat something, you're gonna die."

"What do you care?"

"If you die, we won't reunite the Smiths," she said callously. I held back. Probably because I could barely form words. We stopped at Jerry's Famous Deli, where I came down to earth over a grilled cheese sandwich and a milkshake. We sat wordlessly for a while, Miki staring at me in disgust and occasionally picking at my fries, dragging them through the ketchup and placing them between her beautiful lips. I stared at her.

"Eat!" she demanded.

The force-feeding worked. I ordered a Bloody Mary from the bar, which worked better. Soon, I was able to speak and think with a shred of lucidity.

"Do you think there's heavy security?"

"Those neighborhoods have their own police force," she claimed. "Which is why you probably shouldn't be seen there twitching like that."

I guiltily sipped my vodka and tomato juice, telling myself the vitamins from the vegetables would restore my health and sanity momentarily. The power of positive drinking, as Lou Reed used to sing.

"I'm sorry, Miki. I got lonely. I missed you," I explained.

"I was only gone a few hours," she said. "Keep an eye out for it!" We were driving through the towering palm-lined streets of L.A. with a star map on the dash (Carole Lombard's house circled in red pen), trying to find Morrissey's abode and making up . . . sort of.

"I know, but I got sad because—"

"I was barely gone and you're doing coke and fucking some I don't know what. Girl!" she shouted. Miki was pissed. "Why was she calling you Ian? And why the fuck can't I leave you alone for a few hours without you freaking out about it? Huh?"

"I'm gonna shut up now, okay?" I said, hoping she'd know that I knew I was being needy. That, coke-poisoned as I was, I carefully censored myself before finishing my thought. That I didn't want to admit that I was dangerously attached to her. That when she wasn't around I'd numb myself any way I could. That yeah, even though I'd probably numb myself any-way, at least now I knew what I was doing it for. Now I knew what I was missing. That everything else I thought I wanted, everything I felt—even when I felt high—was forever compro-mised. That I wanted to be inside her anywhere, her ear, her mouth, because outside her was no longer close enough.

"I feel like a fucking stalker," I complained as the rental car idled outside Morrissey's house. "But you know, I'm not a stalker. I'd never stalk anyone."

Miki and I weren't exactly sure what to do as we stared at the huge white house with its rounded towers, Mexican tiled roof, and large blue double garage doors. We could make out an iron gate at the top of the steep staircase that led to his front door. Everything else, the windows, the yard, was ob-scured by trees.

"This is how his fans meet him," she said. "I've heard stories. Sometimes they wait for hours and he'll just drive up and get out and they'll say, 'Hi, Steven,' and he'll just say hello. And sign autographs. I mean, he doesn't invite them in for tea and biscuits, but he's supposedly very friendly."

"We should have bought coffee and donuts," I suggested mockingly.

"For Morrissey?" she wondered.

"No, for us. Then at least we could pretend we were cops." I sneered. My coke high was wearing off and in its place a poison headache was creeping in. We sat there for an hour, barely speaking. Occasionally a car would pass. Neighbors, probably. Used to seeing goofy fans parked outside this particular location.

"Why don't we just ring the bell?" I asked.

"You're gonna ring the bell?" she challenged.

"No," I admitted. I wasn't nearly drunk enough to do that. Without booze I was pretty much a coward. Miki would have to hold my hand to get me anywhere near that bell. Not in the dark anyway.

"Let's ring the bell, Joe," she finally said.

"Are you sure?" I asked.

"Yeah." She unlocked the door and got out. I followed. She wasn't holding my hand or anything but she was leading the charge and that was good enough. I got out and followed her toward the stairs. Step by step we climbed them like a couple of senior citizens. Deliberate. Terrified. Purple-haired Dorothy and the strung-out Scarecrow at the door of the Great and Powerful Moz. There was a buzzer on the side of the tall metal gate. A small black button. It might as well have been the doomsday device or something. Neither of us knew the ramifications of pressing the thing. I looked at her. She looked back at me. And both of us looked at the panic button. A bird flapped suddenly in the tree overhead and we both nearly pissed ourselves.

"We're just here to say hello because we're in town . . . and you'd . . ." she started.

"We'd really appreciate it if he agreed to reunite his old band," I finished. She laughed. The tension eased slightly. Then, without tipping me off, she hit the buzzer.

"Damn," I whispered. She turned to me and smiled mischievously. It seemed like we were friends again. The hours-old rift dissolved in a wash of adrenaline and frustration.

Nothing happened. We stood there for another five minutes, waiting. Silent. Then it was my turn. I pushed my finger into the button a bit longer. Then again. Then again. Three sustained buzzes.

"Do you think he's in there and he's not coming out cause he sees us?" I asked.

She didn't answer me directly.

"Hello? Is anyone in there? We're not, um . . . we're sorry to bother you," she called. "We're not crazed fans."

Yes, we were. Crazed people anyway. I didn't correct her.

"We're journalists."

"I think he'd prefer crazed fans," I whispered.

She hit the button again, then sat down on the step and asked for a cigarette. I'd left my pack in the car and offered to go fetch them.

"Don't leave me here," she pleaded with a nervous laugh. She followed me down to the rental car and we lit up a couple of smokes, then walked back to the gate together, puffing away. Staring up at the tower's window, imagining a reclusive pop star inside, watching us through a slit in his blinds. Wishing we'd go away. It made me wonder what the hell we were. We couldn't be real journalists cause we had no objectivity. We couldn't be pure fans because for better or worse, we had actual credentials. We were in limbo.

"We have to figure out what the hell we're doing, Mik," I said. "We have to get serious. This isn't working because we never decided like . . . who we are."

"What do you mean?"

"I mean, do you know who you are?" I asked.

"Are you still high?" she wondered.

"No. I mean, yeah. But I'm thinking clearly. I mean, I think I'm thinking clearly. This isn't the way to do this. We're either reporters or we're not. We either have dignity or we don't," I raved.

"Reporters pick through people's garbage, Joe," she pointed out.

"Do you think we should pick through his garbage?" I asked.

"To find what?" she countered.

"I don't know. Maybe something to bribe him into agreeing to a reunion. Dirty pictures. Or . . . I don't know. Meat."

She laughed. "Meat!" she shouted.

"If we found meat in Morrissey's garbage, that would ruin his career," I pointed out.

"Look, Mozzer, we know what you're up to, we found the meat," she exclaimed, imitating some cartoon gangster.

"Now here are our demands," I added, easily adopting the same tone.

"And our suggested set list."

We were riffing yet again. Loose. Friendly. We'd just about forgotten that we were still sitting on Morrissey's walkway stairs, now under the cover of the early autumn darkness. The moon was hanging brightly over us and our trespassing.

"Is there anything you haven't done that you wish you'd done by now? By thirty?" I asked.

"What do you mean?" she wondered.

"Well, we haven't met Morrissey. Like that. Like I haven't read the Bible. I've never . . . eaten Spam," I offered.

how soon is never?

"You've never read the Bible?" she asked.

"Or eaten Spam," I repeated.

"I've eaten Spam. And read the Bible," she said.

"How's the Bible?" I wondered aloud.

"It's all right," she answered, and grabbed another cigarette.

"And Spam?"

"Salty," she replied. "Do you not eat Spam cause you're kosher or something?" she asked. It never occurred to me that the differences in our ethnicity and religion were an issue. Growing up in a neighborhood full of Jewish people, I assumed that everyone in the world was a Jew. Then, after Bennington, I was so comfortable around all manner of cultural and sexual and ethnic diversity, I just assumed everybody else was too. But maybe Miki wasn't.

"Floyd's not Jewish?" I joked.

She shook her head.

"What's up with you and him, anyway?" I asked. She stared at me blankly. "Look, I know it's none of my business but you never talk about him. You're hardly ever with him, at least not when I'm around. You don't live together. He doesn't seem to mind that you're running all over the world with me. I don't even know if he even likes the Smiths."

"He likes the Smiths," she volunteered. Nothing else.

"I'm curious about him, that's all. I wanna know what kind of guy he is," I pushed.

"Why?" she asked, irritated.

"Because I'm curious what kind of guy you go for cause it's obviously not the kind of guy that I am," I hinted. "Is it because I'm a Jew?"

"No," she replied immediately.

"Cause I'm only half Jewish." I was completely Jewish, obviously.

"Which half?" she asked.

"Whichever half you want," I quipped. "The good half if you're into it. The bum half if you're not. Just tell me what to do, Mik. What do I do? How do I get you? There's got to be something." I inhaled deeply on my smoke and in an effort to purge my headache and my heartache, I began singing loudly: "Please, please tell me now! Is there something I should know?"

"He's not gonna come out if you keep singing Duran Duran." She laughed. I laughed. Then without forewarning, without even any internal starting gun or signal for my own benefit, I leaned in and tried to kiss her again. Right there on Morrissey's stoop. She pulled away and I ended up kissing the air. She stared at me. I unpuckered.

"Joe, what are you doing?" she asked.

"Nothing."

"You have that girl's lipstick on your neck, Joe," she said. "Cherry."

I jerked my arm to rub it away a bit too quickly.

"We should go," she said. "He's not coming. We can try the Cat and the Fiddle bar later. I hear he shows up there sometimes." She got up quickly. Walked to the car. I sat there for a minute, hating myself. Hating her. Hating myself again for watching her ass as she left. Wondering if anything would be different if I weren't so impatient and addicted and spoiled. If I were clean and charming and Irish. If I were anything at all but what I am. I wondered if I'd ever know. Or if I'd already blown it. Or if I'd ever see her naked. Was there any point in trying to change? What if I did and she still wasn't ever going to be mine? Would I be able to get back to who I was before? And what the fuck is the deal with Floyd? Maybe he found dirty photos or meat in her garbage. Or maybe she loved him. Maybe it was that simple. She loved Floyd and she didn't love me. All these thoughts flew around my aching head until one thought chased them away and made me jump: I was alone on Morrissey's property. I hurried toward the car but didn't get in.

"Come on, Joe. What are you waiting for?"

"It's over," I said. "I don't want to do this anymore."

"Joe, we can't give up," she insisted. "We're so close."

"No. We're not."

"How can you say that?" she said. "How can you be so negative?"

"I can't do this anymore, Miki. I can't!" I finally shouted.

"Why not?" she yelled back.

"Because I don't want it anymore."

"What?" She was truly shocked. "How can you say that?"

"I'll tell you how."

"Yeah, why don't you tell me how you can say that after all we've done?"

I swallowed hard.

"Because there's no point. Even if we did get Morrissey, even if they did reunite, nothing in my life is going to change. I thought it would, but I realize now it won't. I have to accept the way things are. That's all. They've fucking accepted it."

"Who?"

"The Smiths."

"No, they haven't!"

"Yes, they have, Mik. They have. And if they haven't already, they will someday, but not if we keep trying to prevent it."

"Morrissey said—"

"I don't care about Morrissey! I don't care about the Smiths anymore!" I turned back to Morrissey's house and stomped my foot and shouted, "I don't care about you!"

I turned around and stared at her. I could see her hands shaking as she gripped the steering wheel.

"I love you, Miki."

"I know. I'm trying to deal with—"

I stopped her.

"No, listen. I'm in love with you. All I want in the world anymore is to be with you. To spend my life with you. That's my dream. I know that now. So what happens if we reunite the Smiths and we can pretend without shame that we're sixteen again? Would anything really change? No. Because everything should be perfect then and I know it wouldn't be. It would never be. I'd still want to fucking die because the dream of being with you is so much stronger, so much more beautiful to me than anything else I've ever felt. I don't even wanna be sixteen anymore! I wanna be thirty . . . with you. And if I can't do that, I've decided that I want to deal with a realistic, depressing, complicated, fucked-up world on my own. Cause that makes sense. Me getting old and being lonely, it makes sense because I won't have you. At least it makes sense. I'm grateful it makes sense. I wasn't before all this. I fought against it and I was unhappy and ashamed, but if I can't be with you . . . then at least I'll understand why I'm miserable."

I lit a cigarette and stared at her. "I couldn't even enjoy a Smiths reunion, Miki. I can't even enjoy the songs anymore. It used to remind me too much of the band breaking up. Now it reminds me too much of you. There's too much pain there! Those songs . . . they're fucking ruined! And that's why the Smiths don't reunite! That's why they can't reunite! That's why they shouldn't fucking reunite! That's why we can't *fucking unite*! There's too much pain here now."

"So that's it?" she said. She looked teary as well.

"This is a good thing. It's kind of the first mature decision I've ever made, actually. I'm lost and sick and old and sad and I totally accept it!"

"Accepting hopelessness is a good thing?"

"It's a real thing, Mik. Anyway, it's the only way things are ever going to change."

how soon is never?

I stubbed out my smoke and quickly lit another.

"I can't believe that after all this, you're giving up." She started the car. "You're such an asshole."

"I'm not giving up," I said. "I'm growing up."

She drove away and left me alone in the dark. Thirty years old. Standing in front of Morrissey's house. I was pissed off and a little scared. The Smiths were never going to reunite. I was never going to kiss her again. And I was never going to find my way back to the Sunset Marquis. But for the first time since I'd met her, I didn't feel pain when Miki left me behind.

i will share you

Okay, I know it sounds like a pretty good ending but I have to admit, I didn't say that last bit about growing up aloud. It didn't come to me quickly enough. It actually came to me as I tried to make my way back to Sunset Boulevard on foot (you know, since the Mozzer wasn't home to let me use his phone to call a cab or anything). I had a lot more time to think, walking in L.A. I just like to tell myself that those were my last words to her before she drove away. It didn't matter if she heard them or not. I finally believed it. The only thing I wanted in the world was gone. Really gone, as I soon discovered. As in back to New York City on the red-eye. Without me. As I sank into that big bed, which still smelled like Cherry and coke and sweat, I fell into the easy sleep enjoyed by those free souls who no longer have anything to lose. Nothing they cared about, anyway.

But that was a lie too.

Miki quit *Headphones* over a year ago. I went to her going-away party out of respect but we hadn't said a lot to each other after L.A. We'd already said too much, I guess. Gotten too close too quickly. I never wanted to look at her and think that she was a stranger so I just pretended she wasn't there. It wasn't ideal but it seemed like the right thing to do at the time. When she split, it just made feeling nothing easier.

I hadn't listened to the Smiths at all since that last day in front of Morrissey's house. I wasn't back on some Guns N' Roses kick but I had definitely shelved my beloved albums in favor of random and innocuous background noise. But one night, a couple of months ago, Tom and Gregory dragged me to Don Hill's again. I didn't know it before agreeing to go out but the Salford Lads, a Smiths tribute band, happened to be on the bill that night. The quiffed-up quintet had been playing around New York for about a year, and I'd always wondered what they were like. They opened their set with a swell version of the single "Ask." That's to say, I recognized it quickly but soon realized I wasn't going to feel any of the old shivers. The lead singer, despite his hairstyle (blond), looked no more like Morrissey than I did back in high school. I excused myself to go to the bathroom, intent on sneaking out the side door and fleeing before they finished their set, but as I pushed through the crowd, I noticed that Miki was there too. She looked happier, younger, and looser than I'd remembered. So much so that I immediately wondered whether or not she still frowned in her sleep. She saw me too. For a second, I worried that things would be awkward, or worse, confrontational. We'd left so much hanging there in L.A. But when she wordlessly got up and walked over to my side, I felt a warmth between us that had been missing since those early days out on the fire escape. She stayed there for a good minute or two, still without saying anything. Just tilting her head toward my chest. I didn't speak either. I believe we read each other's minds again that night. She knew what I was thinking. I knew what she was thinking.

It was the same thought . . . *This is what it would have been like if we'd succeeded. A Salford Lads show.*

She wrote down her new number on a piece of paper and pressed it into my hand. Then she went back to join her punk rock friends and I walked into the street. As I heard the Lads' rendition of "How Soon Is Now" echo down Spring Street, muted by the metal club walls, I imagined that they were actually the reunited Smiths. I pictured Johnny, Mike, Andy, and Morrissey up there, trying to pretend they were still young. Faking it as they struggled through the classic. Morrissey had a hairpiece. Johnny played the chugging drone with his walking cane. Mike had an oxygen mask. Andy pretty much looked the same. They'd save nobody. I walked down Hudson Street toward my apartment as it started to rain. I took out the scrap of paper that Miki had written her number on and thought about throwing it away. The raindrops dripped on her inked phone number and it started to run. I carefully folded it and put it back in my pocket. The city felt beautiful and clean and full of possibility. I decided I would call her one day. When I let myself into my apartment, I dug through my record collection and pulled out *Hatful of Hollow* and cued up the same song the Lads had just covered. I sat down on the edge of my bed and lit a cigarette and listened. I don't know if it was the rain or Miki's smile after so long or the fact that it wasn't the Salford Lads but I heard it like I'd heard it for the first time almost 20 years earlier. And it didn't make me hurt for losing her. It didn't even make me hurt for Morrissey losing Johnny. It just made me happy. This music was hardly ruined. It was and always will be perfect. And I realized as I fell asleep that as long as I can still hear that, I would never be truly lost.

If it hasn't already, this will happen to your generation too.

On March 3, 2004, Marc Spitz interviewed Morrissey for a *Spin* magazine cover story at the Beverly Hills Hotel in Los Angeles. They discussed Morrissey's latest album, *You Are the Quarry,* the current state of pop music, the Smiths, and *How Soon Is Never?* The full text of that interview is included here.

MARC SPITZ: If you could just say anything . . .

MORRISSEY: I will speak in this tone permanently.

MS: I've met many of my heroes . . . but this is, uh, you know, you must be, uh . . .

M: Well, I have. I don't continue to, but I have. I've been in certain situations where I've found it quite difficult to speak. But let's not dwell on that [*laughs*].

MS: Do you have any advice?

M: There's actually no advice apart from dunk your head in the pool and hope for the best.

MS: I'm going to refer to these notes, but I hope this will be more of a conversation . . . Forgive me if this seems a little stilted in the beginning.

M: Absolutely fine.

MS: First of all, I should say off the bat that I've only listened to the record [*You Are the Quarry*] twice, but I think it's a very, very solid Morrissey album. It's a great record, the songs are very strong, and I enjoyed listening to it.

M: But if the songs were very weak, would you say, "The songs are very weak"?

MS: Would I lie to you, you mean?

M: Yeah.

MS: Uh, no.

M: I think you would.

MS: You think I would?

M: [*Laughs*] Yes . . . yes.

MS: No, I mean, OK. I should just get into it. I mean, I'm obviously a huge fan. I mean, if it was an atrocious record, I probably would've told you.

M [*Whispering*]: Yes!

MS: I think it's a great record.

M: Mm-hmm.

MS: It's a long time in coming.

M: Mm-hmm.

MS: And I was very—it was great. But so upon the few listens I detected a recurring theme and maybe I'm wrong but there is a theme on the album of strength of survivors' resilience and I don't know if that's accurate or . . .

M: I think it's inevitable at this stage, really. It's inevitable that I feel that way. It is practically twenty years, twenty-one years on. Which is alarming and surprising to me more so than anybody else.

MS: Yeah. So you feel like a survivor?

M: Well, yes.

MS: You've weathered a lot.

M: I have, yes. I mean, so many slings and arrows that, um . . . and I still appear to be here.

MS: A lot of your heroes, whether it's James Dean—and correct me if calling them your heroes is inaccurate . . .

M: It's inaccurate. [*Laughs*] It is.

MS: "A lot of the people who used to mean something to you, or might still mean something to you"—is that accurate?

M: Well, James Dean really isn't in that category.

MS: Marc Bolan or the Dolls—

M: Well, yes, they—

MS: —all seem to be symbols of self-destruction.

M: Yes. Yes.

MS: And I'm wondering, since you're still here, you're still vital, you're still making music, you've not perished, if you lived vicariously through them?

M: Well, I, I, I was never a reckless or exciting person. I never

had an exciting private life. So that's perhaps why I've survived whereas the people you've mentioned haven't. They
lived to some degree of excess. I never have. So that's why
I'm in reasonably good shape these days.

MS: It's amazing—you might be the only one in rock and roll
who hasn't. You know what I mean? I mean, even I have.

M: Well, most people do if they get the chance. They just
throw themselves over the edge and they're happy to do it.

MS: It's just not in your nature?

M: No, I'm far, far too dull to join in the fray.

MS: Right. Is there something about them that appeals to you
because you are, so self-described, "dull"?

M: No. Not really, I mean. There's not really a happy ending
for anyone, I don't think, in music. Everybody eventually
self-destructs somehow. Or it appears that they do. And
every life ends. And it's usually with a terrible scream.

MS: [*Laughs*] Or a sigh.

M: Or a sigh. Yes, yes.

MS: Well, but your music, I think, will probably outlive you
and me and further generations, and it's definitely survived
thus far very, very well. I made a point in my notes that if
you listen to something from the same year, whether it's
a-ha or Adam Ant, it sounds almost kitsch, whereas the
Smiths music doesn't. To what do you attribute that? Is it
because you were never a fashion band?

M: I think it's several things, but above all, I think, it was and
is the tone of realism, which is hardly ever engaged in pop
music. When people begin to make music they always
adopt some kind of persona that's actually quite alien to
them. Whether it's in order to become "rock and roll," or
whether it's to become entertaining. Or it's to become a
performer. And I've never remotely felt like a performer.
I've always simply felt as if I was just secretly me.

MS: There's no shift at all?

M: No shift.

MS: Not when you take the stage?

M: If only there was, I'd be a happier person than I am today. There's absolutely no shift at all.

MS: Because with someone like Freddie Mercury or David Bowie they go through the door and a different persona comes out the other end.

M: Well, it's pure show business. It's absolute show business. And David is, David's showy. Um. Never could personally. You know.

MS: Do you think that that is why, in the interim between your records an entirely new generation—which is ten years removed from my generation, and I think you're ten years older than I am—has embraced your solo stuff and the Smiths stuff? What do you think it is that speaks to them?

M: Well, it's something I've noticed, but it's fascinating because year after year it seems to absolutely catch the fourteen-year-olds. And capture their imaginations somehow.

MS: It's a rite of passage almost.

M: Yes, yes, it is.

MS: Like zits.

M: Well, in your case perhaps but not mine. But it's, it's, it's fascinating. It's fascinating. And I think it really is just that obviously, within the Smiths, as I was often told, I represented the voice of teenage angst. And then the word "alienation" was thrown at me all the time. And I think for all teenagers that's a reality. And they do feel estranged from life. And they want to. And if they can't help it, then they willfully feel that way. And I don't honestly think my position has changed that much really. I still feel beyond the gates.

MS: You still have some sort of empathy for them?

M [*Whispering*]: Yes. Oh, yes.

MS: That's why then, maybe, they instinctively appreciate that or maybe pick that up.

M: Well, I think it's also a time in your life when you gravitate toward realism, and there's often a somewhat dark realism. Because you want truth. And you want people to stop talking to you as if you were a child. And you want people to give it to you straight. And I think my singing voice has always sounded like a real voice. It's never sounded like something that's been heavily treated and I don't sound like a person who's terribly happy.

MS: [*Laughs*]

M: God knows how that started, given my natural exuberance.

MS: It's almost a phenomenon. Because the fans not only embrace the music, many of them embrace your image, they style their hair like yours.

M: Have I got an image?

MS: I mean physical—

M: Oh that. Yes.

MS: Or they put your badge on their lapels.

M: Well, that's not really a phenomenon, you know.

MS: Well, it is. I would not do that for Jethro Tull or Yes or music that my older brother listened to.

M: No.

MS: It's phenomenal the way it crosses generations. And in my opinion it's because the music is timeless. And like you said the reaction/connection to the listener is authentic so it's gonna be authentic no matter what the year is or who the listener is.

M: Yes. Well, I do agree.

MS: But at the same time we're all getting older. As a man of a certain age, is it awkward at all to have friends who are fourteen?

M: Not really, because it's not as if I take them home and bake them pies or anything like that. So, no, not really. I can put it in perspective always. And I'm very thankful that anybody should listen. When I've often been told that nobody should.

MS: Are you still surprised that people do?

how soon is never?

M: I've always been surprised.

MS: Are you insecure?

M: Mmm. Over self-judgmental.

MS: Because a part of you must know that you have a talent.

M: Uh, when you say talent, I just imagine somebody with pearls dangling free and tap shoes and so forth, so . . . yes! Perhaps I'm in that category.

MS: You mean like juggling?

M: Yes.

MS: Well, that's not what I mean.

M: I think vocation, more so than talent.

MS: What do you mean by vocation?

M: Well, it's . . . that's a spiritual drive, to be honest. I mean I have no interest in playing a musical instrument. I have no interest in being able to dance properly. So I don't—

MS: Is it true that you only dance on stage?

M: Not even there. I just simply move, and it seems rhythmical and people at the back think it's dancing. News to me.

MS: Gut response maybe?

M: Absolutely.

MS: How well do you think you're aging physically? Are you vain?

M: Well, I think we all are. I think that's unavoidable really.

MS: Because you look great.

M: Well, passable. But I mean nobody wants to be told they look grotesque. So I think we're all vain to a certain degree.

MS: Because you look at someone say, like Mick Jagger, and you know they're dyeing their hair. On the airplane here I read this whole debate over whether Madonna had Botox injected into her forehead. Everyone is vain to a certain degree, but if you were in the public eye I imagine it might be a bit difficult.

M: Well, it's difficult to the degree that if you're repeatedly photographed, people are constantly commenting on how you look. I mean, if you're a bus driver or if you are a tree feller, then people don't constantly comment on how you look.

MS: And I don't pull out and reference photos of you in your youth.

M: Exactly. But the thing is, if you are in the public eye, it seems to be acceptable for people to repeatedly tell you that you either look great or you look terrible. And that doesn't really apply in any other walk of life. But simply because you make music you're appearance is repeatedly—freely—commented upon and you're supposed to accept whatever people say. And if you don't look great, then for some reason, this must be voiced. And it must be said.

MS: Yeah.

M: I mean it's only the feint luck of the draw that I'm not today a milkman. So why should—? And if I had become a milkman, would my appearance be important to anybody? Would it affect their milk?

MS: Perhaps the people you deliver milk to. If you showed up looking a fright, they might look a second time at the milk before drinking it.

M: Only a novelist would say that.

MS: To what degree does that affect you at all? Would you ever consider dyeing your hair or having surgery? I mean, you look great.

M: Thank you.

MS: But I'm—

M: I've read on several occasions that I obviously dye my hair. Which is very amusing to me because I haven't since I was twelve years old. And so. It's very, very difficult because some people do say I look appalling. And I did an interview for *Index* magazine recently and the photographs were done by Wolfgang Tillmans. Do you know him?

MS: I saw the issue.

M: Hugely respected photographer. And probably the most dreadful photographs I've ever, ever seen. I mean, he has bits and pieces hanging in the Tate. The most shocking photos. I mean, I looked ninety-seven years old.

MS: Ninety-seven?

M: Yeah. They were actually taken in torrential rain, so obviously I did look terribly grim.

MS: In England?

M: Yes. But I did receive some letters saying, "Oh dear." I don't think I ever presented myself as human or physical perfection. If you look at very, very early photo sessions, I was just saturated with spots. 'Cause I had quite bad skin because the diet I had at the time was absolutely restricted to chocolate and potato crisps. I'm not kidding, it really was. Before a major concert I would have a bar of chocolate and some potato crisps.

MS: Was this just an idiosyncrasy?

M: No, I thought I was eating quite well. I thought I was covered. And I was absolutely emaciated in those days.

MS: So it's, I guess what you're saying is that it was sort of always—

M: Well, no. I was never. I've never tried to be physically attractive. So therefore I don't feel I'm in the running to be pulled down if I'm not, if I don't look superhuman.

MS: I just wonder if people have such an attachment to the way you look—

M: I don't know why. I mean, people will say to me, "Well, you look terrible in that photo session." And I say, "Well, I wasn't trying *not* to look terrible."

MS: I think you're in great voice, I think that's more important.

M: Yeah? Well, not bad, I mean, never any cigarettes. And alcohol in moderation.

MS: The song "Come Back to Camden," on the new album—

M: I'm very proud of that, I think it's—

MS: I mean, the vocal performance is, it's, you know.

M: Please complete the sentence.

MS: But do you—?

M: I wouldn't have bothered to make the record.

MS: Do you, do you do anything?

M [*Whispering*]: Nothing.

MS: No training?

M: Nothing.

MS: Just—

M: That's all.

MS: Avoiding cigarettes and—

M: Yeah.

MS: And—

M: Avoiding bad air, and I get as much sleep as I can at night-time.

MS: Listening to later Frank Sinatra records, he sounds a bit more gruff and kind of whiskey-damaged.

M: Sixty a day. Sixty a day. And in Marianne [Faithfull's] case, 160 a day. [*Laughing*] And not terribly great to begin with.

MS: It adds a certain quality to the voice, but you still sound like it's '83, '84. It's very clear.

M: I'm blushing. I didn't sing this well in '83 and '84.

MS: Really?

M: I don't think so.

MS: I thought you sang pretty well.

M: [*Adopts gruff voice*] Ah, well.

MS: When listening to this record, I kind of cocked my ear to see if time or anything had made you a bit different. But maybe you're right. Maybe it all about accomplished, experienced, exercised vocals now.

M: It's so easy when you become known in music to begin to spread yourself thin amongst people. Go everywhere, be everywhere, be seen everywhere and try to do everything. And my reaction was always to take one hundred yards, to step one hundred yards backward and to retire, in effect. And I think that has preserved me somewhat. And I don't, I don't rush to meet people. I'm very, very careful about

how soon is never?

where I go and how I tread and so. And for that reason, I've begun to think that I'm just simply a really monotonous person. But maybe I'm not. Maybe I'm fascinating.

MS: I think you're pretty fascinating.

M: Well . . .

MS: Is your singing an ability, or is it something you have to work on, because you said that you're better—

M: Well, I was always stood by so-called crooners like Matt Monroe and Vince Hill and, even to a lesser degree, people like Doris Day and people who could really sing and belt out an emotional number. And I was never stood by rock and roll singers, apart from David Johansen in his you-know-what days. But otherwise, I wasn't attracted by hell-raising. It was always the older generation of stately crooners that attracted me. And when that gets meshed into the perversity of how I write or see the world or present myself, then, it's a curious package.

MS: Are you at all aware of the sort of emo movement? Have you ever heard that term?

M: No. I was born yesterday.

MS: Because this is more of a throwback to an earlier question. Obviously your music is the cornerstone of this genre. And you're referenced a lot by these bands.

M: Yes. Fascinating to me. Absolutely.

MS: Because they don't sound like you at all.

M: Yeah, but I don't sound like the people I lived for when I was younger, so maybe they can't sound like me.

MS: Not too many people can. What they say about emo is that it takes the naked emotion of the Smiths, of your music, and marries it to the raw power of punk. And I don't know if that's accurate or if you acknowledge that statement as valid. The bands don't even acknowledge this. They don't like to be called emo the way people twenty years ago maybe didn't like to be called New Wave.

M: Well, I mean, there's lots of people who will wiggle away from any kind of categorizing. And I've always been one of those people. But I think there is certainly a modern trend to expose the emotions, more so than ever before. And whether it's as far-reaching as groups like System of a Down or—

MS: The Deftones, or something like that.

M: Yes. Everybody is inverted commas "coming out," and I don't mean sexually. Coming out, throwing their emotions out. And everybody seems to know what they want and what they need. They don't necessarily attain it or have it. But they know what they want from life, and they know what they want to say. And I think that's a part of what—

MS: It almost kind of "outs" metal or punk as very repressed in a way.

M: Yes.

MS: Very sort of arrested.

M: Yes.

MS: Would you agree with that?

M: I would agree with that, but then I see, I always thought our society was terribly repressed. And certainly pop music was terribly repressed and— But I feel now that there's, there are more honest statements. People are simply saying what they want to say. And then Eminem does—

MS: Do you like Eminem?

M: Well, I, I, I certainly appreciate the lack of scruples [*laughs*].

MS: I read an interview where somebody tried to compare you to him. And you, I think you might've even had a response to it.

M: Probably best not to remember . . .

MS: Do you still have a distaste for hip-hop?

M: Yes, I do. I've never come across anybody who could convince me that it was useful.

MS: Please don't take this the wrong way, but one of the thoughts that occurred to me when I listened to the new album, that in its personal politics it was a bit more like hip-hop in its golden era.

[M makes a face here.]

MS: I know, I'm sorry.

M: You are kidding.

MS: The late '80s, some bands would speak about themselves, they would speak about the world around them. Whereas now, it's pretty much a singles genre where it's all party records. Thematically, but not directly, in terms of its bold-ness and its directness, there are elements of hip-hop en-ergy. I would never obviously call you a hip-hopper.

M: I think you need to spend a week at boot camp or some-thing like that, really. Because that's—

MS: We'll move on. Seven years since the last record. I know that this is something that people are gonna say in every in-terview that you do. It's almost like a Patti Smith thing . . . Your legend has almost grown in your absence.

M: It seems to. It seems to.

MS: To what do you attribute that?

M: I think with people such as myself it doesn't really matter. You don't need to be throwing music at the public con-stantly. And there are certain artists who are absolutely timeless and they're not dependent upon the media to sup-port them. They're not really dependent upon anything be-cause the audience that they attracted in the first place came to them for the right reasons. And they understood. And the music was always very important to the audience. I've never been in a period or a stage whereby the people I was singing to, the people who were listening, were listen-ing to me for frivolous reasons. It's always been very, very personal with the audience. And the upside of that is that the audience will remain interested forever. The downside, of course, is that the people who don't like you are also very passionate about disliking you and want to get rid of you.

MS: But it's strange that you don't have to do something

every few years to say "Here I am, remember me." A lot of artists feel pressure to put out product all the time.

M: Well, that's because a lot of artists aren't really terribly good. And I'm not being funny. Most people have nothing to offer. So they really depend upon anything that the record company can distract the public with in order to convince. I'm not one of those people, I don't think. Maybe I'm deluded. But I don't think I am. My success, if you want to call it that, has never had anything to do with the record company. Ever. Ever. Ever.

MS: So there isn't much of a difference in your perspective, between '97 and now?

M: Absolutely not.

MS: Really?

M: No.

MS: Lyrically, this record sounds like someone who has been observing a lot, and maybe been holding his tongue, and now it's bursting forth. A lot has transpired politically and culturally in the world since 1997, and you always struck me as a sort of intimate but at the same time aware lyricist.

M: Yes.

MS: You have things to say, but you've not put out a record in which you say them. Now, this is sort of the tally of your opinion of the last seven years as far as your life and all of our lives. Is that accurate to say?

M: Well, yes, it's very difficult when you cannot release an album. I think everything in pop music, if you are a timeless artist, comes in waves. And when you don't have support from the media, it doesn't really matter what you're saying or what you're doing, they'll never listen to you. But it is fascinating how my name is now bandied about so much. And I think a lot of people in the media have realized that. And I always knew that it would happen, to be honest.

MS: Was there any one incident where you said, "I have something to say, I'll put something on the Web. I'm gonna release a single."

M: No.

MS: And this is another—sorry—hip-hop example. The Beastie Boys take like six years to release records, but when Bush invaded Afghanistan and Iraq, they released their commentary on that right away.

M: Yeah.

MS: It must be hard for someone like you to sit back after so many years of having a direct outlet.

M: Yeah.

MS: Because I'm assuming, and correct me if I'm wrong, I'm assuming you express your personal feelings through the lyrics.

M: Yes. Well, it's always been absolutely, and exclusively about me, really.

MS: Well, it's just, and if you look at the sort of trajectory, or the discography if you will, these seven years are a huge gap in the—

M: Well, even though it was very frustrating, I absolutely believe in fate, and I knew it had to happen, and I knew it would end. And it has.

MS: It was destined . . .

M: It was absolutely destined, and I felt as if I was being carried along by something and perhaps all the better that there was a gap.

MS: Mm-hmm.

M: Because the last album I released wasn't a showstopper.

MS: *Maladjusted.*

M: Well, the sleeve was dreadful.

MS: It was kind of, very sporty.

M: Well. By accident, it looked like a mushroom, or a leprechaun.

MS: Your standards must be very high.

M: They're just absurdly high, really. It was designed by the record company, it was dreadful. And the record company was collapsing when it was released and there was just a terrible dark cloud above it.

MS: Were you dispassionate about it?

M: Not really. But it was the third album produced by Steve Lillywhite. He knew that he was the fourth choice. The first three people refused so it wasn't done with any great gusto or exuberance. Unfortunately.

MS: Do you consider yourself a proud person? Because I think to wait seven years and release something like *Your Arsenal* would be great. Go out on a high note. But to wait for a new album seven years after something like *Maladjusted* . . . did that double your frustration of not having a record deal?

M: Yes, it did. Because I also find that certainly in the media, all writers, or shall we say just most writers, say exactly the same thing. So if they recognize a cloud above you, then they'll say, "Oh, yes, there's the cloud."

MS: "He's lost it."

M: Yes.

MS: Many critics wrote Bowie off too.

M: Well, I only said that *Maladjusted* wasn't a showstopper. I didn't say it was absolute crap [*laughs*].

MS: Fair enough. How do you think you are aging? Are you happier? Were you ever clinically depressed?

M: I think I was medically depressed, that's how it was recognized.

MS: Medically depressed? And you got therapy?

M: No, no, I think I was quite clinically depressed. I feel so much happier now.

MS: Is that just a natural sort of . . .

M: Well, I think with age, you can put things into perspective and realize how absurd people are. And when you're younger, you're somewhat in awe of people who are in so-called authoritarian positions. And as you get older you realize that most people in life are absolutely absurd, and especially people in authoritarian positions. And you realize that most people haven't a clue about what they're supposed to be doing. When you're younger, of course, you feel that, well, if this person is a lawyer or an accountant or a high court judge, they must actually know something.

MS: Or a police officer . . .

M: Yeah, or a police officer, but in reality, they absolutely don't.

MS: Yeah, they probably just saw a job opportunity.

M: Absolutely, absolutely.

MS: Um, they can still screw your life up, though.

M: Well, unfortunately yes, but that's the fascist society we live in, and I don't know why you're laughing.

MS: Well, I guess to keep from crying or something.

M: Feel free to cry, you'll feel a lot better.

MS: So, you just feel generally less vulnerable.

M: Well, the dull reality is that as you get older, the less people pick on you.

MS: We have talked a little about the cycle of generations embracing your music. There's a line on the record, "The critics try and break you down and then they make you." The British press over the years has occasionally been brutal to you, yet in your absence their sentiment has been "Oh, well, we miss him. We had a kind of a good thing with him, and the music scene is sort of lacking without him." Perhaps the press have come around a bit, begrudgingly at first perhaps, but now with a belated respect or a belated appreciation. Have you noticed that?

M: Well, yes, I have.

MS: The *NME* named the Smiths the most influential band of the millennium, and they also published a best-of collection of your interview quotes in one issue. And Manchester voted you like the greatest person from Manchester. That must be gratifying, right?

M: It's very gratifying, it's very gratifying because these things happen without anybody pitching for them to happen.

MS: Is that what you meant in the lyrics of the last song on the record ["You Know I Couldn't Last"]?

M: Not necessarily, but when I considered that so many of the critics I have are very passionate about trying to destroy me or have been, then they don't realize that the part of the passion that they give and the destruction is actually, certainly quite helpful to me. Because it wouldn't be helpful if absolutely everybody adored the sight of me. That wouldn't be useful.

MS: They make you into a polarizing topic of discussion, someone who can't be brushed aside because everyone has a different take on you. Is that what you're trying to say?

M: Well also because the criticism against me is so passionate, it implies that I must at least be someone important. Otherwise, nobody would bother chasing me, hawking me, and trying to assassinate me. So, it's an absurdly . . . disguised respect. Or misfired compliment.

MS: But do you appreciate it nonetheless?

M: I only appreciate it because it also implies that they realize that you can take it.

MS: You accept the compliment.

M: Well, you don't accept the criticism, but you can take the criticism, and they wouldn't do that, for example, to Tammy Wynette or . . .

MS: [Laughs] Well, they couldn't now.

M: They couldn't. Well, they still can, they still can.

MS: There's definitely expressions of longing still on this album. Do you still—

M: That's simply part of having a poetic instinct.

MS: So it's just a constant, your internal sensibility?

M: Because when you do have a poetic instinct, you view life in a very intense way. You might not necessarily be an intense person, but you certainly view everything in a very deeply, analytical way. And let's face it, modern life isn't really something that bears much scrutiny.

how soon is never?

MS: We talked about how things rattle you a bit less as you get older. You're also a bit less guarded when it comes to relationships as you age. This has been my experience. When I was younger I had a lot of trouble with intimacy. And the older you get, you start to feel like "Well, the hell with it," and you let your guard down. I'm wondering if, and I don't mean to get too personal, but do you still feel alone, do you still feel unloved?

M: Um, I did feel it very intensely in the '80s, but I don't feel it now because I absolutely don't care anymore. But when you're younger, you're constantly expecting everything to work itself out, and you're constantly waiting for something to happen and you're constantly trying to make something happen. And it doesn't, and now it still doesn't, but I actually really do not care.

MS: You don't at all?

M: No.

MS: Do you think that one day you'll just meet someone, and it will change your life?

M: No, no, I don't believe that at all, I don't actually believe in, as you so eloquently term it, "one day." I think that today is all there is, that there isn't anything else. Just this minute, and here we are in it.

MS: [Laughs] I guess that is a romantic way of looking at things, you know, "My prince charming will come one day," and it is not very realistic. But I'm wondering, strictly in reference to your lyrics, if that's something you would even be open to if it happened?

M: I don't think so, to be honest. I don't think so.

MS: You function well.

M: Better.

MS: Yeah.

M: Yes. I can't actually think of anything that anybody could give me at this stage that I would jump off a building to grab, really, honestly.

MS: Well, it fills up some time, fills up your day, having a relationship.

M: Believe me, it doesn't.

MS: But you must have had some downtime over the past
seven years.

M: I've got my work at the L.A. Animal Police. That takes up
all of my time. And I still prefer horses to humans.

MS: Is your animal rights work very time consuming?

M: Yes, yes, it is.

MS: For thirty years now you've been a vegetarian, probably
one of the more famous vegetarians.

M: Well, I'm not looking for any award, or anything greater,
and I hate to be wagging the finger, the wagging, nagging
finger, I don't want to do that, but I just still find it really
shocking to eat these animals. I've never heard one single
good reason or excuse for eating animals. I don't think anybody can think of one.

MS: Well, I think it's because most of us were raised by our
parents eating meat. You have to make a choice.

M: A mere detour, a mere detour.

MS: Can we talk about the first song on the album, "America
Is Not the World"?

M: Yeah.

MS: We're living in a climate now where you can't criticize
America without people pointing their finger and saying
you're unpatriotic, especially after 9/11. In that song you
mention that you love the country, and I think it is almost
an act of love to criticize it when something happens like
President Bush trying to rewrite the Constitution against
gay marriage.

M: Well, this is the problem, this is the problem—there is
some twisted mode of thinking whereby people consider
George W. to be America, and as far as I can see, he does
not represent America.

MS: Well, he's our president.

M: I know, but the president isn't always right. And this dreadful American era is unthinkable.

MS: It's almost worse than when you were railing against Thatcher.

M: Well, it's worse because George W. has such an old-fashioned idea of who a president should be, and he's not popular, and he was never popular. And he gained his position by pressure, and he hasn't earned any respect. And he's been very destructive, and a lot of people have died under his name unnecessarily. And people don't like him. And it's just astonishing to me that at this stage of the game somebody like George W. can actually become president. It proved how absurd the political game is and how it's not at all representative of what the people want or need.

MS: And it's a power thing, too, his father was president . . .

M: Well, what else is politics ever about other than ego and power? And there is George W. He is married himself, but he opposes gay marriage. I mean, it's pathetic.

MS: It's like book burning is next. You laugh while knowing it couldn't happen . . .

M: And this is the danger, it really, really is the danger. How could America have come so far, a very intelligent country, so many fantastic novelists and essayists and theorists and so forth, and yet, George. W. is the president. It's absolutely pathetic.

MS: He might not be the president much longer.

M: No, he won't be, he won't be.

MS: So what do you love about America? What does it represent to you?

M: I think the landscape is very underrated. I think it's a beautiful country visually.

MS: Oh, definitely. Not just this hotel.

M: No, not just this hotel.

MS: And you've seen most of it on tour, right?

M: Yes, I've seen everything, from Toledo, Kalamazoo, to . . .

MS: Toledo's not so hot.

M: No, I know, but it has its interesting corners. But people never think of America in terms of being visually stimulating, I don't think. It is. And architecture, I find the architecture in this city to be beautiful. The people can be very amusing, and the clothes can be very fantastic. But the danger of the moment is that the prevailing image throughout the world is always the obesity and the appalling television . . .

MS: The trash.

M: . . . and the absurd Oscars. That's always the prevailing image, and George W. and political figures who as soon as they cease to become president, they're absolutely forgotten. Ronald Reagan, who remembers Ronald Reagan, who remembers anything he did or said?

MS: They'll probably put him on a coin.

M: Well, fine, but that's meaningless.

MS: And is Blair in his pocket now?

M: In Bush's pocket? Oh, absolutely. Blair is totally forgettable. Totally egotistical and destructive also.

MS: In regard to the song "Irish Blood, English Heart" I have a question. I asked my friend Brendan, who's originally from Manchester, whether it's a struggle living here, and whether he had to make an effort to preserve his Englishness. Is that a word, Englishness?

M: Yes.

MS: Do you ever find that it is a struggle living here? Someone asked Brendan the other day if he was from England, because they didn't detect an accent. And he freaked out about it. Does America absorb you after a while?

M: Yes, it does.

MS: Is this song a reassertion of your Englishness?

M: No, I mean I'm not fighting against America at all, in that regard.

MS: Well, just reasserting your Englishness is not necessarily anti-American, it's a personal thing.

M: Mine is so deeply rooted, it will never go away. I could never be Americanized. I could never say American words, I could never use American expressions, I never have, I never will. But it is very sad when you see British people here and they do have American accents—it's a human tragedy.

MS: How does that happen?

M: Maybe they want to be American.

MS: It's an envy? I never thought of that.

M: Oh, believe it, believe it.

MS: In your opinion, what does "Irish Blood, English Heart" represent? It's political, it's defiant, but it's also proud and personal.

M: Well, people often ask me if I feel more English than Irish because all of my family and all of my family roots are Irish. And the answer is that I am Irish blood, English heart, and that is a type, that is a category, if you like, and there are a lot of people in England who are of Irish blood, English heart.

MS: What are some of the qualities of that?

M: Well, you take the qualities of both countries and you pretend that you have them.

MS: Is there a sort of like a . . .

M: That was a joke by the way . . . obviously not.

MS: Right over my head. Um, is there a sort of stubbornness? Is that accurate?

M: I'm not exclusively English, and I'm not exclusively Irish. I'm a little bit of each, and I'm sick to death of the two-party political system in England and conservatives in Labor, which never helps people. And I don't understand why the British people as a whole are not sick of this. It never helps people. The political system in England is pathetic, which wasn't your question, I know, but here we are talking about it.

MS: But the song's lyrics address that.

M: Yes, they do. But then the political system everywhere is

pathetic, isn't it? I mean, who in American politics repre-
sents your views and feelings, thoughts? Name one person.

MS: In American politics?

M: See, you can't name one.

MS: Yeah, at this moment, it's hard because anything seems
better than Bush. So even someone like Kerry, though I
don't know much about him, seems like a savior. It's kind
of a loaded question.

M: Well, there really isn't anybody in American politics whom
you ever see addressing an audience and you say, "Well,
that person really is for me."

MS: Right, everyone goes back to JFK. He was probably the
last politician people connected to.

M: Well, it is a compliment in American politics if you're as-
sassinated, isn't it, because it does mean you're a good person. People always assassinate the good, and they never
assassinate the bad.

MS: Do you return to England frequently?

M: Oh, yes.

MS: But you enjoy living in Los Angeles.

M: Yes, I do.

MS: But there are so many crazy people here in Los Angeles.
Fame makes people crazy. I'm sure that you've seen some
crazy people. Why does fame make people crazy? Why does
fame make Michael Jackson crazy, why does fame make
Phil Spector crazy? Do you ever want to take a break?

M: Well, you may be astonished to hear this, but I know a lot
of American people who are not deranged . . .

MS: Famous American people?

M: Well, some. And they're not deranged. Michael Jackson,
one assumes, was halfway there to begin with. And who
was the other person?

MS: Phil Spector.

M: Well, I think they're the wrong people to drag out, they
really are, but I don't think that's American.

how soon is never?

MS: You, for example, are an activist in causes that you believe in, but you've never tried to unleash a clothing line or
fragrance on your fans, and there are devoted fans who
would buy. People have this sense of infallibility, and Los
Angeles is the capital of it.

M: Well, they're devoted, but they're also severely critical.
Maybe that's because I am that way. I think there's a lot of
sanity in America. But the core of American society, i.e.
television, is so twisted and is so a triple-edged sword always and it's constantly trying to present a very creamy image to the world. This is why we think America is basically
a crap nation. And politically America is total crap. And
they won't allow strong women any visibility. There are so
many enormous questions to ask, but please don't think
that there aren't lunatics in England because there are.

MS: In the past seven years you've developed a great following among Mexican fans too, and I don't mean to say that
your only fans are fourteen-year-olds and Mexican people
and emo punks . . .

M: And see, I'm thankful that it's anybody.

MS: But it seems sort of unlikely that that Mexicans would be
drawn to you.

M: Which makes it all the more interesting.

MS: You must have talked to some of them.

M: I've often been asked why. I have no idea. I have no idea. I
assume it's a burst of volatile emotion and the laying of the
heart on the line. I don't think of any other reason.

After a short break Marc Spitz and Morrissey discuss How Soon
Is Never? *and Morrissey asks if Joe Green is an autobiographical
character.*

MS: It's fiction. It's obvious there are elements of truth and
I've fictionalized many things, but to what level it's autobiographical, you know, I'm still figuring, I've not sat down
and read it, the final version. I read it while I was editing it.

M: Well, did you make those journeys to England?

MS: What do you think?

M: My aunt in Scotland who read your book can't work it out.

MS: Really?

M: Do we get to know the truth, or is this beware-the-novelist time?

MS: Yes. I did many of the things in the novel and there was some research done too. This is awkward. I tried to interview you in like '99 when you were on tour, and we did talk to some of the other members of the Smiths. And there was a girl, and we did travel, but as far as like the actual things happening, you know, it's [laughs].

M: I think I know what you mean.

MS: Yeah?

M: I think.

MS: I hope that if you read it that nothing upsets you.

M: Well, I get very nervous about reading the Smiths things because they're always so glaringly inaccurate, and they're always written by people who've never met me at the time that they write. So, I often wonder, well, what could they possibly know? I mean, it's all very well if they're writing from an appreciative position of the music. Well, people don't write that way. They have to have the searing inside knowledge about everything, and I often wonder how they can possibly feel they have that if they haven't met me or they haven't been involved.

MS: Right. Well, in my book, you're not a character. There's never any real discussion of you, or you don't really say anything because we didn't meet you.

M: That usually doesn't stop me, honestly. And I'm not being funny. Everybody knows and understands the real me more so than I do.

MS: I think it's clear in my book that the story is filtered through my take on things, er . . . the narrator's take on things, not mine. But I would never speak for you.

how soon is never?

M: I can only look at you with one eye closed when you say that.

MS: Oh, really?

M: Yeah. Well, it's the nature of the literary beast, isn't it?

MS: Honestly, I feel like someone else wrote that book. I have a distance from it, which is maybe a literary thing and you can understand this. It is definitely deeply personal in places, and now I'm just a little bit frightened because I'm talking to you about it [laughs]. It *was* as much about me as about anything, and it was never . . .

M: It usually is.

MS: Have you read it, or . . . ?

M: Well, as I said, I try to avoid reading things about the Smiths because I just assume that they're gonna dramatically upset me.

MS: Oh, okay.

M: But I know lots of people who've examined it, and they give me the filtering information.

MS: Yes.

M: I trust them.

MS: Was it thumbs up or thumbs down?

M: It was . . . I'm not telling you. [*Both laugh*] You're indulging yourself.

MS: Well, you agreed to the interview, so it can't be that bad, right?

M: A detail [*both laugh*].

MS: Wow. Well, regardless, it's still . . .

M: I don't want to make any big hint. It won't be good for you. You'll suffer in the long run.

MS: Thank you, I'll guess. Someday I'll come to understand why, I hope. This might be a good time to talk about that phenomenon because I, to be honest, I don't want you to reunite with the Smiths anymore. At a point, I did. I think a lot of people still do.

M: I don't want to. Do they?

MS: VH1 now features a show where they reunite '80s bands

like Kajagoogoo and Romeo Void, and it's like a culture of nostalgia is happening. What do you make of that? There are fourteen- or fifteen-year-olds who are never going to get a chance to see the Smiths live, so it would be a nice thing for them. But what do you think of this weird retro kitsch culture?

M: Well, it's very easy to analyze.

MS: Bands reuniting, and my book, to an extent.

M: Well, I think people generally reach for things that they can't have. Also, I think the Smiths re-formation has just become the thing to say, really, with a lot of people. And they say it without really thinking about it, and they don't really quite realize how much time has lapsed.

MS: It wouldn't be the same, would it?

M: Well, how could it be, who would ever want it to be?

MS: Right.

M: But, also I think people who ask the question don't quite realize the intensity of, for example, the Smiths' court case, the aftermath, and the way I was victimized throughout it. So it's a nebulous comment. And I don't really hear it anymore, I just can't quite think why anybody would assume that I would want to reunite. What would I be doing, for heaven's sake? What's the point?

MS: I guess some people might assume that time will heal some of those wounds. Maybe there's not really enough time elapsed, maybe they'll never be healed . . .

M: There isn't enough time in infinity.

MS: There are certain members of your old band who seem to be kind of capitalizing on that retro thing—they show up at these conventions or the Smiths DJ nights like they're Adam West coming by Batmobile. It cheapens the legacy a little bit. I don't want you to talk trash about them . . .

M: No. Well, they haven't changed. Their position has never changed, their outlook has never changed. That's how they were, and that's how they are.

how soon is never?

MS: Right.

M: And that's why there was a great division between them and Morrissey and Marr.

MS: Has the court case ruined some of the memories? You must be proud of the music.

M: I'm very proud of the music, and that's all it ever was really for me, the songs. There was nothing else.

MS: You still play some of them, right?

M: Less so, less so. I'm very proud of the music.

MS: But you mention in your bio from the new album that there are no links to the past on this new record. And it just didn't seem like you're someone who dwells on the past. Like you said, you live in the moment.

M: Yes.

MS: They almost won't let you forget.

M: They won't, I accept that, but it is a very distant place, very distant. And I'm not twenty-two, I'm not twenty-three. And a lot of people don't seem to realize that. But they must.

MS: Is the court case resolved, or are you still suffering from that?

M: That's not remotely resolved, that's not remotely, no . . .

MS: Really? It's just going to go on and on?

M: It will go on and on and on, yes.

MS: There are many songs on this album that do sound, I think this is an accurate statement, lighter. I think I've heard all your albums. The album is airier.

M: It's airier.

MS: It is windy in some places.

M: Yes.

MS: How would you describe it?

M: I can't describe it, I never could describe the music. I absolutely never could. I don't feel that the concerns, or the lyrical concerns or the outlook I have, are shared by many other people in music. And that's always made me seem a bit marginal—but that happened to be there. I don't feel, I still absolutely don't feel a part of anything, at all. So, I think the music reflects that.

MS: Did you have a vision for the sound, the production?

M: Yes. I had said earlier to you that I listen to people like Martin Rowe and that's how I see myself, which you don't have to burst out laughing, which you haven't, but it is absurd, I know. It's an absolutely insane idea, an insane notion, but that's the one I have.

MS: Well, comparing you to anyone in general seems like an absurdity, so if you compare yourself to someone, it doesn't seem that outrageous.

M: Wow, that's, that's a great compliment. That's a great compliment.

MS: I don't know if you agree or not, but I think there are few people whom you can classify as unique, and that's why your music has meant a lot to me and why it means a lot to people, is because I don't think there is a precedent, and I don't think there will be.

M: Well, what you just said is all I could hope to ever hear from anybody. There's no further to go. That's incredible.

MS: Do you have, don't take this the wrong way please, take it however you want . . .

M: Oh, GOD. You had to kill me.

MS: I'm sorry. At this point, do you care about commercial appeal, or do you feel like there's a certain number of people who will buy every record you make. I heard that "Irish Blood, English Heart" is the American single, but one of your most hooky pop songs is also on this record, "I Like You."

M: Yes.

MS: Which could easily be another crossover hit. Do you have anything commercially to prove? Do you, across the board, like creative integrity, credibility?

M: It really is both, because although integrity comes first, I also realize that absolute nonsense sells, absolute nonsense makes the charts throughout the world, and I see absolutely no competition at all. So, therefore, I don't feel that anything is impossible. I feel absolutely everything is impossible. And I think that any old twit can make the charts, and any old twit can sell sixty million because those old twits DO.

MS: Success used to be all about the songs . . . maybe not, maybe that is revisionist history, but there's a reason why so many Motown singles went to number one—because they're really well crafted.

M: Yes.

MS: Almost art.

M: That's not the case these days.

MS: No.

M: I think public taste has widened, and it's widened because people like me, in my small way, forced it to be more open. It's not because of record company executives. Public taste has absolutely sprung open, and now anything is possible. It's totally open for anybody to infiltrate. And if you examine the British charts, help me if you do, but any old piece of utter twaddle screeches into the top ten with no problem whatsoever.

MS: They're all covers, mostly, right? You cover a Simon and Garfunkel song and put a slow beat behind it, and it's a hit. Was that always the case? Because I know you grew up collecting these great records.

M: No, it wasn't always the case, because certainly in the '60s and the '70s pop music in England was for everybody, and the pop chart was for everybody, and your parents bought pop music, and there were very, there were middle-aged people in the charts, and the middle-aged people would get to number one. And that's why all the people that you liked, whether it was the New York Dolls or T-Rex, were very threatened, so therefore, when they rose in the top ten, it was very, very inspiring because they were battling against all these older people who were terribly, terribly conservative. It's not like that now, it seems that everybody who is successful in England is, and I use the word through the most gritted teeth, is *independent*, and this is the acceptable sound now. And there's absolutely no other form of music, really, that makes the chart. There are no balladeers. There are no older people. They've all disappeared. And even the absolute giants of the '80s like Phil Collins and Queen and so forth, that whole spectrum of people has just completely disappeared. Peter Gabriel, you can complete the list for hours. They've all disappeared. It just seems to be now inverted commas, independent artists.

MS: Give me an example.

M: I can give you seventy-five examples. I hate to name names, though. But they're like political prisoners. You know who they are without mentioning their names.

MS: Do you still like rock and roll, loud rock and roll?

M: Like who?

MS: The Smiths and your earlier solo work is often dismissed as mopey. These people don't realize how aggressive and rocking a lot of that stuff is. I was listening to *Rank* the other day. And the version of "The Queen Is Dead" that opens the record is like a freight train.

M: Well, it's stonkin', it's stonkin', as they say in Torrence.

MS: Stonkin'?

M: Yeah, stonkin'.

MS: Do you still like loud guitar? Do you like the feeling of playing a rock show?

M: I think the music has always been somewhat aggressive. It's never been an arts and crafts fair, and I'm happy about that. But I don't really know what you mean about rock and roll. I don't know who you mean. Well, I think just of rock and roll as a, not as a lifestyle, but like as a life-affirming energy, maybe.

MS: Are there any songs that have a special place for you? These are my "winding down" questions.

M: Well, the winding down reply is that they all do.

MS: Really?

M: They really do. It all means a lot to me, it really does. Yes, I can very easily see highs and lows, and once you make the album, you unfortunately see how it could have been better and you see the flaws and so forth, but so be it. Nobody's perfect.

MS: A lot of this record almost feels like a summation. The song "I'm Not Sorry" sounds like your "My Way" [*both laugh*]. Do you feel like you've done well?

M: Yes I do. I feel like I have done well, against a multitude of odds I might add, but nobody's ever helped me, which is, once again, I don't mean to sound like somebody drilling a hedge, but they haven't, and I've never been promoted as far as I know. Do you think I have?

MS: I think that people are aware of your music and who you are. It's getting out there somehow.

M: It is, yes, it is. But I think it's always been word of mouth. But yes, I am very proud, I am very proud. I don't feel as if I've done anything wrong, and any faults I have are simply basic human foibles. I'm not Flash Gordon.

MS: And you don't change at all when you walk through the stage door? I don't mean to sound incredulous, but . . .

M: Absolutely not, absolutely not.

MS: So there's no reason to even ask you if you'll still be doing this in twenty years, because if you're still alive, you'll still be doing it.

M: Well, I'm absolutely a variety musical. I am like a child who was born in a trunk. It's just that in my case, the trunk wasn't opened for forty years [*laughs*].

MS: Let's talk about the closing song on the album. How do you feel about your fans? I guess it might be a good way to close the interview.

M: Well, I never call them fans, I never have.

MS: Um . . .

M: It is such a demeaning word, it's like fawning. That's a terrible word. I mean you immediately picture a seal sitting on a big plastic ball.

MS: Uh, what do you prefer?

M: To what?

MS: To call them?

M: To call what?

MS: Your fans?

M: Oh, either the audience or, if I'm really forced to be pompous, I would say followers, listeners.

MS: Appreciators?

M: Yes. I can't stand this expression "the kids." And sometimes I've given interviews in America and I would talk about the audience and they would print the words, they would print the term "the kids."

MS: Will they let you be and move on? They're so attached, you know what I mean?

M: They are, yes. People are constantly trying to pass me notes—"You must call me straight away," and "You must take me with you."

MS: Is it strange to be on the other end?

M: Rib tickling. Rib tickling. I would never have believed it, never. And part of me still doesn't.

MS: Part of me didn't want to meet you. Some of my friends said, "I could never meet him, I would be terrified." And others said, "Well, he's just a real person, he's just a real person." What I'm saying is, will they ever let you be a real person?

M: I don't think so because the image they have in their mind is so fixed. A lot of them realize that I change and move on and grow older, but they won't let me do it without severely criticizing me and "How dare you be what I don't want you to be?"

MS: You couldn't wear a Hawaiian shirt or a straw hat if you wanted to.

how soon is never?

M: You know, I can do anything really, but I have to be ready for rotten tomatoes.

MS: Are you ready to get back into it? Touring and everything, talking to people like me?

M: Mmm, I haven't been anywhere. I haven't been away. I've always simply been here, sitting here. It's all the people that go away.

MS: The pace must be accelerated, though, when you go on tour . . .

M: Yes, it does accelerate.

MS: It must screw with your daily schedule.

M: Yes, it does.

MS: It must be exciting.

M: It's amusing, really, it's very amusing.

MS: It must be hard to watch the decline of pop music. Well, I'm sure you've seen it decline.

M: Well, it's heartbreaking, but equally it gives you something to kick against, and you realize you're always going to be the dissenting voice. You're always going to be the one at the back who is saying no.

MS: I think we're done. I don't know what to say. This is a high point of my young life.

M: Well, you're not that young.

MS: No, I'm not. I'm thirty-four.

M: See, it's all down hill from now on.

MS: Can I just shake your hand?

M: Oh, yes.

acknowledgments

SPECIAL THANK YOUS TO:

My mother and father for giving me life. The Smiths and WLIR for saving it.

Carrie Thornton for her genius, her patience, and her gift for knowing exactly which of my tantrums to take seriously.

Jim Fitzgerald for his genius, his patience, and his gift for not taking any of my tantrums seriously.

Amanda Haas for letting me sleep on her oddly shaped couch in Los Angeles, accepting my no-good personal checks, setting me up in her sunny kitchenette, and saying, "Just start it."

Jason Gordon for his vision and for that night at Lit.

Kirsten Ames for not giving up on me and teaching me that wearing sunglasses and drinking and smoking during important meetings tends to throw certain entertainment industry types.

Brendan Mullen for being my mad punk rock uncle and vetting the Manchester chapters.

Maureen Callahan for encouraging me while reading sections of the first draft over her tea cup.

Tracey Pepper for being my "rock mum."

Sia Michel for teaching me how to say "I wrote a motherfuckin' novel" with conviction.

Danny Fields for convincing me that I already had all that I needed.

Ron Richardson for saving me from retail heck.

Jonathan Lisecki, Kari Bauce (you should have danced with Joe Strummer when you had the chance), Jackie Baer, and James and Camille Habacker for being my best friends and saving me from post-retail heck again and again.

Emma Forrest because sometimes a boy needs another Jewish pop-obsessed novelist living just up the street.

Ronald Eugene Shavers, wherever you are.

Elizabeth Goodman for dealing with my post-novel depression and making it all seem romantic.

And every girl from my high school graduating class for not sleeping with me.

I COULD NOT HAVE WRITTEN THIS BOOK WITHOUT THE FRIENDSHIP, ENCOURAGEMENT, AND HARD WORK OF THE FOLLOWING PEOPLE:

Jim Walsh, Bill Adams, and everyone at Three Rivers Press; everyone at the Carol Mann Agency; Jadrien Steele at I.C.M.; Alan Josephberg, Nicole Miller, Gary Kaplan, Alan Light, Sarah "Ultragrrrl" Lewitinn, Jere Couture, Esq., Alex Ross, Douglas Gillock, Zeke Farrow, Andersen Gabrych, and all the Panic Players; Jessica Lynn for picking me up off the street and cleaning me up as best she could; Stacey Reilly, the Poledouris family, Lara Behnert; Vicki Weathersby, who will one day admit that she's been a closet Smiths fan for quite some time; Nick Bodor, who should take "Best" off the jukebox and put *The Queen Is Dead* back on . . . and everyone at the Library; Andy Bodor; everyone at WXOU "Radio Bar"; everyone at the Jane Street Tavern; everyone at the Slipper Room; whoever turned my phone back on at the Riot House; everyone at the Sunset Marquis; everyone at Morrissey-solo.com; David Greenberg, the Salford Lads, Damien O., Kateri Butler, Rob Sheffield, Jaan Uhelszki, Timothy Haskell, Mark and Ian Hundley, Chuck Klosterman, Ben Cho, Andromache Chalfant, Tim Buggs, Matt Connors, Andy Goldberg, Marti Zimlin; Ryan Adams and Ryan Gentles for introducing me to John Porter; Jason Roth, Andy Gensler, Greg Milner, Nathan Misner, Julie Pietrangelo, Craig Marks, Gilbert Gottfried for posing for the cover, Dave Moodie, Michael Hirschorn, Stuart Cohn, Mark Pellington, Andy Greenwald, Gideon Yago, Nicole Barnette, Julie Bowen, El Vez, Richard Blade, Julie Farman, Chloë Sevigny; James Tod and Leslie for taking care of me in London while I wrote chapter 4; John Bourke, Frank Calabrese Jr., Frank Calabrese Sr., Jonathan Marc Sherman, Peter Dinklage, Pleasant Gehman, James Iha, Valerie Clift, Bonnie Thornton, Adam David, Brendan Blake, Angela McLuskey, Mick Rock; Heather Schomp; and "Fletch."

marc spitz **about the author**

is a senior writer at *Spin* magazine. His work has also appeared in *Maxim, Nylon,* the *Washington Post,* and the *New York Post,* as well as on MTV, M2, and VH-1. Spitz is the co-author (with Brendan Mullen) of *We Got the Neutron Bomb: The Untold Story of L.A. Punk* (Three Rivers Press, 2001), which if you haven't read, you really should. Seven of his plays, including *Shyness Is Nice, Worry Baby,* and *Gravity Always Wins,* have been produced in theaters of varying size and cleanliness levels. Spitz lives in Manhattan with two cactuses and a few cockroaches. He is 33.

also by
Marc Spitz

Too Much, Too Late

1-4000-8293-5
$14.00 paper
(Canada: $21.00)

Rock Out.
Break Out.
Burn Out.

Sixteen years after forming their high school band, The Jane Ashers, Sandy Klein and his buddies are still in the garage, approaching middle age and rocking out purely as a hobby. But when one of their kids' friends raves about the band in her blog, The Ashers acquire millions of teenaged fans, a record deal, and a massive hit single overnight. Finally, their rock dreams are coming true. . . . Right?

The Untold
Story of L.A.
punk

Taking us back to late '70s and early '80s Hollywood—pre-crack, pre-AIDS, pre-Reagan—*We Got the Neutron Bomb* re-creates word for word the rage, intensity, and anarchic glory of the Los Angeles punk scene, straight from the mouths of the scenesters, zinesters, groupies, filmmakers, and musicians who were there.

**We Got the
Neutron Bomb**

0-609-80774-9
$13.00 paperback
(Canada: $20.00)

THREE RIVERS PRESS • NEW YORK

Available from Three Rivers Press wherever books are sold
www.crownpublishing.com